Nature Preschools and Forest Kindergartens

Nature Preschools and Forest Kindergartens

The Handbook for Outdoor Learning

DAVID SOBEL

with contributions from

Patti Ensel Bailie, Ken Finch, Erin K. Kenny, and Anne Stires

Redleaf Press®
www.redleafpress.org
800-423-8309

Published by Redleaf Press
10 Yorkton Court
St. Paul, MN 55117
www.redleafpress.org

First edition 2016
Cover photograph by AP Photo/Ted S. Warren
Interior design by Wendy Holdman
Typeset in Palatino and Avenir
Interior photos on page 57 by Bob Bailie; 98, 98, 100 by Mauren Campbell; 161 by Ken Finch; 37, 80, 81, 150, 154 by Lia Grippo; 149, 173, 196 by Claire Harris; 88, 131, 133 by Riley Hopeman; 206, 220, 231, 232, 233, 234, 235, 240, 241, 243, 244 by Erin Kenny; 37, 48 by Rachel Larimore; 50 by Stephanie Lorek; 28, 38, 40, 46, 61, 146, 208 by Jocelyn Mathewes; 198 by Karen Olsen; 31, 47, 77, 111, 127, 140, 194, 201, 215 by Molly Steinwald; ii, 8, 9, 11, 14, 15, 17, 21, 24, 32, 102, 126, 129, 139, 144, 145, 193 by Anne Stires; 94, 96 by Mary Temple; and 115, 116 by Erica Wilson.

Printed in the United States of America
22 21 20 19 18 17 16 15   1 2 3 4 5 6 7 8

Library of Congress Cataloging-in-Publication Data
Nature preschools and forest kindergartens : the handbook for outdoor learning / [edited by] David Sobel ; with contributions from Patti Ensel Bailie, Ken Finch, Erin K. Kenny, and Anne Stires. — First edition.
     pages   cm
  Includes bibliographical references and index.
  ISBN 978-1-60554-429-8 (pbk. : acid-free paper)
1. Science—Study and teaching (Early childhood) 2. Science—Study and teaching (Elementary) 3. Nature study. 4. Outdoor education. I. Sobel, David, 1949– editor.
  LB1139.5.S35N38   2015
  372.35'044—dc23
                                                                    2015018991

Printed on acid-free paper

Contents

Preface

It's been an honor and a privilege to work with a number of inspired and industrious colleagues to write this book and to launch the Nature-based Early Childhood Certificate (NbEC) program at Antioch University New England in Keene, New Hampshire. Each of the contributing authors either teaches a course in our new program or has been a featured speaker at our annual In Bloom: Promising Practices in Nature-based Early Childhood conferences. I thank each of the contributors to this book for their inspiring words and work.

Anne Stires, author of chapter 1, is the founder and director of the Juniper Hill School in Alna, Maine. The school provides exemplary nature preschool and forest kindergarten programs for midcoast Maine children and families. She is a pioneer of the nature-based early childhood movement in New England.

Patti Ensel Bailie, author of chapters 3 and 10, helped launch the Nature-based Early Childhood Certificate program at Antioch University New England and now teaches early childhood education at the University of Maine–Farmington. She was the first person in the country to get a doctorate focusing on nature preschools, and she is an acknowledged leader in this rapidly emerging field.

Ken Finch, author of chapters 7 and 8, is the former director of Green Hearts Institute for Nature in Childhood, one of the first conservation organizations devoted to restoring and strengthening the bond between children and nature. He has led two of the largest nature centers in the United States and is a former vice president of the National Audubon Society. He has been a tireless advocate for nature preschools throughout the country.

Erin K. Kenny, author of chapter 11, is the cofounder and director of Cedarsong Nature School on Vashon Island in Puget Sound, Washington. Erin is one of the earliest originators of the forest kindergarten approach in North America and is a frequent keynote speaker on nature-based early childhood approaches.

Acknowledgments

It has been great good fun, and refreshing too, to spend hours outside with young children and innovative early childhood teachers. We flop down and watch the Pooh sticks drift down the marshy stream under the bridge, we throw pinecones at balanced rock targets, we build stick forts, we thrash the mud with sticks, we lie on our backs and watch the birds flit from branch to branch. We sing "Little Jack Frost, Get Lost" and "Itsy Bitsy Spider" and "Come Walk with Me," and things are right with the world. Children are happy and ruddy-cheeked and active. And I wonder, "How did we stray from this path?"

It has been a kind of homecoming for me, a return to my first incarnation as an early childhood teacher, able to laugh with children rather than always thinking about what we need to teach them. While feeding the goats with a bunch of four-year-old boys last week at the Wild Roots program at Stonewall Farm, I realized how much four-year-old boy kids are like little goat kids. They all want to gambol onto the picnic table, butt heads, nibble everything, splash in the water, trip-trap off into the high grass. This is what these little creatures should be doing; this is what constitutes healthy development. And I am thankful that there are hearty educators with the energy and grit to don all those layers of warm clothing and keep putting mittens back on those cold hands.

Therefore, thank you to all the children and teachers who have gotten down on the ground with me in San Francisco, Ottawa, Wyoming, North Carolina, Washington DC, midcoast Maine, Michigan, Boston, upstate New York, and all across New Hampshire and Vermont while writing this book. Thanks to all of you who believe, as Thoreau claimed, that "in Wildness is the preservation of the world." May you instill the kernel of wildness in all your children.

Much appreciation to the Storer Foundation, which has supported the growth of the nature-based early childhood movement across North America. Very specific thanks to Sara Wise, my Redleaf editor, who helped to elegantly prune the manuscript into a graceful form. And similar thanks to my research assistant and godsend, Tricia

Hurley, who created a masterful system for tracking down parental permissions for the pictures of children who appear in this book.

Finally, thanks to my colleagues in the Education Department at Antioch University New England, who are committed to making the world a beautiful and wondrous place for children.

Introduction

There's a new movement afoot in the land of early education, and that movement is nature-based early childhood. The nature-based early childhood movement has twin origins. The nature preschool movement started in North America around the time of the original Earth Day in 1970 and has quietly spread its mycelium underground for forty years. Now the mycelia are budding and sending up mushrooms around the country. The forest kindergarten movement similarly surfaced in the 1960s in Scandinavia and then flourished in the 1990s. Now there are thousands of them throughout Norway, Sweden, Denmark, Germany, the United Kingdom, Australia, and New Zealand, and they're cropping up in many Asian countries as well. Forest kindergartens started showing up in the United States in the last decade, and each week I hear about a new one. Clearly, their time has come. This book is a beginning operator's manual for all those interested in starting a nature-based early childhood program and for those interested in "naturalizing" existing early childhood programs.

The book covers the gamut from history to current practice, from theory to brass tacks. The first and last chapters of the book get us out into the elements. They provide portraits of a day in the life of two exemplary programs in the United States. The following early chapters explore how nature-based early childhood approaches are a response to the digitalization of children's lives and the academification of formal early childhood programs. The middle chapters frame some of the organizing principles of curriculum in nature-based programs. There are lots of vibrant examples of good practice and curriculum in here. The later chapters get down to the nitty-gritty—business planning, policy development, managing risk, assessing possible sites, and evaluating your program. Hopefully, you'll learn what pitfalls to avoid, how to compose an elevator speech, whether kids should be allowed to climb trees, and which outdoor gear to suggest to parents.

Before you launch into the book, I want to let you in on a bit of my personal history. Why am I excited about this healthy new approach to early childhood education? Why am I writing this book now?

Many moons ago, actually about 559 moons ago, I founded an early childhood program with Tina Staller, a gracious dancer and teacher. We were both graduates of a short-lived but wonderful teacher education program located at The Prospect School in North Bennington, Vermont. Antioch New England Graduate School accredited the program for a few years, so our degrees came from there, and when a branch of the graduate school moved to Harrisville, New Hampshire, we went along to start The Harrisville School. Harrisville, and most New Hampshire public schools, didn't offer public kindergarten at that point. Preschools were few and far between in the rural Monadnock Region, so The Harrisville School served four- and five-year-olds from five surrounding towns.

Up on top of a hill at the end of a steep dirt road on the shabby campus of a long-closed boys' school, our little school was a beehive of progressive education busyness. With precious few school administrators or state educational bureaucrats looking over our shoulders, we created a thriving little school, based on the principles of the integrated day from British infant schools. We implemented a child-centered curriculum and created a school that felt like home, preserved the magical world of early childhood, and gave children ample opportunities to play in and explore the natural world.

We spent lots of time outside, wandered in the woods, used vegetables from parents' gardens to make snack, made pottery, built a playground from scratch, and crafted mud pies. It wasn't quite a nature preschool or a forest kindergarten as described in this book, but we were often immersed in the natural world. While mostly working with young children, we also taught a course for aspiring teachers. For one of those classes, I took a group of adults into the woods behind the school for an afternoon of water play. We found a little stream, dammed it up, created a little village, created miniature people—and then we left it intact. The next day, I brought my four-year-olds out for a walk in the woods, and we came upon this little village. Right away, all the children jumped in to play in this stream world. There was no question about where this had come from; the children seemed to intuitively know that fairies and gnomes had made this village just for them. And this convinced us teachers that what we were doing indoors and outdoors with children was exactly what they needed.

After three or four years of early childhood experience, I migrated into higher education with a focus on elementary teacher preparation. That's where I stayed for much of the next three decades, with only infrequent forays into preschool and kindergarten. My focus turned to the emergent practice of place-based education, using the fabric of local natural and cultural places as the warp of the curriculum in schools. It has been rewarding to see hundreds of independent, charter, magnet, and inspired public schools take up the mantle of place-based education and forge an approach to teaching that assures academic achievement through engagement in real-life problem solving on school grounds, in neighborhoods, in their communities. John Dewey's vision of schools as "laboratories of democracy" is thriving in many of these schools.

On the other hand, the No Child Left Behind movement, the compulsive descent into high-stakes testing, and the resurgence of mind-numbing didactic teaching in too many public schools has been disheartening. It's like *Invasion of the Body Snatchers*. Where did all these aliens come from who have inhabited the bodies of superintendents and administrators and turned them into mindless drones? What happened to good old-fashioned developmentally appropriate, child-centered education?

While the body snatchers have been taking over public schooling, nature preschools and forest kindergartens have been growing in the shadows. Nature preschools, often housed at nature centers, put an emphasis on engaging children with the natural world, having them outside about 50 percent of the day, and balancing this with a progressive early childhood indoors curriculum. Forest kindergartens are even more committed to children being outside—often 75–100 percent of the day—and put more emphasis on social-emotional and physical development. As stated earlier, they're both enjoying a growth in popularity. And even though the body snatchers are making relentless headway in taking the fun and play out of kindergarten, preschools are still somewhat free of the scourge of downward creeping academics. It's still accepted pedagogy, strongly supported by the National Association for the Education of Young Children, to believe in the value of play-based learning. And more and more early childhood educators are recognizing the benefit of open spaces, fresh air, and natural world play in creating the "readiness to learn" that all kindergarten and first grade teachers know is the crucial foundation for schooling.

I hope you'll join the movement to reconnect children with the natural world in early childhood. This early bonding experience with nature can serve as a foundation for environmental values and behaviors as children mature into responsible adults.

Juniper Hill School. Map of school grounds, meadows, and woods.
Cartography by JHS third and fourth grade classes.

CHAPTER 1

A Winter Day in the Life: An East Coast Nature Preschool and Forest Kindergarten

ANNE STIRES

Early on a February morning, Juniper Hill faculty members greet each other with smiles and hugs in the kitchen of our winter-chilled schoolhouse. The school operates out of a 1762 farmhouse sitting on forty-two acres in Alna, Maine, that once belonged to my paternal grandmother. Shimmering icicles cling to the evergreen boughs and winterberries decorating the door. They welcome us and fill our noses with an image of the winter woods. We move from room to room, settling our gear in the cubby room with the painted-forest floor mat. The large kitchen, etched in my mind since childhood, is our gathering place and includes our daily check-in about weather, general plans and activities, and noteworthy information about families or individual children. We get ready for the day here, filling thermoses of hot water for the yurts, making tea for ourselves, and packing our backpacks with water, extra clothes, and a refreshed first-aid kit. We talk about our lives, shedding emotion from personal stories, thus giving one another support so we can walk into our day with young children clean and present.

All the teachers form a circle. Holding hands, we say a blessing, sing a song, or share a word to take into the day. We light a candle and honor the time as often as possible, especially if we are heading into a particularly busy week, are holding a school family in our hearts, or have difficult meetings on the horizon. The elementary teachers, Julia and Christina, head up the hill at 8:20 a.m. to greet the Roots and Sprouts children (first through third graders) in the Welcome Woods. Meanwhile, the preschool/kindergarten teachers, Lucy, Kimberly, and

I (teachers of the four- to six-year-old children's class called the Seeds), spend a few minutes layering on our own winter gear and gathering last items for our entire morning spent out of doors in all weather.

The temperature on the thermometer reads minus-six degrees Fahrenheit. The air is still today, and the sun is out—the wind will pick up in the afternoon, and for now the sun is still very low in the sky. The windchill will bring the temperature well below what the thermometer reads. This is the tenth straight day in a row with mornings well below zero degrees. Children in our neighboring school communities have spent the last two weeks indoors all day with no recess due to laws governing cold temperatures and "safety."

Instead, nearing the end of February at Juniper Hill, we prepare for yet another day of active learning, connected exploration, and dynamic play outside.

"Will you remember the Kelly Kettle, Lucy? And are their mugs packed?"

"Kimberly, please put some extra hats and gloves and wool socks in the red backpack—we are liable to have someone with cold toes in boots that are too small or a child with mittens that are not snow or ice proof."

Once the materials for the morning are gathered and prepared (*Bear Snores On* by Karma Wilson, a fireside tale about friendship, a lesson plan from Danks and Schofield's *The Stick Book* for optional activity time, the warm clay bucket and shovels, and the story collection journal), we check our own layers.

"Did you wear your new extra woolies or silks today, Anne?"

"Woolies, yes! But it is getting hard to keep them clean and ready each day given the consistent lows. It is amazing to have taught in the outdoors for fifteen years and have this be the first winter I have had what I have needed to stay warm!"

We three teachers replace the liners to our Sorel boots or Mukluks, reattach wool mittens to the waterproof overmitts, and pull neck warmers up over our faces. At the door, we look at each other once more—"Ready?"

Lucy notices that someone was out already early this morning and shoveled a new path up to the Welcome Woods for us. Perhaps it was one of the wonderful parents we are so blessed to have in this school community? Often the older children shovel a route down the hill, but today they will not need to, as someone has chipped in to help. Kimberly pulls the tow sled for the backpacks and shovels for the children to do their good work in our outdoor classrooms, just as moles are doing their good work under the snow. Lucy carries the backpack, which houses everything from an outdoor bathroom shovel to the first-aid kit, water, and extra clothes, to the teachers' observation notebooks and the last of the family newsletters to hand out. As we round the top of the hill (along what is actually the old driveway from the 1930s, steep and straight), we see the Roots and Sprouts beginning to gather together at the sound of an icicle bell. We wish them a good day and greet them by name as they pass. The Roots and Sprouts have already greeted the Seeds students who arrived early or with their older siblings, giving hugs and smiles easily to their reading buddies. The fourteen elementary students range in age this year from six to nine—but they all look us teachers in the eye as they pass, smiling, and say, "Good morning," or "Buenos días!" I even hear a few of the students greet parents of the Seeds students who have just arrived by their first name! "It is an amazing thing," I had a parent say to me recently, "to be a part of a school community where the students greet me by my first name and ask how I am. I am not just an unknown adult or the mom of one of their friends."

The Roots and Sprouts begin their academic studies at 9 a.m. with Morning Meeting and shared jobs at the Yurt, the rounded shelter that serves as the indoor space for our group. Their day is split almost equally in half, with the morning spent indoors in integrated lessons and miniworkshops in reading, writing, and mathematics. The time is punctuated by movement and group games outdoors halfway through the morning. Lunch and Active Play are also outdoors in the Porcupine Woods (the older children's main outdoor classroom) no matter what the weather. Only torrential rain, unsafe exposed skin temperatures, and lightning will keep them inside for lunchtime. However, torrential rain and freezing temperatures don't keep them inside for Active Play. After such a big out breath (physically active behavior) during big weather or simply being outdoors for many hours, read-aloud storytime and optional handwork (such as knitting and sewing) allows for "breathing in" (quiet and reflective behavior) time. Science and social studies lessons make up the rest of the afternoon. The elementary day ends at 3 p.m.

Building a Learning Community through Play, Adversity, and Resilience

At the top of the hill, a few of the Seeds' parents have arrived, and they are talking with one another by the information kiosk at the drop-off

area. They discuss the upcoming school conferences and a local family dance event that weekend. The Seeds' faculty splits off: Kimberly begins to greet children who have just said good-bye to their parents, while Lucy heads into the woods to welcome the children who have skipped and slid down the long, tree-lined path to play in the Welcome Woods classroom. I talk with parents after they have said good-bye to their child. I keep these interactions brief, but they provide a daily check-in for parents' questions about outdoor winter gear: "I saw Sophia with a pair of overmitts that seem to work really well—can you send me the link for those?" or "Thank you for reminding us about the 4:2:2:1 ratio for warmth layering in the latest newsletter! We are looking forward to the parent portal so we can continue to share clothing and ideas with one another."

It's also an opportunity for parents to update teachers about events going on in their child's life outside school: "I am going to be away for the next five days, and my mom is coming to stay with the kids. Can you help her get situated to Juniper routines if she makes mistakes?"

or "The last time Eli threw up was forty-eight hours ago, but I kept him home yesterday for rest day. I cannot believe how fast he bounced back. This same thing is traveling through other schools, and it is lasting far longer! Thank goodness for outside time and building immunity."

Kimberly and I both ask the parents and the children about sleep, breakfast, and warmth. "It is so good to see your face today, Ben! How did you sleep last night? Did your exciting dream about flying come back? I noticed you did a drawing about that during rest yesterday. Perhaps you could tell the class about that dream when you are playing this morning."

"The winter boots we sent home with Clara seem to be really working to keep her feet warm and dry. What do you think, Aimee? Isn't it astounding how fast children's feet grow? I am glad we had an extra pair here to send home." By identifying children and parents by name, looking them in the eye, wishing them a good morning, and connecting to something that happened with them either at home or school, we are connecting with the family on a deeper level than if we merely greeted children in our classrooms after they arrived off the bus or waved good-bye as they were dropped off in what some schools call the "car line." Often the teachers will bring families together by letting

Juniper Hill School. Enjoying the snowy winter landscape every day.

them know about a connection their children made the day before or about a common interest in supporting the school. The morning-time rituals are vital for the children—and for the parents also. We build community every morning by saying, "I *see* you," thereby adding blocks to our growing structure of caring and respect. As Nel Noddings (2002, 2), professor emeritus in the Graduate School of Education at Stanford University, writes in her preface to Ruth Charney's book *Teaching Children to Care,* "The time spent on learning to care is not wasted; it is not time taken away from academic instruction. Kids who are friendly, happy, and cooperative tackle their academic work with more confidence, and both teachers and students enjoy greater success. They are not adversaries but partners in caring and learning."

I watch with a small group of lingering parents as the last three children—a six-year-old girl and two boys, ages four and five—wait for one another, look up at Kimberly's smiling face, then reach for one another's mittened hands. They walk into the Welcome Woods together to greet Lucy, who bends down to adjust the girl's balaclava so she can see better, zips one of the boys' coats, and gives each child a hug. Lucy tells them what some of the other children are playing: "Lowell, Will, and Willie are a beaver family living under the ice, but still gathering logs for their lodge. The group you can hear snarling and growling in the grove of baby hemlocks and pines are in predator play—I believe they are making ice wands and potions with dead leaves, evergreen needles, and bark. There is another group of friends already climbing the fallen tree and shoveling off the otter slide." The three children take in this information and begin to make choices.

The "otter slide" was discovered accidentally. The children were exploring under our enormous pine snag climbing tree in late January, when all of a sudden one of them whooped for joy. "Everyone! Come here! There is a magic slide in the woods, and it is an otter slide!" After a short thaw period and then a solid freeze, ice had formed a sheet on the south facing woodland slope. It remained a popular play feature until the beginning of April.

The pure joy of discovery continued as all the children began sliding down the otter slide on top of one another into one large pile below. After two such slides, the group came up with guidelines for safety and cooperation. Michael, our oldest boy, found a large stick to use as a gate. The self-appointed gatekeeper now stands at the top of the hill and gives the all clear for sliding. A teacher already—and silently—had found her way to the bottom of the hill and quietly removed potential large hazards before any sliding began. The group

of "otters"—on their own—established a side route to walk up after a child who was walking up the main slope lost her footing and then another friend slid into her. Again, teachers observe, but intervene only if there are dangers the children do not see—thereby increasing the likelihood of the benefits of risk. Group communication, personal resilience, and a growing understanding of physics are just a few of the positive benefits of risk worth mentioning with regard to the otter slide.

Meanwhile, all six of the children who are a predator family are different species. There is a boa constrictor, an alligator, a crocodile, a tiger, a lion, and a polar bear. It doesn't much matter to them that they are all different species of predators from around the globe (though none from Maine). Together they are a family. One child says, "We all love each other and we take care of each other and that is why we are a family. See that is a baby snake and a baby polar bear, and we are the moms and dad lions and a tiger. And those guys are the brother and sister crocodile gators." If only our world was as accepting of such a diverse family! I make a note in my observation notebook with the date, the names of the students, the nature and theme of the play, and then transcribe a few of their conversations.

Young children naturally become animals and animal families and then connect their own lives to the lives of animals. In his book *Beyond Ecophobia*, David Sobel (1996) discusses the importance of children first *developing empathy*. He writes,

> Empathy between the child and the natural world should be a main objective for children ages four through seven. As children begin their forays out into the natural world, we can encourage feelings for the creatures living there. Early childhood is characterized by a lack of differentiation between the self and the other. . . . We want to cultivate that sense of connectedness so that it can become the emotional foundation for the more abstract ecological concept that everything is connected to everything else. (13)

As I finish this group observation and transcription, I notice another group of students racing through the Welcome Woods in a desperate hurry to find King Winter. One of the youngest boys runs into a stick being used by another child as an "ice drill" to break up the thick layers of ice that formed overnight on a woodland puddle. The running boy stops and addresses the child with the stick. "Hey! You need to do a safety circle [a teacher-taught safety technique] when you have a stick. Maybe you forgot, but you just hit me a little by accident. Can you please next time do a safety circle, and then you will know if you are hitting me?"

The children all have sticks of varying shapes and sizes, with features as varied as the family of predators. All of them move through the trees with their sticks pointed down just as they have been shown, taught, and reinforced. I ask them to stop for one moment after witnessing their work, and I ask them what their sticks are to them. "An ice blow gun." "A torch to light our way." "A sting ray 66 to guide us to King Winter's palace." "A knife with two blades." "A sword for protection in case we meet monsters or dragons on the way." Every day sticks become treasured items of play, used for stirring potions, as building tools, for raking, for shoveling, for mining, as magic wands, as utensils for cooking, or for playing with as little people. The list is endless (I take down lists from time to time, and a recent one included pistol 24, ax, shock gun 25, bubble gun, sword, ice shooter, pick ax, sting shooter, digger, cloud sweeper, pistol scraper, magic snow wand, and fire/mud/ice/water/air shooter). As Fiona Danks and Jo Schofield (2011, 6) write in *The Stick Book*, "The stick is perhaps the best-loved toy of all time, the starting point for endless adventures for generations of children all over the world." Why do we even need toy stores when children have bottomless uses for sticks alone? These young students seem to have everything they need in the woods for hours of creative learning, problem solving, and play-based inquiry. We never hear them say, "I'm bored," or "There is nothing to play with!" David Elkind (2009, 1), professor emeritus at Tufts University, concurs, stating in the introduction to *The Wisdom of Play*, "For children, [play] is a way to learn about self and the world through self-created experiences. . . . When we [as adults] appreciate the important role play serves in a child's learning about self and world, we give children the time and opportunity to engage in the self-initiated play that is the surest way for them to fully realize all of their intellectual, emotional and social potential."

The Sacred Fire Circle

Once the children settle into their varied and creative imaginative play themes, Lucy, the teacher, begins making a fire in the sacred fire circle. In December, as we approached the first day of winter, we told a story about various mammals getting ready for winter—a shrew, a mouse, a squirrel, and a raccoon. The children gather sticks every day that are the size of those four mammals' tails and lay them in sorted piles outside the fire ring. In the Seeds group (ages four to six), the children help lay the fire, but only an adult lights the fire. When the children join the Roots (ages six to eight), they learn to make their own fires from start to finish, gathering wood and tinder and laying the kind of fire they want—applying all the safety techniques they learned as a Seed. By the time they are Sprouts (ages eight to ten), the children gather, make, light, and tend their own fires, as well as learn to cook over them. They also carve their own sticks for cooking and making racks.

As a young Seed, interest and excitement is built through asking questions, observing, modeling, and helping. Lucy sits inside the fire ring, and children begin to gather around the ring inside the sacred fire circle. Most sit on seats made from tree stumps, quietly singing, or simply watching Lucy as she builds the fire. You can hear a five-year-old girl start to chant, "The Earth, the Air, the Fire, the Water: Return, Return, Return, Return," which we sing when we gather for story circle around the fire. The sacred fire ring is a quiet, no talking zone. There are two doors in a large woven nest-like structure that the children helped build in the fall. They know that they need to enter

Juniper Hill School. Roasting bread on a stick.

and exit out the circle from those openings and that only slow walking is allowed inside the sacred circle.

Lucy offers bread on a stick for the children to cook over the fire. Our Snack Elf passes out honey nuts, popcorn, and apples for snack and cups for tea. Kimberly pours the tea water from the Kelly Kettle into the brewing thermos that contains the wild tea and garden herbs. Earlier in the morning, a few children chose to walk with her to gather hemlock, pine, and wintergreen to add to the dried mint, lavender, and lemon balm loose tea that we made with the children from our school garden. We sing the snack blessing as more children filter over. We always make sure that all the children eat a snack rich in protein on these cold days and drink at least a mugful of tea to warm their bodies from the inside out. I read *Bear Snores On.* The animals in the story brew tea, eat honey nuts, and pop corn (from a school family's farm).

Skate Experiments

Meanwhile, Kimberly and I are observing and writing—when our hands will tolerate mittens being off!—about the children's play at Troll Rock, near the Rhythm Log and Hemlock Home, and the Bad Cinnamon Tree and the Potion Stump. We also ask questions that prompt the children to think about why or what or how things happen. For instance, six-year-old twin sisters experiment with stick shapes to use for skating on the ice in Beech Grove (a stand of young beech trees frame an open area in the circle of eighty-year-old pine trees, with very little understory except for ledge rock). The ledge allows water to collect and freeze, and the hill of rock provides good sledding opportunities. The two girls begin pushing round, short sticks with their hands and run along in downward dog yoga pose, saying, "Slipping dog, slipping dog. Look at me, Soph . . . I am an ice skating dog!"

"Hey, Freya, what would happen if we just stood up on these sticks?" They try this, and the sticks roll out from under their feet, and one of

Juniper Hill School. Skating on bark surfboards.

them falls down, while the other catches her balance. "Why did that happen?" I ask. One of the girls responds, "Hmmm . . . it is round like a ball. It is like standing on a ball, which is very hard to do, even though clowns can." Then Freya suggests, "What about these pieces of bark, Soph?" Each takes two large flakes of pine bark that some of the children have been collecting from underneath the snow. After several unsuccessful tries they figure out how to strap the bark on their feet with the elastic from their snow pants and try to skate . . . but then the bark cracks apart. They have attracted a small crowd of observers. One of the students in the crowd offers his "shields," two flat pieces of wood. A few boys have been excavating these shields from a large fallen tree at the edge of the Welcome Woods. "Try these," he suggests. The two girls start singing a surfing song and push off with one foot, and then try to balance both feet on their "ice surfboards," as they call them now.

"You are so good at that!" I hear a child call out. "Yeah! You are! Can I try?" Each child experiments differently, turning the board upside down or sideways to see if that works better—which they discover *on their own* that it doesn't. I am continually amazed at the length of time a particular activity can engage the learning interests of the children, and how the activity can sustain itself regardless of age, gender, and number of students. Invariably, things morph into other activities, as this one did when they discovered large pieces of blue-green lichen dropping onto the ice. They all yelled, "From King Winter! Time for Spring salads!" The surfboards immediately became salad bowls, and the children began chopping fallen leaves and needles to go in their salads and mixed snow in as the dressing, using sticks as their knives and stirring tools. One child even used a pointed stick to pull off bits of rotten log to top the salad off with "pulled chicken BBQ." And Mrs. Thaw's Café was born.

Spontaneous STEM Learning

All STEM (science, technology, engineering, and mathematics) learning begins with inquiry. Children are natural problem-solvers. They are also natural scientists, engineers, and mathematicians—they are constantly wondering about everything, then experimenting and answering their own questions. And, according to scientist Rachel Carson (1965), they need a knowledgeable adult to act as their support and guide. At Juniper Hill School in the nature-based early childhood program, we believe it is important to ask the children, "Why is this?" and "What do you notice?" and "What do you think happened here?"

I turn away from Mrs. Thaw's Café and the delicious salad I just ate and witness a group of six fully bundled children in brightly colored balaclavas, neck warmers, mittens, and full snowsuits pulling a log across another log. "Ahh! Don't you see? Come over here, Carmella. You need to be on this side. No, Eli, you stay over there because then we can see if it is even." Two children are on each side of the log, and the two others watch and wait as they are instructed to sit elsewhere to balance out the seesaw. "Yay! We did it!" announces one of the leaders. "Up, bump! Up, bump! Up, bump!" chants another. The log all of a sudden rolls to one side and pitches the half dozen children off the log. They laugh and get right back on, switching the order, moving the log and trying a host of other combinations of sizes, weights, and lengths of the log in relation to the fulcrum.

On the other side of the Welcome Woods, another science and social studies event is underway. Through a small grove of hemlock, fir, and pine sits Troll Rock at the edge of a power line cut. Also sitting there are five puzzled children with two twenty-five-foot tree logs, six to eight inches in diameter, on their laps. They are discussing something very important. Kimberly, who had been observing the group, calls me over and fills me in. The group has been trying to work out how to balance the logs together across the top of Troll Rock as a "worker

Juniper Hill School. Outdoor play translates into STEM learning opportunities.

team." Freya stands up and commands, "Here, I know what we are going to do with this cannon. You hold this end, Griffin. You too, Eli. Me and Ben are going to the top of the rock."

Freya and Ben, clearly self-identified as the leaders of the mission, take one end of each of the logs and lift them up, with help from a few others, and place them on the side of the rock fulcrum. All five children slide their hands down to the bottom of the logs on the opposite side as if someone told them to do so all at once. They work together, wordlessly, to push the logs one at a time up the rock until they reach the top. The two leaders scramble up the side of Troll Rock (a very large glacial erratic that stands as tall as any of the teachers) and take their places. They call out, "Okay, now . . . Ready!" No one discussed this series of commands, and yet the children on the ground all seem to know what to do.

They lift the end of the log that is on the ground up above their heads and push. "Heave, ho! Heave, ho," they shout in unison. Freya calls out, "A little more to me, to the right, I mean the other way, left! It is almost in. There! It is locked now and will stay. Good job! We did it!" Ben and Freya slide down Troll Rock into the arms of their team. They all hug one another and run off to bring some other friends in to show off their work. These balancing and constructing activities illustrate STEM learning at its best—children posing their own problems and then solving them. When we say play is a child's work, this is what we mean. The seesaw activity begins as play and ends as work as the children figure out how to locate the fulcrum, create the right balance of weights on either side of the log, and tinker with a variety of variables. Similarly, the Troll Rock activity develops both engineering skill and team collaboration.

Peep Village

It is now midmorning; the temperature has risen to twelve degrees. In the sun and near the fire, I begin an activity in Hemlock Circle, a sheltered place bordered on two sides by a rotting log and a large boulder. I do not purposefully call any of the children over. I start by placing a golden stick that I found a few days ago in the center near my feet, along with the book *Children of the Forest* by Swedish children's book author Elsa Beskow open to the page of the hobgoblin on the mountain. I reach into the clay pail and pull out a fist-sized chunk of clay. I start molding, slowly at first. A few children gather around me with hands on my shoulder or crouching low on the snow.

"Once long ago . . ." I begin in a quiet voice, telling the local origin myth of the Peep Village. "There was a village of little people. The Peeps, as they were called, had a happy and peaceful village, helping each other to build shelters, gather food, and make merriment. The community had a school, and musical dances, and a farm for growing crops. This village trip-tropped along . . . until one day a storm cloud darkened the sky. It darkened the sky for three days, and then the wind began to blow cold and fast. The Peeps rushed around, helping each other to secure their wares. Then the rains came, melting the snow, but flooding the farm, causing potential upheaval for the whole village . . ."

I continue by sharing the already familiar story of the protective hobgoblins, or the spirits of the forest, who help the Peeps get through seasonal transitions.

"And so the hobgoblins are born again, as you might remember from the autumn when the Elders created big hobgoblin masks on the trees in the Peep Village. With the help of the Big People (the children) now, and the Elders (the teachers), we can protect the Peeps as Mrs. Thaw arrives soon. There is likely to be a lot of ice, and wind, and rain as we move into spring."

Tiptoeing and entering the activity carefully, many other children arrive during the story and are anxious for a lump of clay. Some remove their gloves and get to work shaping clay faces of all different shapes, intently watching me work. Other children gather lichen, tree mosses, sticks, oak and beech leaves still on the trees to decorate the hobgoblins' faces. Still others finish shaping the face I started and place it onto a long stick. They work quickly and purposefully; the temperature has barely climbed to fifteen degrees above zero. As the children finish, they wash their hands with hot water from the thermoses and dry them with a soft towel.

With mittens back on, we march to the Peep Village with our hobgoblins on sticks singing, "Off we go. Off we go. Off to the Peep Village. Off we go! Whoa, Peeps!" sung to the tune of "Trot Old Joe," a traditional toddler knee-bounce song. We place them in the snow leaning against the log at the entrance to the Village and say thank you for protecting the Peeps through the change of seasons. Some children even kiss their hobgoblin good-bye!

We all gather easily as we recite a late-winter verse that praises the returning sunlight and the emergence of pussy willows and the daffodils pushing up through the snow, and then we sing "Come Walk with Me" by Walkin' Jim Stoltz.

The Seed students walk, run, crawl, and often hold hands, to the pine trees, where their backpacks hang waiting on branch hooks. We pile many of the packs onto the tow sled, as some of the children have to work hard enough simply to walk down the icy, snow-covered slope. They partner with someone who is wearing the same color as they are, and we create a rainbow to walk down the hill together, singing "When I Walk in Beauty" and "Juniper Hill Magic Places," written by the children and teachers during the winter of 2011.

Juniper Hill, Juniper Hill has lots of magic places
Juniper Hill, Juniper Hill has lots of magic places

There's the Porcupine Woods and the Fairy Woods and the
*   Gnome Woods too*
There's the Porcupine Woods and the Fairy Woods and the
*   Gnome Woods too*

There's the Color Woods and all of the Forts and the Apple Trees
*   in the morning*
There's the Color Woods and all of the Forts and the Apple Trees
*   in the morning*

Juniper Hill, Juniper Hill has lots of magic places
Juniper Hill, Juniper Hill has lots of magic places

There's the Welcome Woods and Salamander Woods and the
*   Magic Woods too*
There's the Welcome Woods and Salamander Woods and the
*   Magic Woods too*

There's the Meadow and the River and Repinuj too
There's the Meadow and the River and Repinuj too

Juniper Hill, Juniper Hill has lots of magic places
Juniper Hill, Juniper Hill has lots of magic places

Indoors Time

At the bottom of the hill, in view of the lower campus, we greet the four directions. "Good morning, North, who brings us winter and cold winds! Good morning, East, who brings us sunrise and moonrise!

Good morning, South, who brings us summer and warm breezes! Good morning, West, who brings us sunset and moonset!" We enter the farmhouse classroom. In the children's mittened hands or in their backpacks, there are a few discovered treasures they bring in for the Animal, Plant, Mineral Nature shelves or the loaded treasure shelf in the cubby room. I greet each child by name at the door with a smile and often a hug. I also shake their hands and wish them good morning. They do the same. I can usually tell right away how a child is doing once I greet them in this way. I also have yet another opportunity to "see" them and to model polite interactions for them.

We have a silent peace circle with a passed candle. With beautiful background music, each child stands up, walks across the circle rug to his or her own heartbeat, and then shares a wish of love for someone or something. We send the love out all together on the cold North Wind. Children are released in song from the circle to indoor work time by their personally chosen nature symbol (fire, maple, fox), "Thanks a lot, thanks a lot. Thanks for the Sun and the Moon. The Grass and the Trees . . ." On the days we have extended outdoor play, a song or story on the Magic Carpet follows, as we get ready for a community lunch. During the middle three days of the week, we explore some indoor spaces where there are activities on the shelf related to our various nature studies. There is a full library, writing/drawing/art area, home play place and peace loft, wooden blocks, and a science corner.

After work time and lunch on those days, the younger children (the Soft Seeds) nap and the older ones (the Hard Seeds) head out to the

Juniper Hill School. Literacy and math activities during indoor Yurt time.

DAILY CIRCLE ACTIVITIES DURING INDOOR TIME

Monday: Community Music Day led by our music teacher, Annie. We play in the Salamander Woods after music and our all-school Community Meeting. This is followed later in the morning by a Peace Circle, when the children walk with a beautiful object from nature to start the year and then begin using a candle when it seems the group is ready (usually midway through the year).

Tuesday: I introduce new works on the shelves (for example, a chalkboard drawing station for drawing items from our nature treasure shelves that are sorted into plants, animals, and minerals; sandpaper tracking boards for doing rubbings; or a special art project such as making quill pens from turkey feathers that we collect!).

Wednesday: Spanish circle with Vero, our Spanish immersion teacher, and then Reading Buddies with the elementary students.

Thursday: Social studies/skills teaching with story or puppetry (for instance, a porcupine family story about helping one another even when it doesn't directly benefit them, to emphasize friendship, building empathy, and kindness).

Friday: Guided visual arts activity outdoors (painting, clay, drawing, 3-D sculpture, collage, and so on).

Yurt for read-aloud time and an integrated main lesson in reading/writing or math. Our afternoon playtime begins an hour and a half later when the younger friends awaken and are suited up and ready for the Salamander Woods.

Back Outdoors to the Salamander Woods

The apple trees now drip with icy rain. The older children rapidly dress in the Yurt, noticing the younger ones are already outside after naptime exploring "the slush box" (which is on top of the covered sandbox). We are nearly ready for afternoon adventure . . . "When we say Salamander, you say Woods! Salamander! Woods! Salamander! Woods!" (The teachers call "Salamander!" The children answer, "Woods!")

"Let's all run (or fly, jump, hop, skip, roll) to the Salamander Woods!" Laughing and running (or flying, jumping, hopping, or skipping), we make our way to another woods classroom, across the snow-covered field, over a rotten log and a winding path, sliding down the icy slope. The woods are smaller here, dominated by hardwoods like oak, maple, beech, and white oak. There are a few large white pine too, most bordering the meadow's edge. There is a large tree that broke off six feet up (it still rests on the stump) and makes a challenging angular balancing log. There is a "boat" and two large forts, both built with nearly whole class participation. There are stumps in a stump circle, which are often (in fall and spring) turned over in search of salamanders. On this particular day, however, some of the students are digging in Chocolate Mountain, as the rising midafternoon temperatures have melted the top layer of snow to slush and loosened the dirt below. The three children, outfitted in primary-colored one-piece rain suits with their winter jackets underneath, begin the excavation. They call out, "The Chocolate Factory will be open soon! Come get the chocolate fudge cookies at the Bakery!" This is the first day since early December that the children have opened the Mountain for business, so there is a flurry of feet and high-pitched shrieks as soon as the announcement is made.

Four girls, fudge cookies in hand, bend down over a series of depressions in the rock candy snow. All of a sudden, one of the older girls, Sophia, drops her cookie and runs over to me, breathless, "Anne! Anne! Come quickly! There is snowshoe hares everywhere! They are hopping and jumping and we can track them . . . !" As if by osmosis, the excitement ripples through the group at the factory. With Sophia in the lead, Allison, Will, Willie, Benjamin, and Griffin (moving with a broken leg as best he can) take off through the underbrush. I hear reminders such as, "Be careful of the tracks, otherwise we will lose the trail," and "Look! Scat! Their poop is everywhere too!" and "How come they didn't eat it?" The children notice running tracks versus walking tracks, where the hares hid, and where they foraged. One four-year-old points out the beech leaf buds snipped off by the hare and even shows us all how the animal stands on its hind legs to do so!

Meanwhile, from a tree nearby, we hear, "Hey! Look at me! I can see the river from here. [Not really.] I can see the whole world from up here! Even my house! [Not really.] You gotta come see!" Several children look up from the Chocolate Factory, but continue their baking work. A few others ask to climb and make their way to a cluster of young beech and pine trees. These trees are nearly ladders, supporting even the most tentative climbers with close-knit "hugging branches," as the children refer to them. In managing these tree-climbing situations, we want to (1) help children learn how to manage risk and understand safety, (2) feed children's innate need for risk with reasonable risks in order to prevent them finding greater unmanaged risks for themselves, (3) increase health and developmental benefits, and (4) build character and personality traits such as resilience and self-reliance (Gill 2007). (For a full discussion of risk management, see chapter 7.)

Juniper Hill School. Mud kitchens are a regular feature of nature-based programs.

Another small group in the large pine section to the east transforms the fort with "porcupine logs." The twenty-foot dead logs with whorls of branches need several workers to move them. Michael, Ronan, Ben, and Lowell engage in an hour of cooperative work moving many large, long logs to repair the group forts after winter's destruction. "Heave, Ho! Lift . . . now! Okay, walk this way!" A series of nonverbal messages follow, grunts, motions, and synchronized movements get the logs across the woods, over downed trees, and through the rope swing area to the partially constructed log homes. The "beaver builder family," as they dub themselves, also begins to connect the lodges "underwater" by digging a path through the sugar crystal snow with the shovels that hang on "tool trees."

Minutes pass. The hush of focused learners, climbers, trackers, diggers, and builders falls over the Salamander Woods. Teachers observing. Children working. The watch on my wrist, with a silent cue, alerts me that the day is coming to a close. I sigh with a smile, wishing for more time, for more moments such as this for all children. A gray, frozen, but unlocking day in a world filled with trees, slush, porcupine logs, climbing, and chocolate dirt. A world that makes children happier, healthier, smarter, and gives them ground for high-standard academics in the years to come. Standing up, I return my observation notebook to my apron and put on my wool mittens. Lucy, Kimberly, and I make eye contact. The end of this day has nearly arrived. To gather the group (anytime we need to), we call, "Juniper, Juniper Hill! Juniper, Juniper Hill!"

When the day is over and all our work is done, we (clap) fly away home.
When the day is over and all our work is done, we (clap) fly away home.
Fly away home to dreamland, we (clap) fly away home.
Fly away home to dreamland, we (clap) fly away home!

We fly home through the woods, over logs, along paths of ice, and across snowy fields; the children return to the lower campus. They move holding hands, running, walking backward, crawling, flying, unfazed by the pellets of icy rain that now pour down; together and singing we make our way to a family Good-Bye Circle in the yard near the main school building.

With a basket of pots and pans and a lit candle in the center, the children stand up ready for our Old King Winter Ritual. Banging pot lids, shaking metal rings on spoons, and stomping their feet, the children call out, "Old King Winter, it's time to go! Take with you these piles of snow!" After saying the verse and stomping around in a circle three times, the children put the noisemakers away. We place a wooden bowl in the center of the circle and pass around a scoop. The children and their families take turns digging one scoop of snow and dumping it into the bowl. Once the bowl is full, we place the lit candle on top. "Melt snow, melt! Spring will soon return!" A hush follows the ceremony as the bowl of snow is removed to the classroom for inquiry the next day. The candle remains and we sit with our families.

"Does anyone have an observation or a note for our journal about our day? What can we share about our play or a notice about nature? What happened with the weather today?" On this particular day, as happens in Maine quite often, the temperature started at six degrees below zero and sunny, only to change to thirty degrees and misting icy rain seven hours later.

The children place their hands on their hearts to share an answer.

"We tracked a snowshoe hare all through the Salamander Woods and even found her scat and even when she probably ate some of it!"

"We drilled in the ice with ice drills that that were sticks in the Welcome Woods."

"We found an *otter slide* this morning!"

"I heard woodpeckers, which probably means the bugs are moving around in the trees."

"I climbed to the highest place I ever climbed today. In a tree."

"We played predator family. Me, Ben, Michael, Ronan, Lowell, and Freya."

"There was chocolate again at Chocolate Mountain so we could make fudge cookies!"

One teacher writes as another calls on the students or asks further inquiry questions. Everyone who wanted to shares at least one note and then our pack leader begins our good-bye song,

May the long time sun shine upon you, all love surround you.
And the good light within you, guide your way home (sung).
May you have Peace—before you, behind you, above you, and
    below you.
From your heart, to your lips, to everyone (spoken).

Children are released into the arms of their waiting parent or family member after saying a clear good-bye to their teachers. I stand up to greet parents and answer any quick questions they may have or share a short story about the day. Kimberly releases students, and Lucy takes the aftercare children to the Apple Trees to climb.

After the teachers say good-bye to the children and families, reflection about the day begins for us. We plan and shape the next day, as well as pull books or materials for activities later in the week. In the kitchen, once again, we wrap our hands around steaming mugs of tea, holding the children's good work of the day in our hearts. With an everyday focus on intention, resilience, play, kindness, and reflection, our community grows strong and deeply connected to one another and the world around us.

CHAPTER 2

The Kindergarten Crisis in the United States and a New Vision of Nature-Based Early Childhood Education

The original image of the kindergarten, the children's garden, is fast eroding. Picture those marble headstones in the graveyard, their once finely chiseled words now worn into illegible gullies by acid rain. Similarly, it's hard to see the original beauty of what kindergarten is supposed to be anymore. Children aren't playing in the garden; instead they're ardently filling in bubbles on worksheets. Many early childhood educators feel that there's a kindergarten crisis in America. The original emphasis on self-directed learning and constructive play is fast being replaced with hours of mandated reading instruction and an alienation from the outdoors. How did it all go astray and why are nature preschools and forest kindergartens shooting up like winter rye on a tilled September pasture? In this chapter, we'll start back in Maine again, explore some of the European roots of these approaches, and then spiral outward to look at a few other nature-based initiatives in this country. In the next chapter, we'll look at how the confluence of environmental education and early childhood education have created nature-based early childhood approaches.

It's one of those misty, just thawing, overcast March days in the woods of midcoast Maine at Juniper Hill, about a month after the day described in the previous chapter. Laid out before me are a panoply of scrumptious goodies—chocolate cupcakes sprinkled with crystalized sugar, a two-layer vanilla cake, popsicles, chocolate pudding. Four young bakery workers are immersed in kneading, icing, mixing, and slipping trays into ovens. There's a beehive of activity here between the fallen log and the face of the mossy ledge. I pay for a decadently rich chocolate cupcake with a piece of coal, the accepted currency in these parts, and take a nibble—it's rich, humousy, with only a bit of grit. Sasha offers Anne a slice of vanilla cake made from two layers of snow that she has frosted together. Anne politely takes a nibble as well.

Since the thaw arrived, these six- and seven-year-old children have been up to their elbows in this bakery activity for the last two weeks, working for hours on end in the muddy woods to create remarkable facsimiles of baked goods. Next week they'll visit Wabi Sabi Cottage tea room where the innkeeper will teach the children to make completely edible cupcakes, pudding, and tea from scratch. Then they'll make a cookbook including the recipes for both mud and chocolate

Natick Organic Community Farm. Making mud and pine needle cookies.

cupcakes. The world of play evolves into the world of measurement, following recipes, writing, the way of tea and economics. From natural resources to natural refinement. As you heard, smelled, and felt in Anne Stires's description of Juniper Hill School in chapter 1, children eat, breathe, and live the natural world for a good chunk of each day. It's one of many nature-based early childhood programs taking root in North America in the twenty-first century.

Nibbling on the chocolate mud cupcake reminds me of an intriguing question that some cultural anthropologists have asked: Why is it that infants all around the world always put things in their mouths? Cultural anthropologists speculate that since 95 percent of Homo sapiens' evolution was spent as hunters and gatherers, the problems of modern humans emerge from the disjuncture between having a hunting and gathering genotype while living in a technological world, disconnected from our biological roots. They examine the *why infants stick things in their mouths* question from an evolutionary perspective. Almost all children, from !Kung Bushmen, to silver-spoon-fed upper-income Brits, to infants living in the favelas of São Paulo, exhibit this behavior between about six months and eighteen months. In other words, it's cross-cultural and biologically driven. Therefore, if every child does it, regardless of cultural setting, there must be some natural selection value to the behavior. Sticking things in your mouth must provide some selective advantage in helping the individual survive longer to pass on her genes.

One possible answer? Young children are genetically driven to do this because it serves as immunization against local bacterial fauna and flora. As the infant sucks on sticks, grass, dirt, and other natural objects, her intestinal system is taking in the bacterial fauna of the local environment and developing natural immunities to those fauna. This interpenetration between the child's body and the natural world is fostered as long as we don't get all flustered when children put things in their mouths. We should support (obviously with some limits) rather than deny their natural inclinations. This is similar to the advantage of having children breast-feed rather than consume milk formula in infancy. Through breast-feeding, the child consumes the antibodies present in the mother's body and therefore internalizes the mother's more maturely evolved immune system.

This healthy penetration of the inner and outer worlds, of the child's body and nature's body, is the big idea here. The child who is allowed to stick things in her mouth and who breast-feeds is enjoying an osmotic, back and forth, interpenetrating relationship with the surrounding natural world. Nature preschools and forest kindergartens are based upon this same premise of interdependency. The intent is for children to live and learn outdoors for a good chunk of the day and to take the fresh air and spirit of the woods/meadows/streams into their minds and bodies. This conviction is in direct response to the erosion of connection to the natural world. Twenty-first-century children spend an average of eight hours a day interacting with digital media and thirty minutes a day outside. Nature preschools and forest kindergartens are an attempt to reestablish a healthy balance of indoors and outdoors in children's lives.

European Roots: The Original Vision

Friedrich Fröebel, the German inventor of the kindergarten (direct translation: "children's garden") in his book *The Education of Man* (originally published in 1826), believed in this healthy balance. As the child emerged from the bower of the family around four or five, he believed the child should step forth increasingly independently into the splash and challenge of nature. The task of the teacher was to encourage and facilitate direct encounters, the interpenetration of the child's body and nature. Fröebel (2009) illustrates what this kind of child/adult interaction should look like.

> "Let it lie," the vigorous youngster exclaims to his father,
> who is about to roll a piece of wood out of the boy's way—
> "let it lie, I can get over it." With difficulty, indeed, the boy
> gets over it the first time; but he has accomplished the feat
> by his own strength. Strength and courage have grown in
> him. He returns, gets over the obstacle a second time, and
> soon he learns to clear it easily. If activity brought joy to the
> child, work now gives delight to the boy. Hence, the daring
> and venturesome feats of boyhood; the explorations of
> caves and ravines; the climbing of trees and mountains;
> the searching of the heights and depths; the roaming
> through fields and forests. (102)

This spirit of trusting the healthy relationship shaped Fröebel's design of the original kindergarten.

Started in Germany in the mid-nineteenth century, the kindergarten idea was imported to North America in the 1870s and 1880s. By the turn of the century, the movement was well established in the United

States. In part I of *The Paradise of Childhood*, a landmark book at the time, Jenny Merrill describes what the exemplary curricula were like in kindergartens. Nature Interests featured prominently, along with Moral and Physical Training, Language, Number and Form, Music and Handwork. Nicely well rounded. More specifically, Nature Interests included:

1. Observations of the sun, the moon, the stars, the sky, the clouds, rain and snow, shadows indoors and out-of-doors . . . the seasons.
2. Care of living animals, as a cat, a kitten, a rabbit. . . . Sounds of animals imitated. Observing life in the aquarium.
3. Care of the caterpillar, its cocoon, the butterfly or moth, ants, flies, spiders, bees.
4. Planting flower and vegetable seeds in springtime; fall planting; watering plants.
5. Naming plants, flowers, fruits, grains, autumn leaves, dried grasses and grains used in decoration, pictures. Sorting and arranging seeds, shells and pebbles.
6. Observing nests and other homes of animals. Learning names of natural objects . . . as acorns, cones, chestnut burrs, milkweed pods, mosses, etc. Note. The children handle and play with these natural objects, learning their names, colors and uses: there is no formal study of them.
7. Walks and excursions if possible. (Merrill 1916, 2)

Family Nature Play. The daring and venturesome feats of girlhood.

Fröebel's vision waxed and waned throughout the twentieth century and then reemerged in the 1950s and 1960s in the form of Skogsmulle, an outdoor education program developed in Sweden. Nature educator Gösta Frohm incorporated gnomes, fairies, and other mythic creatures into the teaching at Skogsmulle. She created the character Mulle, a cheery and innocent gnome-ish character with a pointy cap and multicolored clothing, who told fanciful stories that

Juniper Hill School. Drawing from nature using a stereo microscope.

captured children's imagination and educated them about the natural world. Mulle had other friends as well. "Laxe helps children learn about water. Fjällfina introduces mountains and high places. The newest and coolest is Nova, who is an alien from another planet, similar to Earth, but totally unpolluted. She arrives in a dragonfly rocket and skis down to Earth on a sunbeam" (Robertson 2008, 3). This blending of fantasy and nature honored the magical thinking of children between about ages three and seven. Seeing the success of this approach with young children, Siw Linde, a Swedish pharmacist-turned-early-childhood-educator, founded the first "I Ur och Skur," Rain or Shine School, in 1985. Two of the founding principles were

> The pedagogical approach is that children's need of knowledge, activities and togetherness is fulfilled by being in nature.

> Children learn how to be in nature and how to protect it. This is achieved by having fun together in the forest, fields, mountains, and on lakes in all kinds of weather, all year round. (Robertson 2008, 5)

By 2008 there were 180 nature-based nursery schools in Sweden, and this pedagogical approach has been expanded so that there are now also eighteen primary grade forest schools as well (Robertson 2008). The Rain and Shine school is even more nature-based than Fröebel's original kindergarten. Here, the forest and its raw materials are the primary learning resources—pinecones and pebbles replace the plastic math manipulatives of the conventional preschool.

Denmark, where formal schooling doesn't start until age seven, has seen a similar flourishing of forest kindergartens. Denmark has conventional indoor early childhood programs, but about 10 percent of the children participate in outdoor schools, and the older children attend five days a week from 8:30 a.m. to 4:00 p.m. Whereas conventional Danish kindergartens focus on developing cognitive and motor skills through drawing and solving puzzles, a Danish forest school is different.

> At a forest school, there are no crayons, no drawing paper and no puzzles—just the great outdoors. . . . There is a curriculum, largely based on the changing seasons. . . . It involves learning to keep warm and dry in the snow, as well as building snowmen. In spring the children look for signs of new life in the forest and learn the names of the main plants and trees. In summer they study the wildlife—deer and birds at this particular school. They learn about changing foliage in the autumn and how animals prepare for hibernation. (Bennett 2009)

The movement has since spread to England, particularly Scotland, and Germany where there are now more than seven hundred German Waldkindergartens, many of which have no heated indoor facility. There's a tool shed, maybe an outhouse, sometimes a yurt, or an open-sided shelter with a fire pit or a tepee. Somewhere to get inside if it's raining hard or the weather is really atrocious. But mostly there's the Forest—with trails, campfire circles, child-constructed forts, stepping-stones across streams, brambly thickets, animal dens, and sand banks—a smorgasbord of explorable places.

And what happens when these carefree Danish kids, who have never sat at a desk, arrive at big school at the age of seven? Where do they find the discipline for comprehension, times tables, and endless writing exercises? Robert Grandahl, a Danish forest school head teacher, suggests that teachers in the local public school find that the forest school students are even more socially adept and ready to learn than the students from conventional preschools (Bennett 2009).

The Good Old Days and the Bad New Days

Perhaps you remember the kindergarten of yore in the good old US of A. There was a smiling, curly-haired teacher with a floral print dress who sang you through the door each day.

"I see Serena, walking through the door.
I wonder what wonders, this day she will explore."

Everyone sat in a circle on the rug and each child had his or her own cubby. Away from the rug there were different areas in the classroom to support different kinds of play and exploration—a big block area, a painting corner, a dress-up and dramatic play nook, a loft where you could cuddle up with a book. There was a door that opened directly to the outside where there was a sandbox, tricycles, a tepee frame. And right inside the door, next to the sink area, was a large terrarium where a little miniature world with mosses, mushrooms, British soldier lichens, and wintergreen provided hiding places for spring peepers and red efts. It really was a garden of delights, where play, poetry, and discovery were encouraged and magic was . . .

Wake up, Sister! Shoo away those dancing sugarplums and wild mice. Snap out of those fantasies and let's get down to work. At-ten, SHUN! Here's how education journalist Laura Pappano (2010) describes a visit to a "modern" kindergarten classroom:

> Elise Goodhue's kindergarten classroom at the Fair Haven School in New Haven, Connecticut, does not have lofts or pillows. Children sit at tables; print is everywhere. . . . "To meet the expectations for first grade, kindergarten has to be like this," she says, explaining that, among other skills, students entering first grade must be able to speak and write in complete sentences, read independently, and be able to retell and comprehend what they read.

Kindergarten is the new first grade. And the academification of preschool is not far behind. Even teachers in kindergarten are required to focus on a narrowing range of literacy and math skills with "studies showing some kindergartners spend up to six times as much time on those topics and on testing and test prep than they do in free play or 'choice time,'" (Wilson 2009, 1). Instruction is teacher-proofed as teachers are required to use scripted curricula that gives them little opportunity to create lessons in response to students' interests. And forget about that easy flow between indoors and outdoors. Many have eliminated recess or physical education, depriving children of the important developmental need to move and develop their bodies.

There are at least three culprits here. One is the No Child Left Behind legislation and the concurrent high-stakes testing requirements in public schools that have crowded out non-test-centered activities, such as recess and arts programming. The second is the electronic digitalization of even young children's lives, which has reduced outdoor free time and imaginative play (screens in the backseats of minivans? Whatever happened to singing rounds and searching for license plates?). The third is the fear of litigation regarding children's accidents on playgrounds. Thus, play as the primary driver of learning in kindergarten has been banished. Despite the substantive research about what's healthy and good for kindergarten children, the fear of lawsuits, abduction, injury, and a misunderstanding of the virtue of play has undone centuries of healthy indoors and outdoors play. This diminishment of play threatens the health and welfare of American children.

Happily, there is a healthy pendulum swing emerging away from the fear mindset. At a meeting of the Juniper Hill School Board a few years ago, the school's attorney, who is also a parent, refuted local concerns about liability issues:

> One of the reasons I send my child here is because the kids get to run around and climb trees. At the local public school, they've gone off the deep end with their concerns. There's police tape on the monkey bars and one of the slides. Children can't go on the grass, and they're prohibited from doing cartwheels. This, in spite of the fact that in the last five to ten years, there has been *not one* lawsuit against a school for playground injuries.

In the face of this indoor-ification of early childhood, nature preschools and forest kindergartens offer a well-needed corrective. This embrace of nature-based education resembles the Back to Nature movement at the beginning of the twentieth century. The destructive logging of the White Mountains in New Hampshire and other eastern forests evoked the recognition of the importance of protecting forests, which led to the creation of the US Forest Service in 1905 and the Weeks Act of 1911, which authorized the purchase of National Forest land. The scouting and camping movements were responses to the increasingly urbanized lifestyles of many families. Similarly now, to get those little tater tots off the couches, teachers of young children are rediscovering the benefits of fresh air and frog catching (and releasing).

What's the Difference between Nature Preschools and Forest Kindergartens?

Just as Danish forest school teachers have to deal with parental questions about children's readiness for "real school," American educators face the same challenge. Nature preschool and forest kindergarten teachers and directors in the United States have to answer the "Will my children be ready for kindergarten or first grade?" question from prospective parents all the time. Sure playing in the woods is nice, maybe even healthy, but parents want their children to know their letters when they walk in that public school door. The way that question gets answered reflects the two different rootstocks of nature-based early childhood education. Therefore, a bit of taxonomy. Though I've been lumping them together, nature preschools and forest kindergartens are probably two different species of the same genus.

Nature Preschools

Nature preschools are native to North America and emerged out of the nature center and environmental education movement. (More depth on this history in chapter 3.) The earliest ones were at the New Canaan Nature Center in Connecticut in 1967 and then the Arcadia Nature Preschool, founded in 1976 at the Arcadia, Massachusetts, Audubon sanctuary in Easthampton. Since then, other prominent nature preschools have taken root at the Dodge Nature Center in West Saint Paul, Minnesota, the Schlitz Audubon Nature Center in Milwaukee, Wisconsin, and the Kalamazoo Nature Center in, you guessed it, Kalamazoo, Michigan. These programs all have beautifully designed indoor facilities, well-established developmentally appropriate curricula, and a commitment to having children outdoors for an hour or more each day. Normally children attend for two to five half days a week.

The Dodge Nature Preschool in West Saint Paul is to die for, designed to look like a great cottage "up north" in Minnesota's lake country. Inside the front door, there's a family area around a fireplace with comfy craftsman couches and overstuffed pillows. Parents and children immediately feel welcomed and at home. Each classroom has exposed beams, lots of nooks and crannies that support different kinds of activities, a separate sunroom, wood-slatted ceilings, a fully operational water table, numerous windows, and direct access to the outdoors. It's every parent's dream of a home-away-from-home for their young child. During the first part of the morning, children build with blocks, make paper dolls, play at being dinosaurs, perhaps there's a bit of drawing and writing. There's a healthy snack of apples, crackers, and honey, a picture book about the wind, and playacting based on a story a child dictated that morning.

For outside time one morning, the children and teachers trundle over to the farm to pick out some new chickens for the tiny hutch on their playground. A fox had dispatched the previous occupant, and so the children and teachers go inside the chicken coop and observe which chickens seem mellow and tame. The teachers scoop up hens and slide them into willing children's arms to test the chickens' amenability to

Wild Roots Nature School. Feeding chickens at Fairview Farm.

being handled. They select two. On the way back, children circle around a squashed garter snake and speculate about how it died. "This is my first time seeing a wild snake outside," says one four-year-old girl with awe in her voice. How fortunate these children are to have hands-on contact with domestic and wild animals on a daily basis.

Forest Kindergartens

Whereas nature preschools are endemic to North America, forest kindergartens have their roots, as we've seen, in Europe. In keeping with the "no paper, no crayons, just the great outdoors" spirit, forest kindergartens have a grittier, wilder feel about them. Join me at the Waldkindergarten on the Natick Community Organic Farm in suburban Boston. It's late November, below freezing, so children arrive bundled up in snow pants, patched down jackets, winter boots, pom-pomed wool hats. The farm is a bustle of activity, as this is turkey pickup day for CSA members. The children meet their teachers at a bread oven adjacent to the farm administration building—they never go inside—and when everyone is there, they trundle back into the woods. On the way, some get distracted tossing sticks into a marshy stream, lying on their bellies on the frosty ground. One teacher takes the time to languish here while the other children and teacher head around the corner.

The outdoor classroom is a sun-dappled acre of towering white pines with smaller scattered oaks. There are a couple of log circles,

Natick Organic Community Farm. Storybook cottage and backpacks.

a low balance beam structure, some homemade hobby horses, the bakery—a sand pile with lots of kitchen equipment, a digging pit, a backpack rack, and child-sized roughhewn tables. The centerpiece is a storybook cottage straight out of Hansel and Gretel. With a field-stone foundation, a steep-pitched roof, a stuccoed exterior and cottage windows, and foot access only, it's fairy-tale-come-true breathtaking. Inside there's a woodstove, more tables, and tiny chairs, Waldorf-inspired toys, herbs hung to dry, feathers, and dream catchers. But the children don't go to the cottage. Instead, they all convene in a circle on the ground and sing chants and rhymes. "Little Jackie Frost pinched my nose, Little Jackie Frost pinched my toes . . ." I'm certainly feeling the pinch as I wonder when we're going to get in out of the cold. But we don't. Waldkindergarten founder and administrator Regina Wolf Fritz explains to me, "The cottage appeals to the parents, but I'm always clear that we spend about 90 percent of our time out in the forest and only about 10 percent inside the cottage."

From circle games, the children move into Forest Gnome jobs—tidying up the bakery, preparing snack, collecting kindling, raking the outdoors block area. It all looks so industrious and self-directed. And this morphs seamlessly into forest play. For a long time. Children dig in the clay pit, continue chopping up apples for snack, huddle at the base of tree trunks and whisper, giving voices to acorn creatures. I watch four boys play for about twenty minutes on a swing suspended from a wire between two pines. Hardly a teacher in sight. One boy stands on the suspended old lawn chair, while another boy winds up the swing, round and round. "Okay, it's ready," he announces. Everyone piles on, a couple on the seat, two more standing, a tangle of arms, legs, scarves. The swing unravels, slowly, then faster, spinning the boys into a blur. Just watching makes me feel mildly nauseous. When the spinning stops, the boys tumble off and some of them roll down the leafy, needly slope below the swing, at one with the forest floor. One jumps up, "Now we need to spin it up again!" They've got an endless appetite for kinesthetic stimulation.

Eventually, they do go inside for snack and a puppet show about animals preparing for winter. (Not always, snack is often outside.) Children get to choose between cheesy pasta and plain pasta and there's herb tea as well. Parents appreciate that a whole foods, often from the farm, teacher-prepared snack is an integral part of the program. Each month there's a different theme—November is Preparing for Winter—but this is mostly conveyed through stories and songs. Curriculum is low-key and subtle. The emphasis is on nature play,

long walks along the aqueduct, food preparation, fairies and gnome houses, and exploration. Whereas at Dodge there's more conscious curricular emphasis, with exquisite documentation as done in schools that follow the Reggio Emilia approach, here ample free play, chores, and vigorous physical activity are prioritized. This is what Leonard Sax (2001) in "Reclaiming Kindergarten: Making Kindergarten Less Harmful for Boys" has in mind when he suggests that

> the 5-year-old boy, instead of beginning contemporary kindergarten, would instead enroll in an alternative kinder- garten in which fine motor skills, math, and preliteracy are deliberately neglected in favor of nonliterary group activi- ties utilizing gross motor skills—singing, dancing, sports, and so forth. (4)

I'd contend that this whole-body approach is best for both boys and girls. In a new film about a Swiss forest kindergarten by Lisa Molomot and Rona Richter (2013) called *School's Out*, a Swiss pediatrician notes that he sees lots of children with attention deficit disorder in conven- tional indoor preschools but no children with attention deficit dis- order in forest kindergartens. Perhaps this is what Erin Kenny (2013), founder of Cedarsong Nature School on Vashon Island, Washington, means when she says, "Children can not bounce off the walls if we take away the walls."

The difference between nature preschools and forest kindergartens is illustrated in two distinctive approaches toward the "Will my child be ready for kindergarten or first grade?" question. Let me be clear that all these nature-based early childhood programs are more alike than they are different. They all honor the primacy of children immersed in nature. But their different histories and styles reflect a deep divide in educational pedagogy and approaches to parenting. Nature preschools work from a cognitive readiness mindset. This is reflected in the beautiful facilities, desks, and slightly more emphasis on formal literacy and numeracy in nature preschools. Forest kindergartens embrace an initiative/resiliency mindset, with an emphasis on minimizing indoor facilities, being out in all weather, and giving children opportunities to solve problems on their own. What's more important in preschool, learning your letters or learning to overcome your fear of tromping through that deep puddle? Or does learning to overcome your fear actually create a foundation for learning letters?

Wendy Banning and Ginny Sullivan address this issue in their wonderful book, *Lens on Outdoor Learning*. Extracting the commonalities from early childhood learning standards across the country—that is, initiative, persistence, invention, problem solving—they show how children's self-directed outdoor play provides opportunities for developing these skills. They contend that these skills are the foundations of academic success. In alignment with these convictions, Paul Tough, author of *How Children Succeed*, is quoted in *Lens on Outdoor Learning*.

> The many skills children develop through play, particularly the self-control practiced and refined in imaginary play, are related to long-term academic achievement. "The ability of young children to control their emotional and cognitive impulses, it turns out, is a remarkably strong indicator of both short-term and long-term success, academic and otherwise. (Tough 2012, 32)" (Banning and Sullivan 2011, 8)

Remember the Danish forest school teacher who said that his students were deemed more socially advanced and most ready to learn when compared to children who went to conventional indoors schools? Social competence and readiness to learn—these might be the most valued currency of nature-based early childhood programs.

The Virtue of Open-Ended Play

Many physicians also support the kind of open-ended, free play that nature preschools and forest kindergartens provide more fruitfully than many indoor early childhood programs. Writing in an article entitled "Resurrecting Free Play in Young Children: Looking Beyond Fitness and Fatness to Attention, Affiliation and Affect" that appeared in the *Archives of Pediatrics and Adolescent Medicine*, doctors Burdette and Whitaker (2005) say,

> The problem solving that occurs in play may promote executive functioning—a higher-level skill that integrates attention and other cognitive functions such as planning, organizing, sequencing, and decision making. Executive functioning is required not only for later academic success but for success in those tasks of daily living that all children must master to gain full independence, such as managing their belongings and traveling to unfamiliar places. (48)

I saw this kind of executive functioning in action at the Juniper Hill School in Alna, Maine, in October 2012 when I watched a five-year-old girl create a nature sculpture on a dead tree on the edge of the Sheepscot River. With no directives or suggestions from a teacher, she peeled off the bark, then tried two different kinds of mud to test their stickiness quotient. Next she collected aspen, birch, and maple leaves and adhered them to the mud-prepared surface in a symmetrical pattern. She framed the whole thing by tying a twisted strand of marsh grass around the trunk of the tree above and below the composition. It took her forty-five minutes; she worked alone the whole time. It was a quiet, elegant composition in the style of nature sculptor Andy Goldsworthy. She was planning, organizing, sequencing, and making decisions. Sounds like executive functioning to me.

Nearby, two groups of boys built bridges across a wet swale—putting down layers of dead branches, fallen leaves, and grasses to create a platform that made traversing the wet spot easier. When one team of boys caught the others stealing some of their construction materials, there was outrage, accusations, and then negotiation. Teacher intervention helped resolve the problem, but only after a lot of conversation about property rights and fairness. Burdette and Whitaker (2005) explain the importance of such interactions:

> Solving these dilemmas and conflicts that arise in play encourages children to compromise and to cooperate. This process can cultivate a range of social and emotional capabilities such as empathy, flexibility, self-awareness, and

self-regulation. Such capabilities, sometimes referred to together as "emotional intelligence," are essential for successful social interactions in adult life. (48)

Furthermore, small world construction, den building, collecting berries, finding your way through untracked woods, following tracks—all the kinds of free play that children create spontaneously—might have long-term effects beyond the cognitive and emotional benefits. Writing in the *International Journal of Environmental Research and Public Health* in an article titled "Risky Play and Children's Safety: Balancing Priorities for Optimal Child Development," Dr. Mariana Brussoni (2012) and other public health physicians cite a US study in which sixty-eight disadvantaged children between the ages of three and four were randomly assigned to participate in one of three preschool programs.

> Two of the classes included at least 21 percent free play and child-initiated activity component. The third class focused on direct instruction of academic skills and allowed for only 2 percent of free play activities. When tested at age fifteen, children in the latter class were significantly more likely than the other classes to experience misconduct, and less likely to participate in active sports or contribute to their family or community. Furthermore, at age twenty-three, problems worsened with significantly higher levels of work suspensions and arrests (Weikart 1998). These findings underline that free play is fundamental to healthy child development, and that restriction of free play in the preschool years might potentially have lifelong repercussions. (4)

Free play leads to lower arrest rates? Now that's a selling point if I've ever heard one. Let's do the math. The average cost of a year-long, three full days a week program at Juniper Hill School is about $6,000. The average cost of a full year of incarceration in the United States is about $31,000. Forest kindergarten sounds like a good investment to me.

Academic preparedness, executive functioning, negotiation skills—these are all great outcomes, but even most far-sighted parents are more concerned about whether nature-based early childhood programs are going to make their children happier and healthier right now or next week. One of the big issues for parents is the gung ho, outdoors in all weather, children-coming-home-muddy-and-wet-every-day orientation of lots of these programs. After three or four hours of being outdoors with children on a chilly but dry day in November, I was ready to get in my car and crank up the heat. It took me awhile to vanquish the shivers. Would I really want my own children doing this two or three days a week?

Remarkably, though, most children seem to relish the opportunity. Look at the *Preschool in the Forest* video on the *Seattle Times* website about Cedarsong Nature School. It's gloomily overcast, the kids are sloshing around in muddy puddles, little straggles of rain-dampened hair are plastered to their faces, they're skritching around in thorny thickets, and yet they seem cheery and unfazed.

Paul Doolan (2011), a dad who sent his daughter to a Swiss forest kindergarten, articulates this difference between the adult and child's perspective on environmental conditions.

> For two years my little girl went to kindergarten in the forest. Not a school in the forest, just the forest. No walls, no roof, no heating, only the forest, a few tools, and incredibly dedicated teachers. In the heat of the summer, in the lashing rain and even in the subzero temperatures of the Swiss winter, she would meet her class at the bus stop outside our house, and they would trek for twenty minutes into their clearing in the forest, free to indulge in the savagery that is unfettered childhood, no computer, or plastic or chalk board in sight.
>
> One day she came home from a day of particularly vicious downpours, her feet inevitably soaked, her eyelashes caked in mud, her cheeks ruddy with the cold and her eyes sparkling with fire, and I said to her it must have been tough being outside all morning in such weather. She looked at me in genuine incomprehension, looked out the window: "What weather?" she asked.

When I walk out into the rain, I feel the need to protect myself. I hunch over, pull my jacket up over my head, quicken my pace to get under cover. Rain is an intrusion, an obstacle. Does it need to be that way? Children who attend nature preschools and forest kindergartens are learning to embrace the rain rather than shun it. This is a good thing.

CHAPTER 3

Nature Preschools: The Cross Fertilization of Early Childhood and Environmental Education

PATTI ENSEL BAILIE

Nature preschool is a unique American species, different from forest kindergartens in Europe. It's the result of the cross fertilization of both the early childhood and the environmental education (née nature study) movements in the United States. To understand what high-quality nature preschools look like, this chapter explores the intertwining of these two traditions. In the spirit of keeping the freshness of children outdoors in all seasons in our consciousness throughout the book, we'll start with a look at a nature preschool in the heartland. In the first chapter, we entered into frigid midwinter in Maine, and in the final chapter, we'll experience drizzly fall in Washington state. We chose these challenging weather conditions to illustrate that nature-based early childhood really happens in all kinds of weather. Sometimes, of course, it's bright and beautiful. Let's follow this path through the pines, around the bend, sun dappling the forest floor and . . .

It's a few months later and one thousand miles west from Juniper Hill School. We're smack dab in the middle of the country on a sunny May day in the Michigan woods. Toads are hopping around the forest floor as preschool children attempt to catch them. Proud of her captive, a small girl stretches out her arm to give me a peek at the pebble-sized American toad in her hand. An even smaller girl touts an even smaller toad in her hands. Other children climb on logs, build structures by leaning long sticks on trees and outcroppings, and participate in a construction project (digging a hole in the ground) that imitates a similar, but larger, construction project happening at the nature center next door.

These children attend a preschool where they begin their day outside in a natural wooded play area behind their preschool building. There aren't any swings or slides or typical playground equipment, just what appears to be an unstructured natural space containing lots of loose parts (large sticks to build with), a sandbox with two large boulders to climb on, logs in various stages of decay, a hollow log to climb through, a wigwam frame, a rain barrel, and a partially built lean-to. One would not know that this was a preschool, except for the set of alphabet cards hanging from the rustic split rail fence. Each card includes a letter of the alphabet (in lowercase, as the uppercase letters are hung in the front play area) with pictures of plants and animals that start with the letter displayed.

Child-sized picnic tables and a circle of stumps with a log bench provide a hint that the children meet there for group time to listen to a story or perhaps share their toads or other discoveries made that morning. A paved path starts at the preschool door and leads out of the play area, through a wooden gate to a woodland trail, and to the left, a boardwalk separates a small pond from the preschool building.

Chippewa Nature Center. The Nature Preschool is housed in a separate building, with enclosed natural play areas and easy access to forest, pond, and meadows.

As the four- and five-year-olds are catching toads in the play area, something catches their attention in the nearby pond. They amble over to the pond and jump in. I'm startled by their effortless entrance into the water. Should they really be doing this? Where's the teacher? Is this a safe activity? But I notice the children seem to be at ease. There is a familiarity about their movement, and they seem to know where to go and what to do. They attempt to catch frogs in the pond, and the children move slowly and methodically. When the water begins to get too deep they stop. Out of the corner of my eye, I notice the teacher is actually nearby and is comfortable with this activity. The children have freedom to explore, and they're all well prepared with boots and rain pants. Their teacher is complicit and asks one of the children to get her boots too. Later she explained their behavior (and hers):

> This morning I had not planned on going over to the pond and getting wet. . . . The kids . . . were finding toads in the back area then they wanted to . . . find frogs. . . . Why can't they just jump over the edge? They've got their boots on. They know where they can walk. We've been working on this for weeks . . . [and they have a] sense of ownership and . . . confidence [that is not often seen in children this young].

Family Nature Play. Easy access to shallow water is a useful affordance.

The children attend the Chippewa Nature Center Nature Preschool in Midland, Michigan. This is one of dozens of nature preschools in the United States. These are state-licensed preschools, housed and/or operated by a nature center or environmental education center. Typically serving children aged three to six years old, these programs are the ultimate bridging of the early childhood education and environmental education fields.

Similar to the Dodge Nature Preschool in Minnesota described in chapter 2, the inside space at the Chippewa Nature Preschool is warm and inviting. Knotty pine paneling, several large windows, leather and rustic wood couches, and a wooden counter dress the reception area. The center hallway rises up two stories, with a cupola-type extension above containing windows that let in natural light. Windows adorn the hallway on both levels, allowing natural light to penetrate the classrooms from above and parents to view their children in the classrooms.

Under the lower windows on both sides are the cubbies where the children have their outdoor gear and nature treasures. The roof of the cubbies, just below the windows that look into the classrooms, is a shelf where teachers can display various art projects, nature items, and documentation of the work that goes on in the classroom and outdoors. Sturdy wooden furniture and nature-themed rugs are found throughout the classrooms, dividing the spaces into various interest areas including dramatic play (complete with loft), art, a plumbed water table, block area, group time, library, discovery area with natural materials and more. Each classroom has a full kitchen with all the accoutrements, and a low counter for the children to sit at. This does not look like the preschool your mother attended!

Chippewa Nature Center. Watery nature reflecting the children's natural state.

Like most early childhood programs, nature preschools contain well-equipped classrooms, professional teaching staff, and support facilities. But unlike these programs, they have access to extraordinary resources that the nature centers can provide, including collections of artifacts, teaching animals, and professionally led naturalist programs. In addition, the teaching spaces include wooded trails that lead to ponds and golden prairies where children find adventure and make discoveries.

High-quality preschools have included nature topics as units of study for a long time: leaves turning color in the fall, geese migrating, bears hibernating, and planting seeds in the spring. Many preschools even include animals in the classroom—a rabbit, guinea pig, or some other furry creature so children might get to care for a living thing besides themselves. In fact, nature has been an integral component of the work of many of the early childhood pedagogical innovators of the past two centuries.

Nature in Early Childhood Education

In addition to Friedrich Fröebel, the creator of the first kindergarten, other progressive educators have emphasized the importance of integrating nature into early childhood education. Maria Montessori believed that nature reflected the child's natural state and that children needed access to outdoor areas where they could take part in gardening. Montessori (1964) relied on agricultural labor or the culture of plants and animals as the means for children to work in nature:

> He still belongs to nature, and, especially when he is a child, he must needs draw from it the forces necessary to the development of the body and of the spirit. We have intimate communications with nature which have an influence, even a material influence, on the growth of the body. (153)

Montessori connected nature education with the natural development of the child, as these cannot be separated in a child-centered classroom.

Rudolf Steiner influenced early childhood nature education through his development of the pedagogy of Waldorf education. In order to allow the child's natural development, the Waldorf classroom was designed to have a warm, homelike atmosphere providing safety through predictable routines. The classroom contains natural

materials such as pinecones, shells, rocks, and wood to be used as
both decoration and in creative play. The years spent playing with
natural materials build a foundation for scientific understanding in
later years. Reverence for the earth and an emphasis on all natural
materials engenders a sense of appreciation and responsibility.

Many nature-based early childhood educators also look to the
Reggio Emilia approach for inspiration. One of the fundamental principles of the Reggio approach is that teachers view the children as
capable, strong, and curious about their environment. Nature provides
a basis for inquiry and development of theories that the children can
test. From children's cookbooks about pesto, to a study of a sculpture

in the town park, there's a Reggio emphasis on engaging children in the surrounding natural and built environments.

Despite all these historical encouragements for nature to play a role in early childhood, the natural world has faded away from much early childhood pedagogy. Since nature preschools in the United States evolved out of the environmental education field, they illustrate a re-embracing of the Fröebel, Montessori, and Steiner impulses.

Study Nature, Not Books: The Underpinnings of Environmental Education

The nature study movement, at the end of the nineteenth and beginning of the twentieth century, and the field of interpretation in the newly established National Parks, advocated for children to have an authentic connection with the natural world. Herein were the underpinnings of environmental education.

Beginning with naturalist Louis Agassiz's first biological field station in America in 1873, public school teachers studied nature by the "natural method," producing the rallying cry for the nature study movement, "study nature, not books" (Armitage 2009). Wilbur S. Jackman, Liberty Hyde Bailey, and Anna Botsford Comstock were central figures in the nature study movement. Wilbur S. Jackman was a science teacher who worked with John Dewey at Chicago's Cook County Normal School in the late 1890s. The Normal School was at the center of the progressive school movement, and nature study was a good fit with the constructivist approach toward teaching science that Dewey articulated. Jackman wrote the seminal book *Nature Study for the Common Schools*, published in 1891 from bimonthly "Outlines in Elementary Science" pamphlets that he had designed for teachers the year before. He suggested that "the teacher must take his cue from nature and from his own immediate surroundings. . . . The work should therefore be planned to suit the changing and recurring seasons" (Jackman 1891, 12). One of the challenges of nature study was the demanding role of the teacher and the difficulty finding qualified teachers. To overcome the teacher's lack of knowledge or understanding, Jackman suggested that "He should without hesitation begin with the simple things around him, and grow with the pupils" (Jackman 1891, 12).

As nature study began to take hold, Liberty Hyde Bailey, a renowned botanist and agriculturalist at Cornell University, published *The Nature-Study Idea*. Bailey's book extolled the virtues of the nature study movement including the child-centered aspect, letting children choose the subject matter, and following the cycle of the year. He recommended that "experience should come before theory" and contact with living things before reading about them in a book (Bailey 1903, 142).

Anna Botsford Comstock, also a member of the faculty at Cornell University, wrote the *Handbook of Nature Study* in 1911. This work boasts over nine hundred pages, reached twenty-four printings by 1939, and is still in print today. Anna Comstock truly embodied the nature study principles. Echoing Bailey and other nature study advocates, Comstock believed that children needed to experience nature first before being given the facts. She wrote the handbook for teachers, suggesting that teachers need to have a love of nature in their heart so the children will love it too. She also advocated for nature study to be correlated with other subjects: "Nature-study should be so much a part of the child's thought and interest that it will naturally form a thought core for other subjects quite unconsciously on his part" (Comstock 1911, 16).

Concurrent with the beginning of the nature study movement in the late nineteenth century, explorers and wilderness guides such as John Muir and Enos Mills were working to protect the vast wilderness of America. As the progressive educators initiated the nature-study movement in schools and homes, it was the explorers and adventurers who gave birth to the field of interpretation in our early National Park sites. Enos Mills lived in Estes Park, Colorado, and was a nature guide and advocate for Rocky Mountain National Park. He founded a nature guiding school and wrote a book called *The Adventures of a Nature Guide* that provided insights into his work. In a chapter entitled "Children of My Trail School," Mills (1920) describes his playful antics and explorations with a group of children.

> They had been explorers in a wilderness, had camped by mighty rivers, had seen wild animals and strange nations. Their imaginations were on fire. This world had become an inexhaustible wonderland.
>
> These children were dealing with real things through interest, and their imaginations blazed with more keenness than it was possible for the powers of legends and fairy tales to incite. They had been to school, had studied, had worked, had learned without realizing it. Their reports amounted to enthusiastic recitations of new, big lessons well learned. Best of all, they were happy, and were eager to go on with this schooling—this developing. (157–58)

Isn't it sad that we've lost this kind of exhilarating learning in most educational settings and wonderful that nature preschools and forest kindergartens are reviving these opportunities for young children?

Mills's school, established in 1920, became known as the Trail School and was a forerunner to nonformal programs that are found at nature centers today. He describes his method, which is similar to the nature study approach, "We try to develop in the child mind the spirit of exploration, so he may enjoy the search for facts, both in books and in the outdoors" (Mills 1920, 165). His program was both child-centered and flexible, led by the interests of the children. Mills found it difficult to find others who could be the same type of nature guide for children: "to find individuals who will do this *without becoming teachy or preachy and deadly to the children* is most difficult. Most teachers, some parents, and many others want us to ignore interest and desire and force the children to memorize something which they consider worth while" (Mills 1920, 172; italics added).

Nature study waned during the First and Second World Wars and continued to fade in the shadow of the space race against the Soviet Union, with the push for classroom-based math and science. Natural history as a curriculum unit was all but extinguished during the peak of the Cold War. But in the 1960s, the nature study and conservation movements eventually evolved into environmental education, as public awareness increased after publication of Rachel Carson's book *Silent Spring*.

Rachel Carson, raised in the nature study movement, was one of the central figures in the history of modern environmentalism. Her mother used Comstock's *Handbook of Nature Study* to explore the natural world with her children in the woodlands outside their Pennsylvania home (Lear 1997). The influence of the nature study movement in Rachel Carson's young life is reflected in her writings, especially *The Sense of Wonder* (1965). Her book *Silent Spring* (1962) brought attention to the dangers of chemical pesticides (specifically DDT) to the general public, and the emergent environmental movement of the 1960s led to the passing of the Environmental Education Act in 1970. This was also the year in which the first Earth Day was celebrated, and the first use of the term *environmental education* appeared.

In concert with this emergent environmental consciousness, the 1960s and 1970s saw the founding of many nature centers, often on behalf of preserving a natural area that was ready to be destroyed by a highway or housing construction project. Environmental educators such as Joseph Cornell developed programs that were experiential in nature and did not focus on the learning of facts, but instead invited children to be engaged in "flow learning"—techniques that emphasized sensory and experiential immersion in nature. Much of environmental education, with a focus on science content, has diverged from Cornell's approach, but his emphasis on experience rather than facts has been preserved in the nature preschool approach. In the late 1960s, middle '70s, and early '80s, the first three nature preschools opened. The field of early childhood environmental education germinated with books like *Environmental Education at the Early Childhood Level* by Ruth Wilson (1996), a professor at Bowling Green State University, who had a dual appointment in both early childhood education and environmental education.

From the nature study movement and the wilderness guides through the era of conservation, to environmental education, there have always been those who advocated for children to experience the natural world with a sense of wonder. Enos Mills, Anna Botsford Comstock, Rachel Carson, and Joseph Cornell each in his or her own way advocated for opportunities where children could connect with nature through direct experience. Mills encouraged "the chief means of interesting children in nature is to expose them—to bring them into contact with outdoor things" (Mills 1920, 181). Rachel Carson (1965) shared her insights:

> I sincerely believe that for the child, and for the parent seeking to guide him, it is not half so important to know as to feel. If facts are the seeds that later produce knowledge and wisdom, then the emotions and the impressions of the senses are the fertile soil in which the seeds must grow. The years of early childhood are the time to prepare the soil. (45)

Environmental education and early childhood education have been partners, to varying degrees over the past century. Common threads weave through the histories of both disciplines. They each have an approach to education that addresses the whole child, provide opportunities for sensory-based learning, include authentic experiences, and integrate subjects across the curriculum. However, the role of nature in early childhood education is primarily focused on child development, and the goal of environmental education is environmental stewardship. The challenge of the nature preschool is to bring these foci on child development and environmental stewardship together.

Environmental education at the early childhood level has the potential for developing an environmentally concerned citizenry that will relate to the earth in a more harmonious way than that of the present generation. (Wilson 1996, 24)

The Nature Preschool

Although the impetus for establishing nature preschools seemed evident, the ability to do so began at a slow pace in the United States. At the same time that a priority was being placed on early childhood education with projects like the creation of Head Start in the 1960s and the HighScope Perry Preschool Project long-term study, environmental education was beginning to play an important role at nature centers. The earliest nature preschools grew out of already existing "mom and me" types of programs. Some nature centers even had young children's programs that repeated (once a month or once a week), but were not officially licensed preschools.

Since the early nature preschools grew out of the environmental programs at nature centers, they emulated that type of program—a theme of the day that all activities revolved around, including a craft that was modeled by the teacher that everyone had to assemble the same way. Often the teachers were not early childhood educators, but rather natural history teachers with little knowledge of early childhood education or developmentally appropriate practices. Since that time (beginning in the 1990s) dozens of nature preschools have sprung up throughout the United States and can be found in almost all states. The programs are diverse in that they range from very small (one class) to large (three classrooms with multiple classes). The directors' backgrounds vary, sometimes with both early childhood education and environmental education experience, but usually having either one or the other (Bailie, Bartee, and Oltman 2009).

There are common threads throughout these preschools:

1. A nature-focused curriculum that includes extensive time spent outdoors in natural areas. Although they are not outside for 90 percent of the time (like the forest kindergartens), these programs usually spend about 50 percent of their class time outdoors (depending on the weather).
2. The inside classrooms are usually filled with natural materials and animals, providing a homey atmosphere that reflects the outdoor environment.

3. An association with a nature center or environmental organization, which provides unique resources that most other preschools do not typically have, such as access to many acres of diverse habitats with hiking trails, wild animals, farm animals, naturalists who provide special programming, maple sugar shacks, apple cider mills, gardens, greenhouses, orchards, apiaries, and aviaries.
4. Nature-based activities happen indoors and outdoors; in whole group activities, small group activities, and individual activities.

The central organizing concept of the curriculum is nature, so everything is based on seasonal happenings in the natural world. The nature preschool programs often take on the goals of their operating nature center, such as providing young children a connection to the natural world so they will become stewards of the environment. But because they incorporate the values of early childhood education, they also have child development goals of using nature as a vehicle for children's development in all domains.

When done well, nature preschools integrate the best that early childhood education and environmental education have to offer. Rachel Larimore, director of the Chippewa Nature Preschool, put it best when she said that the goals of the program are "two-fold . . . to provide a quality early childhood educational experience that's developmentally appropriate, preparing kids for kindergarten. . . . Then the other part is to connect kids to nature. To get them outside and to build a life-long connection with the natural world."

We'll revisit the idea of this synthesis in high-quality nature preschools in later chapters, with a focus on the Schlitz Audubon Nature Center in Milwaukee, where thoughtful early childhood programming is integrated with a conscious attempt to develop environmental attitudes and behaviors.

The Current State of Nature Preschools

As of 2014, the nature-based early childhood movement is burgeoning. The Storer Foundation in Jackson, Wyoming, has established nature-based early childhood as one of its funding priorities. Through their support, the North American Association for Environmental Education has created Natural Start, a website to organize and orchestrate nature-based early childhood initiatives throughout the United States.

Seattle has more than a dozen nature-based early childhood programs. Boston Nature Center's inner city Pathways to Nature program has a waiting list. In Canada, Forest Schools Canada, a network of forest kindergartens and schools, is similarly bringing together initiatives from the Atlantic to the Pacific to Hudson Bay. There's a particularly strong nature kindergarten movement in the Vancouver and Victoria areas of British Columbia and similar urban initiatives in Ottawa and Toronto. Clearly, this is a movement whose time has come.

Moreover, these programs are respected for both their intellectual and social/emotional virtues. Currently, faculty at Antioch University New England and researchers from Program Evaluation and Education Research (PEER) Associates are researching the comparative effectiveness between nature preschools and high-quality indoor preschools in preparing children for kindergarten in Midland, Michigan. The school district is conducting parallel research to compare the effectiveness of their nature kindergartens in preparing children for the early elementary grades. Charlie Schwedler, superintendent of the Bullock Creek Schools in Midland, recently said, "Lots of our students come from families that have hunted and fished for generations, but they're starting to not go outside as much. Nature-based education connects them to their traditions and it integrates everything that they do, it connects their learning to the real world. I know this is a good thing and we're not waiting around for the data to prove it, we're going to keep advocating for this in our schools" (Sobel, Becker-Klein, and Bailie 2015).

Initial findings and studies in Europe suggest that children who go to nature preschools and forest kindergartens are just as well prepared for kindergarten and first grade as their compatriots in more traditional early childhood programs. But these nature programming students are also developing persistence, stick-to-it-ive-ness, and collaboration, and they're more physically active. In short, they're just as smart but perhaps have more grit—more self-reliance, persistence, ability to stay on task. And grit, we're learning, may be a better predictor of school success than academic test scores (Duckworth and Eskreis-Winkler 2013).

CHAPTER 4

The Challenge of Transplanting the European Forest Kindergarten to North America

What happens when you import the European idea of the forest kindergarten to North America? Just as there are differences between British English and American English, there are different underlying cultural assumptions about childhood in Europe and the United States that make for challenging translations. The Waldkindergarten (from German, *Wald* = forest and *Kindergarten* = preschool, which therefore translates as "forest preschool") program at the Natick Organic Community Farm in Natick, Massachusetts, provides an excellent case study.

Let's start with a couple of definitions. In common parlance, Wikipedia offers up this description of the Waldkindergarten.

> A type of preschool education for children between the ages of three and six that is held almost exclusively outdoors. Whatever the weather, children are encouraged to play, explore and learn in a forest or natural environment. The adult supervisors are meant to assist rather than to lead.

From the Scotland Forestry Commission (Robertson et al. 2009) comes a somewhat more elaborated definition. Following are key features of the forest kindergarten:

This chapter is based on a presentation by Regina Wolf Fritz at the Nature-based Early Childhood conference at Antioch University New England in Keene, New Hampshire, on May 15, 2013. Much of the content is drawn from the experiences of Katie Roberts, Kirsten Smyrni, and Regina Wolf Fritz of the Forest Gnomes Waldkindergarten at Natick Community Organic Farm in Natick, Massachusetts. Tables are reproduced with permission. When "I" or "my" is used, this refers to the opinions and voice of David Sobel.

- uses a local woodland, (or other natural area, such as a beach, meadow, pond) preferably within walking distance, and selected based on agreed criteria of accessibility and health and safety
- structured, organized and mostly run by local, qualified teachers
- regular, frequent contact in the same setting over a significant period of time (meaning daily, weekly or fortnightly visits to natural areas all year round in almost all weathers)
- provides child-centered freedom to explore using multiple senses and intelligences, child-led and adult supported
- provides a low pupil-to-adult ratio, through involvement of parents and volunteers
- helps children to appreciate, understand and care for our natural heritage
- provides a real world context for all learning—firsthand experiences meeting of the outcomes of Scotland's Curriculum for Excellence

Salient phrases such as "supervisors assist rather than lead," "almost exclusively outdoors . . . whatever the weather," and "child-centered freedom" suggest where some of the rub is going to be. Think back to the description of a text-rich environment dominated by teacher-driven instruction in that New Haven kindergarten classroom in chapter 2 and you'll get a sense of how different these programs are from mainstream kindergartens in the United States. But even when you're dealing with locavore parents who are choosing this kind of outdoors-based early childhood education for their children, the deep paradigmatic assumptions about childhood still differ between European and American parents.

A Bit of History

In Germany the first Waldkindergarten opened in 1968. Recall that the first nature preschool in the United States opened in 1967, so both of these movements arose during a time of increasing environmental concerns in western democracies. In 1993 the German government recognized the Waldkindergarten as a legitimate form of preschool education, making these programs eligible for state subsidies, which significantly reduced tuition costs for parents. By 2005 there were 450 Waldkindergartens in Germany, and in 2013 there were more than 1000 programs. They constitute about 3 percent of the total number of preschools (Robertson 2008).

The Natick Organic Community Farm is a nonprofit, certified-organic farm providing productive open space, farm products, and hands-on education for all ages year-round. One of their core goals is fostering community goodwill through love of the land. Their co-ordinator of public programs, Regina Wolf Fritz, was born and raised in Germany and earned an engineering degree in horticulture from the University of Hannover. She was hired in 2001 to run the existing school and public programs and create new programs for children and adults in order to broaden the reach of the Farm and fulfill its mission.

In response to financial pressures to make use of all the farm's land, and the national children and nature movement fomented by Richard Louv's book *Last Child in the Woods*, Wolf Fritz proposed the creation

Natick Organic Community Farm. The Forest Gnomes storybook cottage tucked in an oak and pine grove.

of a preschool program to take advantage of ten unused acres of forest land owned by the farm. Louv's advocacy of the benefits of unprogrammed time in nature for children merged with Wolf Fritz's own parenting style, and the result was the Forest Gnomes program, which started in 2009.

As described earlier, the Forest Gnomes program is at home in an open forest of white pine and red oak trees, with a charming Hansel and Gretel cottage used during severe weather, and sometimes for snack and activities. The program accommodates no more than twelve children aged three to six at a time with two educators. The educators are both mothers with backgrounds in early childhood and environmental education. Children come either on Monday/Wednesday or Tuesday/Thursday from 8:45 a.m. to 12:45 p.m. Program elements include a teacher-led morning circle of seasonal songs and recitations, daily free play in nature, Forest Gnome jobs (sweeping, washing dishes, raking, tidying up the bakery), sharing a home-cooked organic meal, walks in the woods and neighborhood, story time, community gatherings, festivals with parents, and farm chores.

European versus American Cultural Attitudes toward Early Childhood

The whole idea of children playing in the forest all morning sounds wonderful. But here's the rub. Whereas European parents are more accepting of free play in early childhood, American parents wonder what kind of balance there should be between play and academics. Is play really a child's work? Are they learning their letters? What if it's really cold? Let's examine the challenges of changing early childhood education that emerge from the cultural differences between European and American parents. To see what happens when you transplant the Waldkindergarten to American soil, Wolf Fritz looks at cultural values in six different categories:

1. Value placed on play versus academics
2. Role of the teacher
3. Safety
4. Concept of fun
5. Concept of nature
6. Concept of childhood

1. Value Placed on Play versus Academics

In spite of the progressive values of many parents attracted to nature-based early childhood, it's hard to resist the lure of the Race to the Top mentality in the United States. We want our children to splash in mud puddles, but we also want them to score well on those first grade entrance evaluations. And deep down, we want our children to go to good colleges, and therefore, it's never too early to get them on the right path. For parents primarily concerned with academic achievement, this means long waiting lists for choice preschools in some cities, and it translates into a mild skepticism about the value of play in early childhood. Sure, play is important, but so is getting ready for reading, writing, and arithmetic. In Europe, Wolf Fritz suggests that parents are more supportive of play and less concerned about early academics. And here we return to that issue introduced in the second chapter—the European attitude is that preparation for school means developing motor, social, and emotional skills, whereas in the United States it means the development of academic skills.

Therefore, many parents in the United States do not trust that a Waldkindergarten program will provide everything their child needs to meet the demands of the twenty-first century. Hence the two-day-per-week model in Natick works well so that parents can get some nature play for children and then enroll them in other more academically oriented programs on the other days. On the other hand, many European countries delay formal schooling that focuses on academic achievement until age six or seven. The schools in Finland have received accolades because their student performance on international tests is among the highest in the world. One possible reason? Formal schooling doesn't begin until age seven, and children spend a lot of time outdoors.

Though current reform efforts in the United States focus on more academic instruction earlier, some early childhood researchers are finding that children learn best through exploratory and play-based activities rather than from didactic, teacher-directed academic learning.

One extensive study done at the University of North Florida found that children who attended academically oriented preschools had lower grades by the end of fourth grade than those who went to play-based programs. Researchers proposed that early academic instruction may actually slow down learning if it's presented before children are developmentally ready for it (Marcon 2002).

1. Emphasis on Play versus Academics in Europe and the United States	
Europe	**United States**
Play is the most important element in early child development.	Play is one of many elements of early child development.
Preschool prepares children for school readiness by developing fine-motor skills, social skills, and emotional skills.	Preschool prepares children for school by teaching academic skills.
Formal school education starts at age six or seven (UK is exception).	Formal school education starts at age five.
(Note: This chart, and all charts in this chapter, are drawn directly from the Wolf Fritz presentation cited on p. 59.)	

In summary, I suggest that a focus on social and emotional readiness for school, as provided for in the Forest Gnomes program, translates into better academic achievement down the line. But it's hard for parents to believe this.

2. Role of the Teacher

In Europe, where early childhood programs center around *play*, the teacher's role is to facilitate playing. In the United States, where the central focus is on *academics* or *knowledge*, the teacher's role is to teach content and impart specific knowledge. Moreover, it's illustrative that in Europe, especially in the British Isles, there's a whole category of profession known as *playworkers*. These are folks who staff playgrounds, afterschool programs, urban park districts, and sometimes early childhood centers. Their job is to facilitate play. When you use the term *playworkers* in the United States, most people don't understand it.

On one visit to a Waldkindergarten program in Germany called Grasshoppers, Wolf Fritz referred to the staff members as *teachers*. They looked puzzled, clearly conveying, *We are not teachers.* The term used for a preschool teacher in Germany is *educator*, meaning to raise or bring up. In the German language, the term *teacher* is used beginning with formal schooling in first grade.

This distinction between facilitating play, as playworkers do, versus instruction, which is what teachers do, is a bit foreign to parents in the United States. This creates another set of challenges outlined in the table below.

My problem-based learning colleagues talk about the paradigm shift regarding the role of the educators from "sage on the stage" to "guide on the side." In the forest kindergarten, this difference is perhaps even more exaggerated. The teacher is responsible for assuring physical well-being, for scaffolding the structure of the day, for preparing meals, for creating the space for things to happen. But then it's important for the teacher to step aside to let children's play experiences unfold, where possible, unfettered.

2a. Roles and Challenges of Being a Playworker/Educator	
To facilitate self-directed play, Educators provide:	Challenges
Safe and stimulating space with many loose parts	No products to show as results of *work*
Time, time, time	Parents want "results" because it helps them to understand what their child has "learned"
A daily rhythm	No measurable growth indicators
Activities that are not result- or expectation-driven	There's a mysteriousness about what's actually happening in the forest
For the physical well-being of the child (body temperature, nutritional needs)	
Emotional support	

The lack of product is an interesting challenge, and there are a range of responses in different forest kindergartens. Claire Warden, a leader of the forest kindergarten movement in Scotland, has created the practice of Talking and Thinking Floorbooks (Warden 2012b). These are a running record of children's comments transcribed by teachers, teacher reflections, and children's drawings and questions. They're done in a large format, durable scrapbook form that documents the day-to-day wanderings and wonderings of the children and teachers. In this way, they become curriculum maps, tracings of the unfolding geographic and mental explorations of the children. This physical document, a much more authentic portrait of learning than isolated skills worksheets, helps to dispense some of the mysteriousness about what's happening out there in the forest.

2b. Roles and Challenges of Being a Playworker/Educator *(continued)*	
To guide and stand back, Educators allow children to have their own experience in the following ways:	Challenges
Observe and refrain from interfering in discovery and conflict resolution.	Observers may misinterpret teaching style. Teacher seen as uninvolved, not caring, not sensitive, not in control, not trained.
Refrain from verbal chatter accompanying play and discovery.	Teachers' decisions to stand back may be seen as failure to discipline.
Allow children their own discoveries, judgments, and joys.	
Let child take ownership of decisions— for good or for bad (autonomy).	

It really is disarming to see children playing in the woods with no adults lurking over them. We're used to seeing and hearing constant adult chiding. "Don't swing that stick, Gabe, you might hurt someone." "Stop squeezing the worm, Maria." "Ari! Use your words, rather than stomping." "Tell me about the acorn you just found." Forest kindergarten educators give children the space to have their own experience.

On the way from the farm to the woods at the Natick Organic Community Farm one morning, I saw these educator behaviors in action. As the group crossed a bridge over the stream, three children flopped onto their bellies to look down into the water. I expected the teacher to say, "We're walking back to have morning circle. No time for this now." Instead she calmly sat down beside them and watched. The rest of the children disappeared around the corner with the other teacher. One of the floppers tossed pebbles into the water; another ran to the other side of the bridge, tossed in a Pooh stick, and came back to watch it emerge from under the bridge; and a third flopper stared, just stared at the water. The educator did not say to the staring child, "Can you see any patterns in the water?" Instead, she just watched. And we sat there quietly, for maybe five minutes, as the children lounged, tossed, and gazed. They were allowed to have their own experience.

Wolf Fritz meets many parents of European origin who seek out the Forest Gnomes program because they crave this restrained approach. They are burned out from experiencing American helicopter parenting at the playground and social events. Instead, they value children not being 100 percent supervised, to not have everything overheard and commented on by adults. This practice is respected in Europe but seen as unsafe in the United States. It helps form children who do what is good even when nobody is watching.

When kerfuffles arise between children, the educators often take a wait-and-see approach. Left to their own devices, children sometimes have the capacity to work these things out by themselves. And isn't that what we want in our children—the ability to develop conflict resolution strategies? Of course, educator intervention is often necessary and the adult serves as mediator, getting both children to explain what happened and to support them in coming to a resolution.

And it's a relief not to hear the teachers make the children say, "Thank you" or "I'm sorry" in a punitive kind of way. On the other hand, the teachers in the Forest Gnomes program always act respectfully to each other. They model thanking each other for help, they volunteer to help without being asked, they apologize to other adults and children when there's been a misunderstanding. They seek to model behavior so that children will do as they do, not as they say.

2c. Roles and Challenges of Being a Playworker/Educator *(continued)*	
To be a role model, Educators:	Challenges
Model and do versus teach and lecture.	Parents want educators to teach.
Emphasize being kind and grateful, instead of drilling "thank you."	Parents feel that teachers do not address issues.
Practice compassion and involve children in acts of kindness, rather than lecturing them about being nice and forcing apologies.	Parents are concerned that educators don't reinforce the interpersonal lessons being taught at home.
Create community through circle time, preparing and sharing meals, working together, and celebrating with families, instead of talking about community.	

Forest kindergarten is different from Sesame Street, Disney World, and birthday parties. In these situations, the adults have pizzazz, they play the lively roles, they make things happen, they put on a smiley face. Instead the educators are sad and happy, and the children are as much the creators of the experience as the educators. As a result, things

2d. Roles and Challenges of Being a Playworker/Educator *(continued)*	
To be authentic, Educators:	Challenges
Behave in a way that is not "put on" or scripted.	Parents expect teacher to be the animator, entertainer, motivator.
React to surroundings and events naturally.	
Convey real emotion.	

happen that adults would never have thought of, such as the mud bakery activity at Juniper Hill School described in the first chapter.

3. Safety

The difference in European and American conceptions of safety and risk was highlighted in a conversation I had with Sharon Danks, author of the playground transformation book *From Asphalt to Ecosystems.* Sharon had recently returned from Berlin where she had been touring playgrounds and meeting with playground designers. She indicated that German insurance companies had done actuarial research and determined that adults who had more active childhoods, in which they were allowed to take more physical risks, have fewer physical accidents. As a result, they file fewer insurance claims than adults who had less active, more physically limited childhoods. Therefore, insurance companies are encouraging designers to create playgrounds with greater risk elements so that children develop kinesthetic competence.

3. Attitudes toward Safety	
Europe	United States
There is no 100 percent safety.	Safety first!
You have to balance striving for safety and allowing growth and life to happen.	"Let's make sure this never happens again."
In order to keep children safe, they need to learn to assess and take risks.	In the name of safety, we keep children away from risks.

In the long run, it will save insurance companies money. Isn't this different from attitudes we normally encounter in the United States?

In regard to safety, many Americans want to minimize all risk, whereas Europeans have a greater understanding of a risk/benefit balance. In other words, it's valuable to accept some risk because it's important to recognize that moderate risk has benefits. Take youth sports for example. We accept the limited risk of potential injuries when a child plays soccer because we appreciate the benefits of aerobic exercise, coordination, and teamwork that soccer provides.

Ellen Beate Hansen Sandseter (2007), a Norwegian researcher in the Department of Physical Education at Queen Maud University in Norway, has found that the relaxed approach to risk-taking and safety actually keeps children safer by honing their judgment about what they're capable of. Children are drawn to the things we parents fear: high places, water, wandering far away, dangerous sharp tools. Our instinct is to keep them safe by childproofing their lives. Perhaps it's a better safety protection strategy to let children take risks.

In the Forest Gnomes program, the educators consider three kinds of risk:

Physical risks, such as climbing, using knives, being close to bodies of water, being in an open space that is not as easily supervised and allows for contact with strangers, and getting hurt in conflicts between children.

Emotional risks, such as letting children deal with conflicts on their own, working through hurt feelings, finding their place in group structures, standing up for themselves, and accepting their role in a multiage group.

Social risks arise out of the dynamics of rough-and-tumble play, war play, the standing-back role of the educator, and the multiage group.

The Waldkindergarten approach treats risk as beneficial for children's development because it gives them a chance to experience their own limits, work on expanding limits where possible, and accept limits that can't be expanded. When children are allowed to climb trees, the teachers find that the majority of children are self-limiting—they know when to not climb any farther. Lou Casagrande, past director of the Boston Children's Museum, described a variation on this theme. A climbing net rises steeply to a height of about fifteen feet in the entrance foyer to the museum. It looked risky to me, and I asked if there were ever any accidents. He responded, "The only time we have accidents is when parents get nervous, intervene, and start to tell their children what to do. They anxiously say, 'don't go any higher, come back down, move your right foot over to the loop just a bit down, now move your hands.' The children absorb the parents' anxiety, they lose faith in themselves, and then they fall. When children are left to climb on their own, they do fine."

This kind of attitude instills respect and teaches children how to evaluate risk. It is better to take small risks and learn than it is to avoid risk and later in life have no tools for risk assessment. Not learning to assess risks leads to either fright or to dangerous behavior, especially in teenagers.

The Forest Gnomes educators also have to deal with American parents' concerns about "stranger danger." In Europe, young children are taught to use public transportation from an early age; in the United States, parents who allow children this freedom are considered irresponsible and derelict in their parental duties. One German Waldkindergarten has the tradition of ending the school year with a five-day sleepover field trip to a farm—without any parent chaperones. Just imagine proposing this in the United States.

In regard to the social risks of war play, it's important to recognize two different perspectives. The sociopolitical view held by many American parents is that war play teaches harmful lessons. Parents assume that children learn militaristic lessons about violence and conflict from their simulated battles. The developmental view of many European parents is that war play meets children's needs. Play, including war play, is a primary vehicle through which children work out developmental issues. In order to accommodate war play and still have all children feel safe in a preschool setting, it is crucial to create safe zones where war play is not allowed. To address the issue of war play, Forest Gnomes staff offer parent education meetings to explain and discuss these different perspectives.

4. Concept of Fun

When American parents send their children to a forest kindergarten, they expect it to be fun. The problem is, of course, that it's not always fun to be in a year-round forest kindergarten program. Parents have

4. Concept of Fun	
American attitudes	**Challenges**
We live in a society that glorifies fun.	It is not always fun to be a Forest Gnome (parents get disappointed).
Pressure for everything to be fun.	It is work to be in a year-round outdoor program (parents question the need to put their children through rough stretches).
At the end of the day, parents ask, "Was it fun?"	The parents' commitment to a program is crucial to its success.

to get their children up and dressed—Mary Janes and cotton socks won't do in a Waldkindergarten in the winter—and get them from their snuggly bed into the cold car. Then the children have to tromp back into the woods in burdensome clothing in the rain, or sleet, or buggy spring. They go on long hikes and fall in the mud. Children come home soggy and dirty and sometimes cranky. If the children aren't having fun all the time, why do it?

The Forest Gnomes educators have found that they have to dismiss this notion of full-time fun as part of the admissions process and then during the year in parent education forums. The emphasis needs to be on appropriate clothing *and* on the development of resilience. At the Cedarsong Forest Kindergarten on Vashon Island in Washington, Erin Kenny's parent information includes suggestions on specific brands of waterproof boots, rain pants, and outerwear that keeps children comfortable. Keeping track of mittens and keeping mittens on children's hands are problems in all nature-based early childhood programs in cold climates and so mittens are always a hot topic at teacher gatherings. (Mittens with long zips are one solution.)

Resilience? This takes us back to the academics versus social skills discussion. Being outdoors during challenging weather provides all kinds of problem-solving challenges—finding warm spots on cold days, older children helping younger children zip their coats, figuring out how to make a roof on the shelter that keeps the rain out. These hard-won successes are sweeter when children participate in achieving them. This breeds the kind of social competence and readiness to learn that are the long-term keys to success. American parents need to understand what they're buying into before they sign the tuition contract.

5. Concept of Nature

The less we face the elements of nature, the more we tend to romanticize it. Many Americans go everywhere in their cars. Europeans walk and bike more, and outdoor experience is a more integral part of their lives. Therefore, they know more what it means to be outdoors for four hours twice a week year-round. American parents often expect a piece of paradise from the program. They expect everything to be harmonious and are surprised by the raw nature of the program, both the rawness of the weather and the rawness of the emotions.

We've addressed parents' surprise at the rawness of the weather above, so let's consider the rawness of emotions here. Due to the underlying "Garden of Eden" preconception about nature, parents are surprised to realize that there are conflicts and a lot of physical interaction. Allowing stick play, for instance, means that sometimes conflict and therefore anger and upsetness emerges. In the *School's Out* video about a Swiss school, there's a scene of boys throwing pinecones at each other. In another scene, a teacher comforts a child who got a bit scorched being too close to the fire. A scene from Claire Warden's (2013) Scottish video, *Outdoor Learning: A Year in Auchlone*, opens with a child curled up sobbing on the ground after a disagreement with another boy. The educator comforts the boy, facilitates the conversation about the disagreement, and the boys go off happily to continue playing. The crux is the need for educators and directors to be honest about the rawness of the experience and the value of the rawness. The goal is not to eliminate emotional ups and downs in children's lives, but to understand that these ups and downs are normal and can be dealt with.

5. Concept of Nature	
American attitudes	**Challenges**
Parents romanticize nature.	Nature as paradise is not the whole picture.
Nature as the wonder drug.	Parents did not count on "inconvenience" of nature.
All parents want their child to be a Forest Gnome on a beautiful, golden fall day.	Unexpected rawness of experience on emotional level.

6. Concept of Childhood

My perspective is that Europeans sometimes think that American parents put their children on a pedestal. (Think of how often parents call their daughters "princess," how they kowtow to every whim.) The parental goal of providing a perfect childhood sounds wonderful, but it comes with a big price for the children. This can lead to children becoming indulged, spoiled, and insensitive to the needs of others.

Forest Gnomes educators often experience parents who find it hard to stand back and let their child work through conflicts. They intervene too quickly and in doing so stymie opportunities for their child's growth and development of a group role.

6. Concept of Childhood in Europe and the United States	
Europe	**United States**
Childhood is an important part of life and prepares children for later stages of growing up.	Childhood is glorified as the time in life when everything should be perfect.
Children have to adjust to the adult world.	Parents adjust to the child's world, and children are catered to.
Children are freer and more independent.	Children are micromanaged and constantly watched.

The big message, then, is that forest kindergartens aren't just about providing a nature-based experience for children, but also about a different teaching and learning style. Programs need to make a conscious effort to educate parents about the joys and challenges of committing to this kind of educational experience. As we've seen, installing a European paradigm in American culture always comes with some resistance. Therefore, one of the compromises they have made at Natick is that though many European children attend these programs four to five half or full days a week, Forest Gnomes educators find that a two-day program works well for their parents.

To summarize the recommendations of both the Forest Gnomes educators and myself, here are some strategies for shaping the American species of the European forest kindergarten:

1. **Educate parents, educators, and policy makers about the benefits of the forest kindergarten concept.** Emphasize the potential cognitive, social, and emotional benefits to most children.
2. **Communicate clearly about what forest kindergarten is, and what it is not.** It is an opportunity to help children to be healthy, develop bonds with the earth, and prepare for formal schooling. It is not the answer to each and every child and family problem.
3. **Demystify and deglorify the forest kindergarten experience.** It won't always be a bluebird autumn day. Children will most often, but not always, want to go to school. They will come home wet and muddy.
4. **Match families with the right programs.** A forest kindergarten program will be right for a lot of children; it won't be right for all children. Be cautious about being overly inclusive and trying to "help" all children. Be ready to encourage parents to consider other options.
5. **Be sure parents are 100 percent on board.** Develop good parent handbooks. Have parents visit the program on wet and cold days. Develop questionnaires that help parents figure out if they're willing to make the commitment before signing the tuition agreement.

To be clear, there are challenges and joys, and when the match is right, parents are thrilled and exuberant. One parent of a child at the Juniper Hill School in Maine commented, "I'm in tears most days. It is really amazing stuff."

And a parent of a Forest Gnome recently said,

> The canopy of trees above, the pine needles beneath their feet, smoke from the fire scenting the air, and the children right at home with the simplest things—pinecones, sticks, stones, sand, shovels—these are their rudimentary toys . . . Unplugged time with the sensory experience of the forest and the secure comfort offered by her teachers. Her imagination is free and wild, her body is exploring its full range of movement, and her face is alight with joy.

When it works, it really works.

CHAPTER 5

The Sticks and Stones of Curriculum Development

The Great Sadness

The great sadness of early childhood education in twenty-first-century America is the collapsing of the curriculum from wholeness to narrowness, from hands, heart, and head to just the head. From Saint Francis of Assisi to Johann Heinrich Pestalozzi to Friedrich Fröebel to Rudolph Steiner to Maria Montessori to John Dewey to Claire Warden, there's been a constant reaffirmation of the need for early childhood education (well, all education really) to address the whole child, not just the right hand or the neocortex. But currently, narrow-minded ideologues have somehow seized the podium and have declared, "Though shalt learn your letters and numbers, above all else! Play and wonder be banished." And many kindergarten teachers, and yes, even preschool teachers, are knuckling under and paying homage to the worksheet gods. Songs and stories, recess and recreation are jettisoned in favor of phonemic awareness and test preparation. Woe is us!

Nature preschool and forest kindergarten advocates are but one faction of resisters committed to resurrecting wholeness in early childhood education. It's important to understand the nature-based early childhood movement as part of the larger cultural movement to bring early childhood education back to its roots. This is an old battle, which has been fought over and over through the centuries. When Swiss education reformer Johann Heinrich Pestalozzi abolished flogging in his schools in the early nineteenth century, the arbiters of educational culture were shocked. But Pestalozzi realized that love of the children we educate is "the sole and everlasting foundation" in which to work: "Without love, neither the physical nor the intellectual powers will develop naturally" (Kilpatrick 1951,viii). Aren't endless worksheets a form of mental flogging that squash the development of children's physical and intellectual powers?

Providing a broader context, Pestalozzi (quoted in Silber 1965) asserted,

I wish to wrest education from the outworn order of doddering old teaching hacks as well as from the new-fangled order of cheap, artificial teaching tricks, and entrust it to the eternal powers of nature herself. (134)

Doesn't this sound alarmingly familiar? Kilpatrick (1951) expanded on Pestalozzi to say,

As "a little seed . . . contains the design of the tree," so in each child is the promise of his potentiality. "The educator only takes care that no untoward influence shall disturb nature's march of developments." (viii)

But what did Pestalozzi mean by entrusting education "to the eternal powers of nature?" What are the evolutionary principles at work in children that nature-based early childhood educators need to adhere to? How do we protect and nourish the little acorn so that it may grow into a steadfast oak?

Nature's March of Developments

The goal in this chapter is to articulate the underpinnings and practice of developmentally appropriate curriculum in nature-based early childhood settings. Through examining some evolutionary theory and accounts of childhood in traditional hunting and gathering cultures, we'll develop a sense of how the young child is biologically programmed to develop in concert with the natural world.

Let's go back a number of decades. In 1972 I helped to start the Harrisville School, now the Harrisville Children's Center, an early childhood center for children ages six weeks to six years. At that time, it was a bit lost and lonely, up a long dead-end road in an old carriage barn on a crumbling estate. There weren't grade level expectations and assessment targets for our preschoolers and kindergartners. Instead, our goals were to balance a reasonable dose of beginning reading, 'riting, and 'rithmetic with rhythm, 'rtistry, and rambling in the woods.

Two children's activities from that time illustrate the force of nature, our evolutionary heritage, expressing itself through the children's play. These activities weren't taught or modeled for the children by adults. Instead, they unfolded spontaneously, sparked by the landscape and the moment. In my early years of teaching, the first activity, drawn from my old journals, involved a group of about ten boys.

22 April 1973

The ever-present spring drizzle had stopped just a few minutes before, so I decided to let the children go outside for recess. Granted they were going to get their feet wet, but it had been raining for too many days to keep them inside again. . . .

Brian and Chip gravitated to the waterworks area and began to create two dams, one above the other. This area is created where a small drainpipe empties out from underground onto a muddy hillside, and a child-sized rivulet courses down the hill, begging to be shaped. Regularly, two or three boys would play in this area. But today, because of the amplified volume of water coming from the pipe, a dozen different boys converged and a massive project began to take form.

The cooperation was admirable. Somehow, all the boys parceled themselves out into specific roles. Some tended the upper dam, some the lower one. There were channelizers, and two boys in charge of controlling the flow of water from the pipe. Then there were the mud and clay collectors preparing the materials for the dam tenders. It suggested many images of beavers and bees. The fascinating aspect was that no one was in charge. There were many conflicting ideas, lots of arguments about whether to heighten this dam, deepen this pool, when to let the water out of the pipe, but they were all worked out without a hitch. Everyone was caught up in the building, the mud and the clay, the flow of the water, the necessity to keep the dam strong. Frequently someone would warn, "Ten minutes till the flood!"

I let things go way past the end of recess, not wanting to intercede, but then finally told them that they'd have to bring things to an end. The consensus was to break down the dams. "Let the floodwaters go! Let the floodwaters go!" they chanted spontaneously. The dams were burst one after the other and the water poured down the hillside to everyone's great delight. I reminded everyone to wash, remove their muddy shoes, and come to the rug for discussion.

Family Nature Play. Children instinctively follow and dam small streams.

There's more to this story, but suffice it to say that there was some inherent primal play impulse expressed here. What child doesn't like to engineer miniature streams like this? How many zillions of times have you seen this at the beach, or after a rainstorm, or with mashed potatoes and gravy? Children aren't taught to do this; it rises out of them from some deep place.

The second activity was equally as spontaneous with no precedent. I walked out to the playground on a spring day a few years later and there was a group of about eight five- and six-year-old girls sitting in a self-organized circle. They each had a big flat rock on the ground in front of them, and then a rounder rock in their hands that they called their "pounders." On the big flat rock they had chunks of crumbly, soft schist that they'd collected from the nearby stone wall. They used their pounder rocks to mash the schist—they called it "making sand." And as they mashed, they were chanting, "Making sand, fast as we can. Making sand, fast as we can."

It looked exactly like a circle of women in a hunting and gathering culture macerating a root, or pounding a grain prior to cooking it. It was as if the old food preparation knowledge buried in their genetic heritage had risen spontaneously to the surface. Again, these girls hadn't seen their mothers do this activity, nor likely had seen National Geographic movies of traditional cultures. But here they were executing this age-old unity of body, raw materials, and song.

In both of these examples, it was as if these children had dropped back into their wild selves. They were completely immersed in the mud, the rock, the water, the repetitive pounding, unfazed by getting wet and dirty, and completely happy to be at one with the elements. I'd contend that this is what Pestalozzi meant by "nature's march of developments." This is children following their instincts to interact with, shape, and transform the natural world, just as children have done in traditional hunting and gathering cultures for millennia. Yes, we need to acculturate children to life in a modern, technological world, but we also need to have them bond with the earth so they can learn to balance ecology with technology. Nature preschools and forest kindergartens aspire to this balance.

Evolution as Pedagogy

We can learn a lot about normal child development, and the kind of activity we want to encourage in nature-based early childhood settings, by looking at childhoods in traditional hunting and gathering societies. Most anthropologists agree that the major shift in human cultural patterns occurred about twelve thousand years ago with the agrarian revolution, a shift from hunting and gathering as the dominant form of food provision to agriculture and animal husbandry. Hunters and gatherers hunted for game and gathered wild plants and roots. They moved seasonally to take advantage of patterns in animal distribution and plant availability. Agrarian cultures stayed in one place and created food by planting crops and raising animals.

Prior to the agrarian revolution, from as long as two hundred thousand years ago when our species Homo sapiens emerged, humans lived in hunting and gathering cultures. That means that approximately 95 percent of our genetic evolution occurred when we existed as hunters and gatherers. Therefore, the behaviors and culture of hunting and gathering peoples are imprinted into our genetic heritage and our early behavior. I contend that we can understand children's behavior, and develop appropriate curriculum for children, by looking at hunting and gathering childhoods. What were the relationships like between child, mother, and other significant adults, and how can we simulate those in early childhood programs? How did children play? And how can we encourage these kinds of natural play? How did adults instruct children in the ways of the culture and can we use some of these traditional practices to breath life into our work with children? Yes, of course, we now live in a postmodern technological world and children need to be literate and computer savvy. But perhaps we get to mature behavior by honoring the early stages of primitive, preindustrial behavior and sensibilities.

For an example, let's look at many traditional children's games— games that occur with different names, but exactly the same forms— all around the world. Capture the flag, hide and seek, tag, and kick the can are all essentially predator-prey games that functioned in traditional societies as ways to acculturate children, especially boys, to the skills and requirements of being a good hunter. Even today, these games develop physical competence, teach patience, encourage rule-bound behavior, and value cunning and innovative thinking. When we discourage running and tag games on the playground, which is happening in many schools, we cut children off from their instinctive drive to physical activity and we cultivate a culture of obesity. Regardless of whether developing hunting skills is a requisite part of modern culture, it is important to encourage children to have physically active childhoods in preparation for an adult life that balances physical fitness with cognitive competence.

In *Nature and Madness*, originally published in 1982, cultural anthropologist Paul Shepard (1998a) succinctly describes the stages of childhood development in hunter/gatherer cultures, both in the past and in the few remaining examples that exist today.

Infancy and toddlerhood:

The experience of such a world is initially that the mother is always there . . . a presence in the tactile warmth of her body. For the infant there is a joyful comfort in being handled and fondled often, fed and cleaned as the body demands. From the start is a world of variation on rhythms, the refreshment of hot and cold, wind like a breath in the face, the smell and feel of rain and snow, earth in hand and underfoot. The world is a soft sound-surround of gentle voices, human, cricket and bird music. (9)

For three- to four-year-olds:

Now the child goes to the fringes of the camp to play at foraging. Play is an imitation, starting with simple fleeing and catching, going on to mimic joyfully the important animals, being them for a moment and then not being them, feeling as this one must feel and then that one, all tried on the self. The child sees the adults dancing the animal movements and does it too. Music itself has been there all the time, from his mother's song to the melodies of birds and the howls of wolves. (10)

For five- to six-year-olds:

The child goes out from camp with adults to forage and with playmates to imitate foraging. The adults show no anxiety in their hunting, only patience; one waits and watches and listens. Sometimes the best is not to be found, but there is always something. The world is all clues. There is no end to the subtlety and delicacy of the clues. The signs that reveal are always there. One has only to learn the art of reading them. There is discomfort that cannot be avoided. The

Wild Roots Forest School. Harvesting wild edibles, with adult guidance, is an appropriate early childhood activity.

Wild Roots Forest
School. Collecting
natural plant materials
for work and play.

child sees with pride that he can endure it, that his body
profits by it so that on beautiful days he feels wonderful. He
witnesses sickness and death. But they are right as part of
things and not really prevalent. (10)

For seven- to eleven-year-olds:

The child is free. He is not asked to work. At first he can
climb and splash and dig and explore the infinite riches
about him. In time he increasingly wants to make things

and to understand that which he cannot touch or change, to wonder about that which is unseen. His world is full of stories told, hearing of a recent hunt, tales of renowned events, and epics with layers of meaning. (10–11)

Herein lies the skeleton of a curriculum for nature-based early childhood programs. From the protected world of infancy, to immersion in the sensory world in toddlerhood, to the glad animal movements of three- to four-year-olds, to hunting, foraging, and understanding clues at five and six, this is what the genetic impulse drives young children to do, and it represents the kind of experiences we should be providing for children.

We can put some flesh on these bones with the recollections of Charles A. Eastman (1902), a Dartmouth-educated physician who spent his first fifteen years growing up in a traditional hunting and gathering band of Sioux tribesmen in the 1870s and 1880s. Describing his education, he recounts,

> My uncle . . . was a strict disciplinarian and a good teacher. When I left the teepee in the morning, he would say: "Hadakah [Charles's Sioux name], look closely to everything you see"; and at evening, on my return, he used often to catechize me for an hour or so.
>
> "On which side of the trees is the lighter-colored bark? On which side do they have the most regular branches?"
>
> It was his custom to let me name all the new birds that I had seen during the day. I would name them according to the color or the shape of the bill or their song or the appearance and locality of the nest—in fact, anything about the bird that impressed me as characteristic. (52–53)

This is an apt illustration of "the world being all clues," as Shepard describes above. The child's mind is tuned to be sensitive to changes in the natural world at this age, and it's the kind of curriculum that children warm to. At Juniper Hill School, the teachers start the day soliciting these kinds of observations from the children. "I liked finding the eel at Deer Meadow Brook. It was scary! It was a whole inch thick." "I noticed the leaves are starting to sound crinkly as we walked down from the Welcoming Place." "At Chewonki, we got to touch the salamander eggs. They felt like jello!" Notice that these comments express children's close sensory attunement to the natural world. But also notice the seeds of math and literacy here—the eel being an inch thick, the elaboration of vocabulary, simile in salamander eggs feeling like jello. By rooting young children's curriculum in the lived, richly sensate natural world, we forge a person–world empathy and we develop the foundation of cognitive skills.

From Narrowness to Wholeness

The dismissing of play from many preschool and kindergarten programs over the past two decades has led to the diminishment of the early childhood experience for children, parents, and teachers. This regretful development, and the alternative, is effectively articulated in a report from the Alliance for Childhood, *Crisis in the Kindergarten: Why Children Need to Play in School*.

> Skepticism about the value of play is compounded by the widespread assumption that the earlier children begin to master the basic elements of reading, such as phonics and letter recognition, the more likely they are to succeed in school. And so kindergarten education has become heavily focused on teaching literacy and other academic skills, and preschool is rapidly following suit. (Miller and Almon 2009, 1)

Miller and Almon continue on to say that this "didactic teaching of discrete skills in phonics, decoding, and word recognition . . . may yield short-term gains in test scores in the early grades," but it pales in significance to the alternative, "the deeper experiential learning whose benefits last into fourth grade and beyond."

In critique of this narrow-minded approach toward an emphasis on reading skills, Miller and Almon cite two failures of early reading instruction. Their first example is this:

> Reading First, the $6 billion federal program designed to help children from low-income families, greatly increased the amount of time children spent being taught discrete prereading skills in kindergarten and the early grades, but failed to improve reading comprehension. (2)

In contrast, other research shows that children who engage in complex forms of socio-dramatic play have greater language skills, better social skills, and more empathy and imagination than non-socio-dramatic players. They also show more self-control and higher levels of thinking. Do we really want to sacrifice the development of thoughtful, more socially competent children for temporary upticks in test scores?

An extensive research project from Germany is even more compelling:

> Long-term research casts doubt on the assumption that starting earlier on the teaching of phonics and other discrete skills leads to better results. For example, most of the play-based kindergartens in Germany were changed into centers for cognitive achievement during a wave of educational "reform" in the 1970s. But research comparing 50 play-based classes with 50 early-learning centers found that by age ten the children who had played excelled over the others in a host of ways. They were more advanced in reading and mathematics and they were better adjusted socially and emotionally in school. They excelled in creativity and intelligence, oral expression and "industry." As a result of this study, German kindergartens returned to being play-based again. (Miller and Almon 2009, 2)

It shouldn't be surprising to recall that Germany now has more than one thousand forest kindergartens, based on this principle of supporting a healthy dose of socio-dramatic construction and physical play every day.

As opposed to the atomistic focus on too-early reading, 'riting, and 'rithmetic, nature-based preschool programs aspire to a curriculum of holism, hands, heart, and head. Yes, I've added a fourth H here to the traditional three Hs that have been at the core of progressive education for almost the last three centuries.

I've added holism, to acknowledge the understanding of ecology and human interdependence with the ecosystem that has developed in the past forty years since the original Earth Day. Whereas for John Dewey the school was a laboratory for democracy, nowadays the school also needs to be a laboratory for earth citizenship. The foundation for this earth citizenship is appropriately laid in nature preschools and forest kindergartens. Just as Pestalozzi said that love of the children is the foundation of education, we need to teach love of the earth as well. This love of the earth, along with the development

Head
Development of cognitive skills, such as literacy and numeracy, and a willingness to apply oneself to solving problems

Heart
Development of a deep-felt sense of empathy, reciprocity and love of family, friends and others

Hands
Development of physical competence in the body and an understanding of how to make things with one's hands in the physical world

Holism
Development of a spiritual sense of unity between self and the natural world and all its creatures

of the physical body and the development of interpersonal love and compassion, are precursors to the development of cognitive skills. A kindergarten filled to the brim with phonemic awareness and devoid of costumes, fingerplays, and natural world romps is a factory rather than a school.

Striking a Healthy Balance

The curriculum in healthy nature preschools and forest kindergartens should neither be all free-form or all teacher directed. Though with younger children it may be fine to err in the direction of open-ended play, there will always be some measure of scheduled orderliness, group activities, dining protocol, and teacher-organized curriculum. In their Alliance for Childhood report, Miller and Almon (2009, 4)

Laissez-Faire, Loosely Structured Classroom	Classroom Rich in Child-Initiated Play	Playful Classroom with Focused Learning	Didactic, Highly Structured Classroom
Ample play but without active adult support, often resulting in chaos	Exploring the world through play with the active presence of teachers	Teachers guiding learning with rich, experiential activities	Teacher-led instruction, including scripted teaching, with little or no play

A conceptual model for Kindergarten curriculum. From *Crisis in the Kindergarten: Why Children Need to Play in School* (Miller and Almon 2009, 5).

describe the "healthy balance" that we should aspire to, saying, "Kindergartners need a balance of child-initiated play in the presence of engaged teachers and more focused experiential learning guided by teachers." To elaborate they cite researchers Elena Bodrova and Deborah Leong (2005, as cited in Miller and Almon 2009), who say,

> In our experiences, we have found that both extremely chaotic classrooms and extremely teacher-directed classrooms are counterproductive to developing self-regulation and other underlying skills in children. Classrooms where children flit from activity to activity support reactive behavior. But when all instruction is whole-group, students become too teacher-regulated. (4)

The diagram above from the *Crisis in the Kindergarten* report suggests the options for curriculum conceptualization.

For the purposes of looking at curriculum in nature preschools and forest kindergartens, we'll have to consider the "classroom" in this continuum as including the outdoor playscapes and forests that serve as the learning environment at least 50 percent of the time. With this in mind, let's look at five examples of "curriculum" that fall along this continuum, examining the pros and cons of all four of these categories.

Juniper Hill School, Alna, Maine

25 March 2013, 28°F at 8 a.m., warming quickly

Knickerbocker Breaker

The day starts with a community sing—local folksingers, all the teachers and children, and some parents. Many of the songs have been modified to reference the Sheepscot River Valley and Alna's ecology. And most of the songs are seasonally specific, about what's happening right now as spring emerges slowly from winter.

> *Mud in the road, wind in my hair,*
> *Mud in the road and I don't care*
> *Snow in the shadows,*
> *But the fields are bare.*
>
> *Sap buckets hanging from a sugar maple tree,*
> *Wild things stirring where no one can see*
> *A big mud puddle that's waiting for me,*
> *And the big black crow is cawing, cawing.*

All the song lyrics are carefully chosen to convey both the children's lived experience as well as specific natural history content of the moment—the differential rates of snow melt in the forest shadows versus in the fields, pussy willows emerging, returning redwing blackbirds. I'd call this **Playful Classroom with Focused Learning**—playfulness in the song and guided movement, focused learning in the content intended to teach seasonal change and phenology.

After snack, everyone dons solid outdoor gear—The Big Five: snow pants, jackets, boots, gloves, hats—and the teacher brings them to a section of the Porcupine Woods that they've just recently started to explore for Outdoor Explorations. There's still six inches of thawing snow on the ground, making surfaces suitably slippery. The children have requested Knickerbocker Breaker, their name for both a place and what would appear to many observers to be a highly risky activity. (The name comes from *Swallows and Amazons* by Arthur Ransome, a British children's book about children adventuring in the landscape fairly unfettered.)

Knickerbocker Breaker, the place, is a schisty ridge fifty feet long, dropping off about twenty feet on one side. The face is more vertical on the near end, and gets more gradual as you proceed along the ridge.

Knickerbocker Breaker, the activity, is about finding different butt-sliding pathways down the face of the ledge. They've been here before so they know the routine. The children clamber along the top until they find the level of challenge they're comfortable with and then start sliding.

Elsa chooses a steep option, plops down, and rockets down the ledge, sliding on melting snow, muddy leaves, peeling moss, bouncing over protrusions. My eyes widen. Is this within the category of "safe danger"? At the bottom she jumps up, giggles, and heads around to climb back up to the top of the ledge.

Zoe sits at the top of an even steeper route. It looks like a double black diamond to my downhill skiing sensibilities. "Lots of fun to try to slide right between those two little trees," she announces. I hold my breath. She plummets down, launches out over

Ottauquechee Public School Forest Fridays program, Quechee, VT. What child doesn't love to otter slide?

a rocky lip and goes airborne, hits the ground and pitches forward, landing on her belly, face mushed into the leafy snow. I grimace in empathic pain and anticipate the crying. But she jumps up and brushes herself off. Her teacher, Anne, has been watching attentively.

"How did that feel?" Anne queries.

"Good, but freaky." Zoe responds. She also clambers back up to the top of the ledge. At the top she grabs another girl by the arm and exclaims, "Audrey, I found the best one!" And she does that same *good, but freaky,* and a little bit dangerous, slide six more times, with increasing finesse each time.

There's much that's instructive in this edgy, ledgy vignette. Using the Kindergarten Continuum above, this might fall in the **Laissez-Faire, Loosely Structured Classroom** category. But in a half hour of Knickerbocker Breakers no one is the worse for wear, in fact they're all exhilarated from the challenge and the speed and probably healthier for it. It reminds me of how I feel after a morning of challenging skiing where I am in my zone of proximal development—slightly above my skill level and appropriately challenged.

I could argue that this activity, and the composite structure of Outdoor Explorations, is more in the **Classroom Rich in Child-Initiated Play** category. Anne is supervising this activity conscientiously, she is "actively present," and there's been a lot of discussion about appropriate risk versus too much risk. It's an integral part of the curriculum to encourage the children to learn to assess risk, that it's okay to push yourself a bit, but not too much. The goal is for children to learn initiative and self-confidence. Note that when Zoe gets flung face down, Anne does not say, "Are you hurt?" or "Don't do that again, that's too dangerous," or "Don't worry, I'll take care of you." She encourages the child to self-assess the situation and decide for herself whether she wants to repeat it or not. Anne has determined that this is "safe danger," that this is "risk with benefits" and therefore worth supporting.

I'd argue that Knickerbocker Breaker and Juniper Hill's Outdoor Exploration component of the curriculum is probably in the **Classroom Rich in Child-Initiated Play** category, but tilting toward the **Laissez-Faire** end of the continuum. Or perhaps we should create another in-between category of **Safe Danger Child-Initiated Exploration** for forest kindergartens that implies attentive supervision but an openness to child-initiated experiences that we adults might balk at, but might be really beneficial in terms of engendering grit and independence in children.

Arcadia Nature Preschool, Easthampton, Massachusetts

27 November 2012, 30°F at 9 a.m. A light dusting of snow, one of the first snowfalls of the year last night

Squirrels versus Snow

Located on a Massachusetts Audubon Society sanctuary, Arcadia Nature Preschool is one of the earliest nature preschools in the country. It's been around for thirty-five years, and its exemplary practices have inspired many other nature centers to follow in their footsteps. It's housed in a small but comfortable separate building and surrounded by river floodplain meadows, easily explore-able woods, and old farm buildings. There's a simple nature playground made with natural materials. Indoors, it's similar to the Dodge Nature Center Preschool in West Saint Paul, but simpler and more homegrown. There's a dollhouse, a water table, baskets of stuffed animals and bumpy squash, bird silhouettes on the wall. Plasticine, paint, and Legos are available. Children cuddle a pet guinea pig.

The theme for the week is squirrels and so the morning circle songs and guided movement are squirrel related.

> *Gray squirrel, gray squirrel,*
> *Swish your bushy tail.*

Children scurry like little squirrels from one side of the circle to the other. Teachers read a set of clues—"bushy tail for balance and warmth," "nest of sticks in tree," and the children have to guess which animal these clues represent.

For the first choice time, there's painting with ferns, dollhouse play, Legos, and a squirrel walk. Four choose to go for the walk. Chloe (name changed) the teacher drapes a set of binoculars around each child's neck and gives each child a clipboard with an observation sheet to record squirrel activity. (Can four-year-olds actually record written or drawn squirrel observations, I wonder?) The children don jackets, hats, and gloves, but no one has snow pants. After some instruction in how to use binoculars, the children head outside. "Let's see if we can see some squirrels and some squirrel tracks!" encourages the teacher.

Quickly, one of the children puts the binoculars to his eyes and realizes "the problem is, when you look through the binoculars, you can't see where you're going and you bump into things." He leaves them dangling around his neck.

But, lo and behold, there's not a squirrel to be seen, not a glimpse of a bushy tail, nary a track. In the meantime, the children are really excited about the dusting of snow (the first snow!) frosting everything. The thin layer on the boardwalk makes for great sliding if you take a few running strides and then glide. Another child is making shuffling steps, plowing up little mounds of snow in front of her boots. Other children are dragging their gloved hands along the railing, enjoying the way the plowed snow cascades down from the sides of the railing. The affordance here is the snow and all the things children can do with it.

Chloe is still focused on squirrels, and so to fill the void she offers some squirrel natural history. "Anyone ever seen a squirrel with its tail on its back to help it keep warm?" None of the children respond. One of the children gets interested in brushing off all the snow that has adhered to the nature trail signage.

In the meantime, the other children have picked up on the affordance of the snow on the boardwalk. "Ice skating!" exclaim the children as they choo-choo back and forth on the boardwalk like trains. The clipboards have been abandoned; the binoculars hang forlornly around their necks.

Undaunted, Chloe wraps up. "Well tomorrow, we'll see differences between what squirrels do when it's snowy and when it's sunny." The children would be happy to keep sliding, but Chloe brings them inside after about ten or fifteen minutes outside.

A bit later in the morning, Chloe takes a different group outside. She leaves the binoculars and clipboards behind. She takes the children to a part of the parking lot that has been not been walked or driven on; it's a palette of fresh snow. She has one child take a few steps and then turn around and walk back.

"What kind of shapes can you see in Melinda's tracks? The children bend over and peer closely.

"Diamonds. Circles. I see little waves!" they exclaim. Then one child looks at his own tracks. "Hey, mine has lots of back and forth arrows," he says, describing the herringbone pattern in his boot. They realize that each of their tracks is different.

Over in the thicket of small sumacs and maples, the children start running and weaving through the saplings. Chloe suggests, "Let's become squirrels and scamper on all fours from one side to the other, looking for food." With no more prompting, they drop to all fours and become squirrels, making little chittery sounds, dusting the snow aside to find seeds to pretend to nibble on. The kids/squirrels are in the palm of her hand.

On the natural play structures, one child plows the snow off the elevated grooved log to make it easier to walk along. Another child delicately licks the snow off of a rope handrail. When snowballs start happening Chloe reminds them that "we don't throw snowballs at people, but it's okay to throw snowballs at trees." That keeps a couple of boys busy for a while.

When one the girls exclaims, "Hey, let's make a snowman," I explain that there really isn't enough snow to make a big snowman, but we could make tiny snowmen. We plop down on the grooved log and I fashion a tiny snowman with twig arms and legs, probably only about three inches tall. She tries to make one herself, but it requires too much fine-motor dexterity. I give her mine and she cradles it in her hands. I'm tickled when her parents arrive to pick her up and she brings the mini snowman home with her.

Now for the curriculum analysis. We've all been here before: The great idea falls flat, the best laid plans of mice and men scatter. Where there were dozens of squirrels yesterday, there are nada today. With apologies to this fine teacher for making an example of her, I'd contend that the first squirrel walk was in the **Didactic, Highly Structured Classroom** mode. Yes they were outside, but this was fairly straightforward teacher-directed instruction. And forgive me for harping on developmental appropriateness but . . . observation sheets while walking with four-year-olds? Better to become squirrels and mimic with our bodies rather than try to observe them and write or draw your observations. And likely it was my presence that led to the teacher's focus on the squirrel agenda and her overlooking of the dusting of snow opportunities that the children responded to implicitly.

To her credit, Chloe reflected on what unfolded and moved back along the continuum to a **Playful Classroom with Focused Learning** approach for her second walk. She realized that children wanted to play with the snow, but she provided guided learning of experiential activities. The children wouldn't have focused on patterns in their own tracks by themselves, but were intrigued via this scaffolded activity. And what a great precursor to looking at squirrel tracks sometime in the future. She seized on children's fascination with becoming animals (rather than observing them) and the children became squirrels foraging for food. They'll be more attentive to squirrels' foraging behavior next time they see them and might observe, "Hey, they're finding seeds in the snow just like we did." And she may even have been back in **Classroom Rich in Child-Initiated Play** mode when she allowed snowball making and throwing, but just gave it a bit of form. Chloe was able to put her own plans aside and see the virtue in recognizing the affordances of the moment (the first snow) and honoring and giving form to child-initiated experiences. This is the mark of a reflective nature-based early childhood educator. The Arcadia educators are well respected for their abilities to tailor their programs to the bird in the window or the squirrel on the limb.

Dodge Nature Center, West Saint Paul, Minnesota

October 2009 about 50°F and bright and sunny

A Tribute to Lori Caramel

Sometimes a piece of curriculum starts and ends with a teacher-directed **Playful Classroom with Focused Learning** impulse. The initial spark doesn't occur in the child, but in the inside or outside world of the school. The following example is drawn from The Willow Room, the five-year-olds' morning class at the Dodge Nature Preschool.

Many nature-based early childhood programs have been enriched through their embracing of the Reggio Emilia approach. One of the salient components of this approach is a commitment to documentation of children's work and the curriculum of the school, often done in an artistic fashion integrating children's drawings, teacher narrative, transcripts of conversations, and photography. At Dodge Nature Preschool, the teachers document their curriculum using this Reggio approach. They create large, almost three feet by four feet, laminated posters documenting Following the Owl, The New Lamb, One Day a Week at the Creek, and other curriculum projects. This narrative is drawn from a poster created by Mary Temple, one of the teachers. Here I incorporate some of the teachers' and children's descriptive language documented by Mary with some of my own reflections.

One morning, *The Willow Room* teachers arrived at school to find that Lori Caramel, the classroom chicken, had died. Lori's body was placed in a box, and the decision was made to bring the children together as a group to talk about what happened.

As the children enter the classroom and begin their day, a few notice that Lori's cage is empty, and they ask where she is. The teachers tell them that Lori died in the night. The news "Lori died" spreads quietly through the classroom.

When the class comes together as a group, (Teacher) Britney explains that Lori had been sick and was an old chicken. Several children share stories of their own pets who have died and family members they have lost. For other children, Lori's death is their first experience with the topic of death. We decide that we will bury Lori in the Butterfly Garden that morning. After the discussion, Britney reads *The Dead Bird* by Margaret Wise Brown.

Here, the teacher truly is taking the lead and scaffolding an opportunity before the children even know that they have a need. The death of a classroom animal is a common occurrence, and savvy teachers recognize that it's important to signify the passing and is an opportunity to teach about life and death. One of the deep principles of ecological learning is an emphasis on cycles, recognizing that all creatures live and die. There is no virtue, and it is perhaps a disservice, in shielding children from death.

Dodge Nature Preschool. Decorating rocks in honor of Lori Caramel.

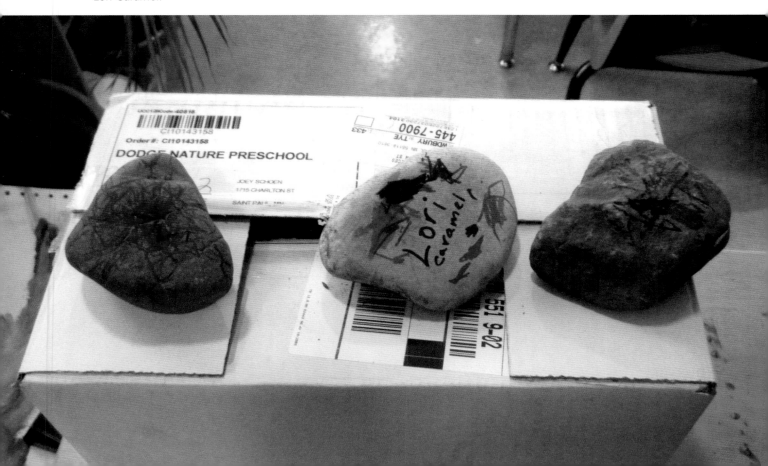

Before going outside, the children decorate rocks in honor of Lori. Some draw pictures on their rocks, some dictate messages from teachers to write on their rocks. (Teacher) Melanie goes to the garden to start digging the hole. She is soon joined by several children who help her dig.

It is now time for the burial. Quinn and Delia carefully carry the box containing Lori's body outside. Greta, Miranda, and Delia carry out the basket of rocks to be placed on Lori's grave.

Creating the rock memories and helping with digging are thoughtful examples of teachers "guiding learning with rich experiential activities." The teachers understand the need to channel the children's sadness and fear into something they can do with their hands and bodies. And what a nice touch to have two of the children carry the box with her body, rather than having an adult do this. This way, the children take part in the honoring of the dead.

At the burial site, the children are given the chance to touch Lori and stroke her feathers. She is placed gently in the hole and everyone helps to cover her with soil. One of the children, Miranda, initiates a song,

> *The rooster is dead, the rooster is dead, they said, they said.*
> *He used to crow in the morning, in the barnyard shed,*
> *Cock-a-doodle doo, cock-a-doodle doo,*
> *Cock-a-doodle doo doo.*

Following the burial, a few words are spoken about Lori Caramel.

Z: You were quite beautiful when you were alive.

R: It's a nice place for her. You can see the farm. We will always remember what happened today.

L: How do we know she's dead? Are her eyes closed?

R: Some chickens have their eyes closed when they are dead and some have them open.

RB: Why did Lori die? Where is Lori?

G: She got sick and old.

This combination of the child-initiated song and the teacher-created opportunity for children to say eulogies is an example of striking the right balance between free-form learning and teacher direction. The teachers are providing the vessel, the form for

Dodge Nature Preschool. Honoring Lori Caramel at the burial site.

mourning, and each child gets to express his or her appreciation, questions, and sadness.

Before the morning ends, a group of children put a rock in the box that Lori's body had been in. They pretend that the rock is Lori.

Z *(excitedly):* Let's pretend that Lori didn't die!

I: Yeah! Then we'll feel better.

Z: It's really just a rock.

I: Yeah. It's really just a rock.

Opportunities to replay the experience help the children acclimate to the chicken's passing. When the emotional processing is not given a form, it lurks beneath the surface unexpressed.

The Dodge teachers anticipated the children's need to mourn. They provided an open-ended script that became a vessel for feelings and a powerful learning experience. Death as curriculum is one of the unique opportunities in nature-based early childhood.

Sabot at Stony Point Preschool and Kindergarten, Richmond, Virginia

November–December 2012

The Dead Log Debate

Sabot at Stony Point is a prekindergarten through eighth grade progressive, independent school located on a historic twenty-eight-acre estate. It's located within the city limits of Richmond, Virginia, but also sits next to one hundred acres of neighboring wooded parkland. There are tall pines and many trees downed by a powerful hurricane. The woods include a long, thin, shallow valley with steep banks and a rocky bottom for exploring. The children call it "the creek" and refer to the wooded area as "the forest."

The Sabot early childhood teachers practice within the Reggio tradition and have thought deeply about how the forest replaces the function of the traditional Reggio "piazza" in their curriculum. (See extended discussion of this idea in chapter 8.) Each year they find themselves committing to more time in the forest piazza. Because of their Reggio orientation, they also conscientiously document the forest goings-on. Recognizing that it's "not just play" going on out there, one of the teachers documented the following environmental debate that emerged over a series of forest days. Mauren Campbell, a teacher, describes,

During our visits to the forest, a decomposing tree has become the source of fascination for most of the children. They chip away at its wet bark for long periods, engrossed in scraping away as much as they can. (The tree is broken at the height of four feet with the rest of its twenty-five-foot trunk supported on one end by the stump and with the other end resting on the ground.) For several weeks, a group of boys has been intent on loosing the tree from its "main support" so that instead of being propped up on one end, the tree will fall flat and roll to a rest.

However, on the other end of the tree, where it rests on the ground, both a chocolate factory and an archeological dig, complete with a history exhibit, have been established. Its workers often offer "pieces of chocolate" to teachers or call them over to look at the newest "piece of history" that has been found. The projects at either end of the tree continued simultaneously and harmoniously

Sabot at Stony Point. Chocolate factory at one end of the decomposing tree and dislodging action at the other end.

until today, when Nora (one of the chocolate factory girls) demanded that the deconstruction of the stump end of the tree stop. The following dialogue ensued:

> **Nora:** It will squish us all. (If they are successful in dislodging it)
>
> **Luke:** Then you should get out.
>
> **Nora:** We're trying to keep it. (By which she means that she and Lydia have been propping up sticks perpendicular to the trunk of the tree to hold it in place to prevent it from rolling over should the boys be successful in freeing the trunk from the stump.)

Drew: If you get out of the way and you're here, it could make a big burst of dirt come up and be like heaven.

Nora: But it's part of the forest. (Meaning they like it just the way it is.)

Luke: It's already fallen. Somebody chopped it down. Maybe Hurricane Sandy.

Now Nora, who senses that her pleas are falling on deaf ears, solicits support from other children.

Nora: Besides, Stella and Sophia (chocolate factory workers) are older than you.

Sophia: It's true.

Stella: It's true. People like climbing on the tree (meaning walking along the pitched top surface of the trunk), and if you take it down they can't do it.

Luke: You could always climb on other things and make another climbing tree.

Annie: It's gonna be a problem for the kids that they can't climb this.

Nora: This is an animal habitat.

Luke: You can always plant more.

Stella: But this is a special tree, people come down here just for this tree. (Meaning children come to this tree specifically for chocolate making, archeology, and walking along the trunk.)

When other deconstructors return from their forest explorations and continue to deconstruct the main support, Oliver offers some new arguments.

Oliver: It's our project that we started, and so we have to finish it. Just like in the *Iliad*, he started the war and he has to finish it.

Sabot at Stony Point. "But this is a special tree, people come down here just for this tree."

Sabot at Stony Point. Reese initiating a nonviolent sit-in.

After this, the deconstructors agree that they won't work on deconstruction while there is another child either climbing on the log or working on the side of the tree to which it will fall. Then, towards the end of Forest Time, Reese, a child who has been affiliated with the chocolate factory workers also becomes interested in the debate. Reese makes a conscious choice to sit on the middle of the log. (Essentially, he has initiated a nonviolent sit-in. As long as he's sitting on the log, the deconstructors cannot work!) He stays there until everyone is called to line up.

What a great example of a natural resources utilization debate! Mining companies versus species protectionists. Shopping center developers versus historical preservationists. Eminent domain versus the rights of individual property owners. Let's consider all the rich skills being developed here:

- learning the process of debate
- learning to take a stand and argue for what they believe in
- using literature and history to support their argument
- recruiting others to help support their position
- recognizing that nonviolent action can be a method for making a point

One of the Common Core Key Points in Writing is described as follows:

The ability to write logical arguments based on substantive claims, sound reasoning, and relevant evidence is a cornerstone of the writing standards, with opinion writing—a basic form of argument—extending down into the earliest grades. (Maine Department of Education 2015)

The Dead Tree Debate is a perfect illustration of developing the oral foundations for this kind of argumentation and writing.

And it's particularly potent because it emerges out of a real, lived experience that these young children feel strongly about. This is a provocative example of a **Laissez-Faire Loosely Structured** activity with the potential to turn into **Focused Learning** or even a **Didactic, Highly Structured** piece of curriculum. Inherent in forest play are the roots of reasoned argument and persuasive essays.

Back in the classroom, the teachers helped the children look at the content of both sides of the argument.

For Deconstruction

Oliver: Persistence is good, like in the *Iliad*.

Drew: Fun to watch when it falls. It'll make a "big cloud of dirt."

Luke: It won't destroy the chocolate shop. There are other trees in the forest that you can climb on. It's part of a natural cycle—it's already dead and might have been knocked over by Hurricane Sandy.

Against Deconstruction

Nora: Leave nature alone. It's part of the forest and animal habitat. It's dangerous. It will squish us all when it falls.

Many: A community connection between children and the tree.

Annie: It'll be a problem for kids that can't climb on it.

Stella: People come down here just for this tree, it's a "special tree." People like climbing on this tree.

I don't know if there was a resolution to this debate, but what's important is to see that we need to provide the opportunity for **Loosely Structured** and **Child-Initiated** activities to unfold as the foundations for **Focused Learning** and eventually **Highly Structured** experiences. Also remember that Rosa Parks's decision to not move to the back of the bus did not just happen one day. She had participated in training in nonviolent action in civil rights at the Highlander School in Tennessee. Similarly, perhaps Reese, the child who decided to sit-in and stop deconstruction, will one day become an environmental activist because of his participation in the Dead Log Debate.

Juniper Hill School, Alna, Maine

March–April 2013

The Chocolate River Bakery

Continuing on the themes of chocolate and mud investigations, let's revisit the mud bakery described at Juniper Hill School in chapter 2. Much of the following description is drawn from the Chocolate River Bakery Cookbook created by the teachers after this month-long project was wrapped up (Stires 2013).

Taking advantage of the thaw and freeze cycle in March in Maine, the first and second graders created a nature bakery and

Juniper Hill School. At work in the Chocolate River Bakery.

café in one of their outdoor classrooms. They wrote a recipe together for their original class cake.

Our Cake Recipe

1. Get some snow.
2. Put the snow in muddy water.
3. Stir the mixture/batter.
4. Carry the mixture to the factory.
5. Shape it into balls, pancakes, or cakes.
6. If the batter isn't wet, cook for 10 minutes. If it is watery, cook it for an hour. Cook for 30 minutes if it is in-between.

Throughout the spring, nature bestowed many wonderful ingredients upon the young bakers: snow, slush, mud, rainwater, even hail. The children created many of their own imaginative recipes for nature treats. The teachers supported this emergent and place-based social studies project with work in fractions, liquid and dry volume measurement, illustration, and procedural writing. The cookbook describes the next innovative step. Note the way that **Child-Initiated Play** evolved into **Guided Learning** and then, at the bakery, **Didactic, Highly Structured Learning.** This is emergent curriculum at its best.

Having developed a full menu, the students were eager to share their baking work with the larger community. They invited friend and neighbor Joan Belcher, the local baker and innkeeper of Wabi Sabi Cottage in Sheepscot Village, to visit the Chocolate River Bakery and sample the children's delicacies. The children were thrilled to talk shop with a real baker.

Joan, a lifelong Maine resident, rises early every morning, dons her apron, and makes homemade scones and cinnamon rolls for guests at Wabi Sabi Cottage as well as for the daily delivery to the Maine Coast Book Shop in Damariscotta. The children learned much through her mentorship. Impressed by the children's passion and curiosity, Joan graciously welcomed the first and second graders to Wabi Sabi Cottage for a delicious soup lunch, a now-and-then baking treasure hunt, and a tour of the bakery.

Joan also helped the class to adapt their recipes for nature treats into recipes for dishes that would actually be edible! In honor of their baking work together, Joan opened her professional kitchen up to the Roots bakers and helped the children throw their families a spring tea party. It was an exuberant celebration of friends and food, and the imagination and hard work that nourish the Juniper Hill School Community.

To be clear, Joan the baker actually took the idea of the original mud concoctions and then designed a parallel, edible version for fabrication in the bakery. The book includes recipes for Nut Bread, Cherry Wary Cake, Ginger Salt Pie, Woodchip Dip, Choking Chocolate Pancakes, and other confections. Here's one of the original woods recipes followed by the Wabi Sabi recipe:

Nut Bread: Chocolate River Bakery Recipe

List of Ingredients

½ cup woodchips
2 cups mud
4 tablespoons sawdust

Baking Instructions:

Put ½ cup of mud in the bottom of the pan.
Put woodchips on top.
Repeat layer of mud and layer of woodchips.
Bake for 10 minutes.

Serve

Nut Bread: Wabi Sabi Recipe

List of ingredients

2 cups all purpose flour
¾ cup white sugar
¾ teaspoon salt
1½ teaspoons baking powder
½ teaspoon baking soda
1 cup chopped cranberries

½ cup chopped walnuts
1 egg
2 tablespoons vegetable oil
¾ cup orange juice
1 tablespoon orange zest

Baking Instructions:

Preheat oven to 350 degrees. Spray a 9-by-5-inch loaf pan with cooking spray.

Combine the flour, sugar, salt, baking powder, and baking soda. Add the cranberries and walnuts and stir till blended. Spoon the batter into the prepared pan.

Bake for 50 minutes in the preheated oven, or until a toothpick inserted near the center comes out clean. Cool in pan for 10 minutes, then remove to a wire rack and cool completely.

Each child got to execute and complete her own recipe. Look at all the fine-motor skill, math measuring, timing, and following procedures precisely learning there is in this professional baking experience. And this was followed by the community service experience of creating a refined luncheon for family and community members—table settings, floral arrangements, invitations, napkin folding, tea brewing and serving, correct food handling procedures—all while clad in white-and-red checked aprons. The messy, laissez-faire play in the woods is transformed into the highly scripted, rich literacy and numeracy experience of baking and lunch preparation.

The Chocolate River Bakery curriculum, along with the preceding descriptions of curriculum, illustrates the ways in which nature play can be transformed into powerful learning. These examples also show the value of recognizing diverse approaches to curriculum across the Kindergarten Continuum. Most of what should be happening in the indoor and outdoor classrooms should strike a balance between laissez-faire and highly structured. Teachers should aspire to lots of **Child-Initiated Play** and teacher-guided **Focused Learning.** But both free-form messing about and highly prescriptive teaching can be good in small measures—½ cup of messing about, 4 tablespoons of didactic instruction, and a dash of silliness.

CHAPTER 6

Language Development: Going Forth Every Day and Becoming

There was a child went forth every day;
And the first object he look'd upon, that object he became;
And that object became part of him for the day, or a certain part of the day,
    or for many years, or stretching cycles of years.

The early lilacs became part of this child,
And grass, and white and red morning-glories, and white and red clover,
    and the song of the phoebe-bird,
And the third-month lambs, and the sow's pink-faint litter, and the mare's
    foal, and the cow's calf,
And the noisy brood of the barn-yard, or by the mire of the pond-side,
And the fish suspending themselves so curiously below there—and the
    beautiful curious liquid,
And the water-plants with their graceful flat heads—all became part of him.

Walt Whitman, *Leaves of Grass*

What would happen if the young child went forth some part of every day, forth into the nearby natural world, whether it be into countryside woods and fields or urban cemeteries and parks, and "became the objects she look'd upon." Became the early lilacs, the song of the phoebe-bird, the chatter of the squirrel, the flap of the pigeon's wing, the shrill of the siren, the glint of a fleck of mica, the water-plants with their graceful flat heads. And through mirroring the flapping, imitating the chatter, describing the wafting fragrance, tracing the leaf venation, and naming the lambs, chicks, and calves, each object "became part of him for the day, or a certain part of the day, or for many years, or stretching cycles of years." Would the child be different if the building blocks of thinking and language were leaves, sand, and mist rather than plastic toys, linoleum, and Glade air freshener?

When the children at Juniper Hill School were asked about what their special moments over the course of the year had been, this is what they said:

> **Ruth:** When I found the peace heart. I found it by my fairy house in the Porcupine Woods. It was a perfect heart and it had a straight line coming down the center. It's a really special rock.
>
> **Zinnia:** It was fun finding the crystal in the Crystal Woods because I was the one to discover it!
>
> **Charlie:** I liked building the boy's fort with Alan and Eben. A phoebe liked the spot that we picked for our camp too, so it built its nest there and laid an egg.
>
> **Sierra:** When I collected a lot a lot of maple blossoms with Charlie. We collected more than one hundred blossoms.
>
> **Audrey:** One of my most special treasures was a really big piece of wood that almost looked like a treasure chest. A treasure for all my treasures. I found it in the Porcupine Woods. I still have it.

A peace heart, a crystal, a phoebe's egg, maple blossoms, a wooden treasure chest. The natural world offers up a trove of treasures for children to collect, describe, save, observe, measure, name, and yes, "become for many years or for a stretching cycle of years." I'd like to advocate here for a language development process that is rich in the fabric of the natural world. It will be replete with the nouns of flora and fauna (*phoebe, maple, chrysalis*), the verbs of movement (*bounding, slithering, cavorting*), the adjectives of description (*heart-shaped, lavender, glittery*), the adverbs of modification (*quietly, roughly, impatiently*), and the prepositions of interaction (*going around, through,* or *over* this puddle).

This is important in a world that is becoming ever more digitized and removed from reality. Even four- and five-year-old children spend up to eight hours a day interacting with screens (television, computers, Xbox, iPhones) and about a half hour outside. This flips the concept of real on its head. What's real is technology and the built environment; the natural world becomes distant and "unreal."

This shift in the foundation of reality was pointed out during a cooking project I once did with kindergartners. We made an autumn soup with garden-harvested tomatoes and served tomato soup for snack. When I asked Angela how she liked the soup she said, "Well, it's pretty good. But I like real tomato soup better. You know, the kind that comes in a can." Real is what comes out of a can, not from the soil. Or consider the 2009 revision of the Oxford Junior Dictionary for schoolchildren when the Oxford University Press cut nature terms such as *heron, magpie, otter, acorn, clover, ivy, willow,* and *blackberry*. Instead they've replaced them with more modern terms, such as *Blackberry, blog, MP3 player, voicemail,* and *broadband* (Flood 2015). When the lexicon starts to eliminate nature words and replace them with technology words, it's an indication that we're becoming more and more isolated from the natural world. Instead, if we root human language in natural systems, we shape a sense of the natural world as the real world, the ultimate source, rather than the man-made world.

One of the simple ways we can do this in nature-based early childhood programming is through consciously tailoring our language with young children. Instead of making analogies between natural and man-made things (this leaf looks like a shovel), we can make analogies between natural and natural things (this leaf looks like a grasshopper's wing). Instead of thinking about our minds as computers, we can think about our minds as complex ecosystems. This is part of our intentional strategy to replace mechanistic metaphors with organic metaphors.

If we consistently analogize the mind to the computer, the person to the machine, we develop a hidden paradigm that the technological world is the source of reality. If instead we use metaphors that emerge from natural history and ecological systems, we acknowledge the true evolutionary sources of our thinking. We say we are one of the creatures of the world, our blood is made up of the water and minerals of the earth, we shape and are shaped by local ecologies. We are born from the earth and we return to it. In *Wild Play: Parenting Adventures in the Great Outdoors*, I said about my own children that "I aspired to have the local landscape mapped onto the backs of their hands. I wanted them to grow up blueberry-stained, trail-weary, watershed-saturated, and with some apple cider—pressed from the apple trees in their backyard—flowing in their blood" (Sobel 2011, 13–14).

Just as blood is the life force of our body, language is the life force of the mind. Therefore, we want children's language to flow along stream valleys, to linger in meadows, to reflect on children's chins like buttercups.

Talking Local

In alignment with the local foods movement, I want to advocate for the idea of "talking local" with our children. Local foods advocates encourage us to eat food that comes from within one hundred miles of where we live. It assures us that our food is fresh, often produced by people we know, and therefore those producers feel a moral obligation to make sure that the food is healthy and safe. In supporting local farmers, we also preserve the nearby agricultural landscape. This practice also reduces transportation costs and therefore the carbon footprint of our food. Similarly, I want to encourage "talking local" with children because it's healthier and more nourishing for their cognitive systems.

In her wonderful book *Teacher*, Sylvia Ashton-Warner (1963) describes her approach toward teaching beginning literacy to mostly Maori students in New Zealand. She used a technique that she called "organic reading," in which she taught first words based on finding words that had emotional potency for each individual child. This was in contrast to using the controlled vocabulary in the reading books that had illustrations and text generated for British schoolchildren (definitely not local), such as "John and Mary see Spot the dog. See Spot run. Run, Spot, run!" Or "Mum makes tea for John and Mary. John and Mary sip tea. Sip, sip, sip." Instead, Ashton-Warner sought out what she called "instinctive" words.

> Pleasant words won't do. Respectable words won't do. They must be words organically tied up, organically born from the dynamic life itself. They must be words that are already part of the child's being . . .
>
> I reach a hand into the mind of the child, bring out a handful of the stuff I find there, and use that as our first working material. Whether it is good or bad stuff, violent or placid stuff, coloured or dun. To effect an unbroken beginning. And in this dynamic material, within the familiarity and security of it, the Maori find that words have intense meaning to him, from which cannot help but arise a love of reading. (33–34)

These first words were emotionally laden—*Mummy, Daddy, frightened, ghost, kiss, wild piggy*—and sometimes violent—*knife, bomb, hit*—but always came out of children's primary experience. Ashton-Warner helped the children create a set of cards of their own words. And while children labored over reading the controlled vocabulary in the prefab texts, they recognized the organic words on their cards immediately.

I want to extend Ashton-Warner's focus on emotionally significant words that relate to the inner world and also advocate for using words from the nearby outer world, the world sensed and experienced on a daily basis. We want to create a bridge between language and the nearby tactile, visual, felt natural world. Leaves are *shiny* or *fuzzy*, the salamander is *tickly* on your hand, the clouds are *wispy* or *puffed up*.

Let's consider an example. Here's a set of conversations I had with my daughter Tara when she was three and a half years old, where my intent was to talk locally with her and build up her understanding of the local landscape through using a local, personalized vocabulary. What follows is an account from my parenting journal (2011).

Family Nature Play. Words that come from the nearby natural world.

10 April 1990 (3 years, 6 months of age)

Tara and I are walking back from our neighbor Mrs. Starr's house through the woods, a way we have never come before. We cross over a little stream, and I say that the big puddles in our backyard go through a pipe under our driveway and come down to this stream. Tara asks where it goes then. I say it goes down near our friend Solveig's house (about a half mile away) and then into a big stream, down to a river, and, after a long trip, into the ocean.

"Then it becomes clouds and rain and it falls into our backyard and goes down and around," I finish.

"Around and around?" Tara asks.

"Yes, just like that, around and around."

"Like a ring?" she asks. (I am not sure whether she's thinking of a wedding ring or Ring Around the Rosie, but both make sense.)

"Yes, we can call it the water ring."

She smiled, and I could see the idea appealed to her. This felt like a nice example of taking something she knew, a ring, to explain something that she was learning about, the water cycle. A tangible image for an invisible process.

That evening at bedtime we were looking at the book Island Boy by Barbara Cooney. It was too long and not really appropriate for her age, but we looked at the pictures and skimmed the story. It's about a boy who grows up on a Maine island, becomes an adult, and moves away to live on the mainland, but then, in his advanced years, comes back to the island. In the end, he dies and is buried on the island. Everyone comes to his funeral.

Tara asks, "What happens after he dies?"

My answer wasn't premade but created at the moment. "His body goes back into the earth to make new soil, and his spirit goes up into the sky to get ready to come back again."

"Like the water ring?"

"Yes, just like that."

Tara's final comment moved me for many reasons. First, I was enchanted by the simple elegance of connected metaphors. The "water ring" was created directly out of her experience in the neighborhood—playing in the backyard puddles, damming the water in the roadside ditch, walking home from Mrs. Starr's house. These concrete experiences, synthesized with a bit of her own language ("Like a ring?"), gave her a developmentally appropriate image for the water cycle. Then, with that image available to her, she could use it to make sense of other processes, like what happens when you die.

For a long time after this, I don't have any references in my journal to cycles or the water ring. I vaguely recall wondering if the image had evaporated for her. Then, six months later, in early November, the image resurfaced.

We had recently experienced several deaths in our families, and Wendy, Tara's mother, was seeking a way to help resolve the sadness. At dinner, in addition to the normal four place settings, she set a place for each departed soul: on each plate was a picture of one of our deceased family members— Wendy's father and mother, who had died when she was young, her sister, my sister, my mother, and my father, who had died just a few weeks earlier. For grace, we invited these loved ones to join us.

After dinner, in the darkness, Wendy and Tara went down to the frog pond by Mrs. Starr's house. Wendy put candles on pinecones, lit them, and floated them out on the black surface of the water. There were six candles, one for each departed soul in the family. As they sat watching the tiny flames floating in the darkness, Tara turned to Wendy and whispered, "The souls go around and around, you know."

"Organic" language and "talking local" create a foundation for language development that is strong and immutable. It's important to build language from the inside out and from the "here and now" to the "long ago and faraway." Just as we talk about food that sticks to your ribs, this kind of language sticks in the child's mind.

The Birth of Language as Pedagogy

In the previous chapter, I briefly explored the idea of looking at child development in hunting and gathering tribes as providing a map or prototype for curriculum in nature-based early childhood settings. Similarly, the early stages of the evolution of language can help us understand how we might best foster healthy language development in nature preschools and forest kindergarten settings. The problem, however, is that while there are still traditional hunting and gathering cultures that provide examples of child rearing in this context, it's impossible to watch the birth of language within a culture. In other words, the emergence of human language as a system of symbolic representation, as opposed to animal language, which is a system of signs, happened millennia ago, and there isn't really a fossil record that helps us see the evolution.

But there is speculation based on the behavior patterns of primates and observations of early language in traditional cultures that provide a possible template. In *Philosophy in a New Key*, philosopher Suzanne Langer (1942) summarizes the theory of Donovan (as articulated in his 1891 article "The Festal Origin of Human Speech") that roots language in dance, ritual, and celebratory song in response to dramatic human and natural events.

> Imagine an early group of humans responding in celebration to the birth of a child, or the sun breaking forth after a thunderstorm, or the plunder of a game animal after a time

of famine. It's a natural human tendency to jump for joy, to exclaim in celebration, to dance in honor.

First the actions of the "dance" would tend to become pantomimic, reminiscent of what had caused the great excitement. They would become ritualized, and hold the mind to the celebrated event. In other words, there would be conventional modes of dancing appropriate to certain occasions, so intimately associated with *that kind of occasion* that they would presently uphold and embody the concept of it—in other words would emerge as *symbolic gestures*.

The voice, used to accompany such ritual acts, would elaborate its own conventions; and in a babbling species, certain syllables would find favor above others and would give color to festal plays.

Now, the centering of certain festivities round particular individuals, human or other—death-dances round a corpse, triumph dances round a captive female, a bear, a treasure, or a chief—would presently cause the articulate noises peculiar to such situations to become associated with that central figure, so that the sight of it would stimulate people to utter those syllables, or more likely *rhythmic groups of syllables*, even outside the total festive situation. (Langer 1942, 130–31, italics in original)

Let me translate this hypothetical evolution into a series of steps that starts in ritual celebration and develops into language over a long period of time.

1. Ritual celebration with movement and chant celebrates the capturing of a bear.
2. Dance movement and song/chant (Ur-sa, Ur-sa, Ur-sa) would be used to refer to the bear after it had been consumed.
3. Gradually the dance movements fade and just the song/chant would evoke the memory of the bear.
4. The melodic chant eventually drops away and just the group of syllables, Ursa, would become the name, the word that referred to the bear.

Langer suggests that language has its roots in ritualized movement and song. My additional point is that language was rooted in the fixing of significant dramatic and local events in the minds of children originally through song and dance. Therefore, if we're going to honor the developmental underpinnings of language, much of early language with children should be wed with dance (guided movement) and song in response to significant events in life and in the natural world. Singing happy birthday to a person illustrates this practice. The ritualized patterns of burial rites preserve many of these forms.

Let's translate this theory into practice. In nature-based early childhood programs, the beginning of the day is often signified and celebrated with movement activities, fingerplays and songs that call attention to and signify the distinctive characteristics of the season. Here, ritual, movement, melody, and words are woven together and the memorization of these patterns is the precursor to reading and writing the written word. Out of wholeness the word evolves.

In the Forest Gnomes program at Natick Organic Community Farm, the November morning circle included the chant and fingerplay signifying oncoming winter:

Rise . . . for baby and family. Lacy scarves used to create an indoor snowstorm.

> *Little Jackie Frost pinched my nose,*
> *Little Jackie Frost pinched my toes,*
> *So I ran to the house and slammed the door,*
> *So Little Jackie Frost couldn't catch me anymore.*

And later as a grace before snack, they honored the fall harvest:

> *Hands together, hands apart,*
> *Hands together, we're ready to start,*
> *For the golden rain and the apples on the trees,*
> *For the nuts, and fruits and berries, we say thank*
>   *you and please.*

In midwinter, at the Rise . . . for baby and family program in Keene, New Hampshire, Erica Wilson describes the movement activity she conducts with the two- and three-year-olds to recreate a recent snowstorm.

> I started out walking around the room twirling a scarf in the air and making wind noises. As children joined in, I handed them scarves and they joined in twirling scarves and making

wind noises. Then I would stop and say, "When the wind stopped all was quiet and the whole world was covered with snow." I laid my scarf out flat on the ground. Without being told to, the children put their scarves on the ground and quietly laid their bodies down on top of the "snow."

After they had lain quietly for a while I would say, "but when the sun came up it melted the snow away." I would stand up slowly with my arms over my head pretending to be a sun and then take their snow scarves from them. The game would start over when I gave them the scarves back. The children loved this game. Vivian Gussin Paley talks about how it is through stories that we can enter the world of the child. Playing this game with the children was one of those rare moments when I felt like I had fully entered the world of the child.

Rise . . . for baby and family. "When the wind stopped all was quiet and the whole world was covered with snow."

In reflecting on how this activity relates to early childhood standards, Erica identifies these diverse components of the learning:

Spreading out the scarves was fine-motor control (physical development).

Seeing how long they could lie quietly was self-control and regulation (cognitive development).

Listening to my words was all about following directions (language and social development).

Maybe learning a little about how the sun melts snow (cognitive development).

Having their imaginations sparked by pretending to be in a snowstorm (cognitive development).

And I'd add that connecting words with movement and images from the natural world enhances the meaning of the words and makes them more retrievable and memorable for these young children.

In early spring at the Juniper Hill School, movement and song similarly celebrate the season.

> *Old black bear, old black bear, is sleeping in his cave,*
> *Old black bear, old black bear, is sleeping in his cave,*
> *Please be very quiet, shhh, Very, very quiet, shhhh.*
> *If you wake him, if you shake him, He'll get very mad!*

> *ROAR!*

Isn't this nicely resonant with the tribal ritual example described above? Bears provoke a similar kind of interest among traditional hunters and gatherers and modern young children.

Prior to this next song, teachers distribute lavender, purple, and gold silk scarves. The children are reminded of the crocus bulbs they planted in the fall and then they're instructed to curl themselves up snug and tight like the bulbs. As they chant along with the teacher, they slowly unfurl and blossom.

> *Deep in the earth, in their dark winter beds, (Children curled up down*
> *   on floor)*

"Someone is calling," the crocus said. (Look up and start to sprout)
In colors bright, they quickly dress, (Put silk around neck like a cape)
Lavender, purple and gold of the best. (Stand up slowly, growing)
Then out in the grass they danced in a ring, (Circle around slowly
*   holding holds)*
And called to the children, "Come it is spring."

By the end of the song, all the teachers and children are prancing and streaming their scarves through the air. It's a movement/song/words ritual celebration of the season providing the fertile soil for language to flourish and gradually evolve into reading and writing.

Rather than jumping into reading at the atomistic level of teaching letters, sounds, and words in print decontextualized from actual experience, it's important for children to have a rich experience of movement, song, and poetry. In all these activities children learn to memorize, to sequence, to translate movement into language, to follow directions, to accelerate and decrease the pace and volume of language, to project their voices, to articulate clearly. These are all the precursor skills of reading and writing, and when we introduce language as integrated with song and movement, it weaves its way into their bodies and minds in an instinctively fluid fashion.

When asked about her favorite song during the year, one of the children at Juniper Hill School said, "The 'Good Morning Song,' because we say 'good morning' to nature. We sing it in Sign Language and Spanish. And I like 'The Earth, The Air, The Fire, The Water' because you sing about the elements. We learned that the elements are connected to your birth." This is an illustration of the effectiveness of this bridge between movement, song, and literacy. The children have learned the lyrics to the "Good Morning Song" in English, Sign Language, and Spanish—what an appropriate foundation for appreciating the diversity and individual character of different languages and cultures.

This "language experience" mode of learning has always been the best way to develop literacy skills in preschool and kindergarten. If we forsake what we know to be most developmentally (and evolutionarily) appropriate, we sacrifice the children's motivation and joy of learning. By wedding the traditional approach of movement- and song-based learning with the experientially rich approach of place-based learning, we maximize the possibilities for cognitive development.

Alphabetizing the Nearby

Learning the alphabet, of course, is an integral part of early literacy, and there are unique ways to approach this in a place-based fashion, both rural and urban. Of course, there's the conventional way to do this—with the individual letters, upper-case and lowercase, posted along the walls of the early childhood classroom. It will be P week. Children complete worksheets writing lots of uppercase and lowercase Ps, trying hard to stay within the lines. They'll talk about some P words—*play, pig, pony, pie*—and maybe look at pictures of P words. Couldn't this be more substantive, more interactive?

Creating alphabet books, based on frequent, recurrent field trips to local places is one possibility. This works both in urban and rural settings. The kindergarten teachers at the Beebe Environmental and Health Sciences Magnet School in Malden, Massachusetts, did this one fall based on walking city field trips. Malden, a city of about sixty thousand, is just north of Boston. All of Malden's kindergarten through eighth grade schools are magnet schools with different themes. Beebe, like most of the other schools, is highly diverse with as many as twenty-five different first languages spoken at home. There's a large English Language Learning population in the school, and teaching English

Beebe School. P and F alphabet cards based on walking community field trips.

I my name is Tina,
I work at the train station,
I help people get on the trains,
And I like turkey.

Beebe School.
T alphabet card based on walking community field trips.

in connection to concrete, tangible things in the real world is a particularly effective technique for second language learners. As Beebe is located downtown, it's just a five-minute walk to supermarkets, shoe stores, the subway station, and Fellsmere Park. Based on these frequent city-walks, the children created their own set of alphabet cards for posting around the outside of the classroom. It's not the natural world, but it's the blooming, buzzing richness of downtown, which offers lots of visual and literacy stimulation. We don't need those prefab alphabet cards!

During that same fall, the kindergartens at the Bradford Elementary School in Bradford, Vermont, went on similar walking field trips to the Town Forest. Here their task was to find forest and field examples of each of the letters of the alphabet. When possible, the object was collected, mounted, and laminated so that the alphabet letter was associated with a concrete object. At first blush, it might seem hard to find every letter of the alphabet, but really only a few letters presented a challenge. Some examples: Ant, Butterfly, Cocoon, Deer, Elf House, Fern, Grass, Horse Chestnut, Ice . . . you get the picture.

I observed a similar endeavor at the Pathways to Nature Preschool at Boston Nature Center just this spring—an emergent list, for each letter for all the things they saw on their walks: A—acorns, apples, B—burrs, bluejays, D—deciduous, dreys. Don't know that last word? The children do. A drey is the twig/stick nest that gray squirrels make in the crotches of trees. Natural world explorations lead to vocabulary expansion.

In a different vein, try walking through the woods to find, in natural settings, each letter of the alphabet. Many are obvious—the forked branch trunk of a tree is a V, a caterpillar is an I, a round stone is an O, the horizontal limb of a white pine makes an L in combination with its trunk.

Some of the sinuses, the rounded or sharp indentations between the lobes of leaves, are V-shaped and U-shaped. Can you identify

Antioch University New England. Which maple leafs have U-shaped sinuses and which have V-shaped sinuses?

which species of maples pictured here have U-shaped sinuses and which have V-shaped sinuses?

Or try this, have every child make a collection of twigs, mostly straight, the longest about ten inches, some half that size. Then provide images of the capital letters and have the children create the letters, using the set of sticks, on a flat surface. Breaking the twigs to make the arms of the E or the rounded shapes of the B and the C is fine. Or encourage children to find rounded twigs. Do it on stiff paper and have the children glue the twigs to the paper to make a twig alphabet. Montessorians have long been advocates of creating letters in sand, in clay, or with natural objects. Giving the letters solid form gets the letters into children's hands and therefore into their heads.

Experiential Richness and Vocabulary Development

Research being conducted at Antioch University New England focuses on the extent to which nature-based early childhood education has a positive effect on children's language development. These are two of the questions we are pursuing:

1. Will the greater sensory and experiential richness of the natural world in nature-based programs lead to increased vocabulary development and more complex language usage?
2. Will the more tangible/real direct connections between natural phenomena and reading, writing, and mathematics lead to greater growth in literacy and mathematics skills?

Let's consider how we came to these questions and some examples of what we've been finding.

Consider the world of the indoor classroom. It's well lit and all the spaces are visible from any vantage point in the space. It's mostly horizontal, on one plane—perhaps sometimes with a loft. The temperature and humidity are kept constant within narrow ranges. There are lots of tables and chairs, whose functions are specified and limited. In a high-quality early childhood classroom, there's a water play area, dress-up center, a blocks area, and perhaps an art corner—an attempt to assure experiential diversity. Every morning the space has been cleaned and tidied up. The dominant paradigm is that the space is orderly and predictable.

In the forest classroom, it's sometimes blindingly bright, sometimes spookily shadowy. There are numerous nooks and crannies, perches and swales, and slopes for climbing and rolling down. It's warm in the sun and cool in the shadows; hot and sweaty in the fall, frigid in the winter. The branches, rocks, puddles, sand, tall grass are flexible, loose parts—they can be assembled in lots of ways. Unexpected things happen—birds come down to investigate, the ants sprawl out of the anthill, a pinecone bonks you on the head, frogs hop into the pond. Everything in the space is a little bit different from the day before. The dominant paradigm is that the space is comfortably welcoming and a bit unpredictable.

We think that this experiential richness creates a significantly different learning environment for the young child—one particularly suited to her developmental needs and one that provides the challenges that lead to language learning.

Think back to the example in the previous chapter of the Sioux boy Hadakah being interviewed by his uncle about his observations. In hunting and gathering tribes, it's important for children to learn about flora and fauna from an early age. Young children accompany their mothers while gathering food. They learn the difference between edible mushrooms and poisonous ones, they learn the difference between insects that will sting you and insects that you cook. They collect the pods of the wild peas and avoid the shiny leaves of poison ivy—"leaves of three, let it be." On hunting forays with their fathers, they learn to decipher tracks in the mud. They learn the character, movement patterns, dens and burrows of fox, coyote, opossum, and raccoon. Children have a magnetic affinity for animals and plants; their brains are instinctively inclined to attend to them.

In fact I would even contend that one of the core structures of language, the one-to-one relationship between a word and a group of similar things, is based on the taxonomy of the natural world. All sugar maple leaves/trees have shared attributes that are distinctively different from the attributes of silver maple leaves/trees and therefore there are two different words, *sugar* and *silver*, to describe them. This sensing of likenesses and differences in flora and fauna serves as the basis for vocabulary development—we need new and different words to describe the difference between the softness of rabbit fur and the velvety feeling of moleskin. We need words to identify the swoop of a hawk as opposed to the flit of a chickadee. Keep in mind that flora and fauna, rain and sun, the hardness or slipperiness of the ground underfoot constituted the majority of sensory experience in this hunting and gathering world. Millennia of genetic evolution programmed us to be attentive to these distinctions (Shepard 1998b). And therefore, young children, in the thrall of their genetic predispositions, are implicitly attuned to the natural world and disposed to describing it with new and different words.

For explicit examples of educators taking advantage of this attunedness, let's turn to vignettes from *Lens on Outdoor Learning* (Banning and Sullivan 2011). This beautiful book captures dozens of examples of children interacting with the natural world and meeting all the prominent early childhood standards through self-directed play and observations.

Oak Apple Gall

The children are on an expedition to a local state park. They follow a trail that takes them through a field, along a gentle river, and through a stand of pine and oak trees. . . . Gabriel finds a round, green, fruitlike object along the path. He picks it up by the stem and takes a closer look. Just then, Rowan finds a larger one. While the two boys begin to compare what they have found, other children begin to notice similar objects scattered all along the path. The children gather in a group with their teacher and talk about what they have found.

"It's a lime. Look, it has a stem."
"No, it's too soft."
"It's squishy. It's lumpy!"
"It is light as a feather!"
"What's inside?" (154–55)

Notice both the children's inclination to identify (it's a lime, it has a stem), and then to differentiate (no, it's too soft), meaning no, it's too soft to be a lime. Then they start to articulate the differences, using an interesting array of descriptive words—"squishy," "lumpy," "light as a feather." This is the mind at work developing cognitive skills and new vocabulary.

The vignettes from this book illustrate children interacting with snow, rocks, garden carrots and potatoes, worms, buttercups, pussy willows, gullies, bridges, tree stumps, and meadows. And each interaction engenders different problem-solving and descriptive challenges. This diversity of experience translates into increased vocabulary as well as physical competence.

Bridging into Literacy

After connecting nature and movement to language, the next step is to connect language to images and the written word. Certainly, the "alphabetizing the nearby" examples above are an early step in the process. Let's explore some of the next steps down this pathway.

Claire Warden's practice of Talking and Thinking Floorbooks is a wonderful example of building this bridge between experience and reflection, between talking and writing. Floorbooks are large-format books made to be looked at on the floor or ground that record children's thinking and problem solving through drawings, children's descriptions transcribed by teachers, children's own writing, photographs, and teacher reflections. These are done on a daily basis and reviewed at the beginning of each day to remind children where they have been (literally and figuratively) and where they might want to go. Warden (2012b) describes the collaborative learning process:

> These books include very large pieces of blank paper that enable children and adults to record their ideas as a group. By giving each person a different coloured marker, it is possible to observe who contributes to the group writing. The adult provides a role model for the process of thinking, listening, supporting, suggesting ideas, accepting challenge, of being a writer, making of diagrams. . . .
>
> [T]he Floorbooks incorporate a wide genre of writing. The adult can scribe for the children to release some of the pressure of secretarial skills during a small group experience; individuals can record their idea in a pictorial form, or writing on a thinking bubble. (9–10)

This careful documentation accomplishes many things. First, the teacher is validating the importance of the children's experience and words through listening and transcribing. Through doing this, the teacher also models translating experience into written language. Following the teacher's lead, the children also start to draw and write their own experiences. Because they're documenting significant emotional experiences, children are motivated to want to write. They want to understand how to write about the fox they saw slipping into the high meadow grass, or describe the slither of the snake across their hand. Once the motivation is there, then children are responsive to learning how to form letters, sound out words, and develop the phonemic awareness about the difference between *b* and *d*.

The close documentation of the Floorbooks allows the children and teachers to capture vignettes that illustrate the evolution of children's drawing, thinking, and writing. One vignette, *Pheasant Death*, describes the series of activities that followed the discovery of a dead bird (Warden 2012b). (Hmm, are we seeing a pattern here—dead birds make for good curriculum?) Following the children's wonderings about what was inside (a different impulse than at Dodge Nature Center described in chapter 5), the staff dissected the pheasant and together they examined its internal organs. One boy, fascinated by the trachea, drew a picture of it saying, "I drew something inside the

Juniper Hill School.
Drawing from nature
induces immersion.

pheasant, it's like a worm with stripes on it." The child's fascination led to wanting to draw the strange-looking trachea, which led to the interesting description of "a worm with stripes on it" written by the teacher and then, potentially, copied by the student.

This close attention to children's language is also evident in the *Alien Rhubarb* case study (Warden 2012b). A bit unnerved by the strange appearance of rhubarb pushing up out of the soil, one three-year-old said, "There's an alien in the garden! It's all coming up, crinkles everywhere, scrunchy, brown, yucky." Look at the picture in the book, and you'll see this is a fresh, accurate description. As the rhubarb flourished, children played with its leaves, saw what happened to picked leaves left overnight, hid in the full grown leaves, and tried to find the largest one. Eventually they composted the leaves. Next year, when the three-year-old was now four, the same boy strode in one morning and said, "It's back, and I know it looks like an alien but it isn't . . . it's rhubarb." The Floorbooks, and an attentive teacher, allowed this evolution of thinking to be captured. And they support building the bridge between children's fascination and the written word.

Similarly, Ginny Sullivan and Wendy Banning (2011) capture some of the same beginning literacy moments in their *Lens on Outdoor Learning* case studies. In *Potato Story* (55–56), they describe preschool children cutting up seed potatoes, weeding the raised beds, turning over the hardened spring soil, digging holes, placing their seed potatoes in the hole with the green sprouts facing up, and finally covering them up with soil. One of the two girls then wonders, "Where is the sign? Let's make a sign. It should say, 'Only potatoes.'" They head inside to make the sign—pictures of potatoes and the written words too. The teacher laminates it, mounts it on a dowel, and the next morning they plant it in the garden. The sign designer whispers, "Good luck. I hope you grow." The physical involvement and hard work involved in planting the potatoes propels students to want to make a sign, which leads to wanting to know how to spell and write "potatoes." Primary experience leads to primary writing.

Reading and Writing Emerging from Nature Study

This same pattern is nicely documented in "Learning to Read Nature's Book: An Interdisciplinary Curriculum for Young Children in an Urban Setting," an article by Alicia Carroll and Bisse Bowman about working with kindergartners at the Young Achievers Science and Math Pilot School in Boston, Massachusetts. Though located in the inner city, this school takes advantage of urban green spaces near the school, including the expansive Forest Hills Cemetery. Let's sneak up and overhear what they're saying:

> Golden leaves rustle gently as the breeze moves through the trees in our urban forest. The children are squatting in the deep green star moss, poking their small trowels underneath the moss with great care. Suddenly, a voice is raised in excitement, "Look Ms. Alicia! Look what I found! What is it?" The excitement was catching, and the rest of the Kindergarten children gathered around Amir, looking into his cupped hand. Lots of theories were shared.
>
> It looks like it's something that's dead.
>
> It could be a dead bug.
>
> It might not be dead you know. I think it could be sleeping.
>
> You know, it's that time of year when animals . . . go to sleep?
>
> You mean when animals hibernate, like bears?
>
> Ms. Alicia, what is it?
>
> I don't know. How could we find out?
>
> (Carroll and Bowman 2006, 19)

This vignette takes place on a ten-square-foot study site on the edge of Forest Hills Cemetery where teachers Alicia and Bisse brought their class for regular fall explorations. This activity is one part of the school's commitment to developing student competence in math

Family Nature Play.
"Look what I found!"

and science conjoined with a strong literacy component for inner-city youth. Doesn't it boggle your mind when principals say, "Well we'd like to spend more time on science, but we've got to do ninety minutes of reading, ninety minutes of writing, and ninety minutes of math each day." When was it that math and writing stopped being an integral part of science?

This kindergarten unit, grounded in the beginning cemetery woodland exploration, included separate word walls for science and math words, creation of Big Books documenting their field trips, nonfiction and fiction books about small creatures, such as *Under One Rock: Bugs, Slugs and Other Ughs* by Anthony D. Fredericks, and multiple visits to the study site in the cemetery. It was on the second trip to the study site that Amir queried, "What is it?" and teacher Alicia's, "How can we find out?" was the springboard for a two-and-a-half month research and literacy project. The children responded by suggesting that they could look in books about creepy-crawlies, ask other people, perhaps watch a TV show about bugs. Alicia instructed, "That's called *research*. It's a 'big' word that's used to describe what you do when you are trying to find out about something." And then they were off.

Setting Up a Research Center

This was the beginning of a very exciting phase of the study! A learning center, labeled "The Research Center," was set up in the classroom. In the center of the table were the small, plastic terraria that contained Amir's pupa and a few other specimens. We set up a bin of different books containing nonfiction for a range of readers, ranging from books with large pictures and almost no text, to Science Rookie Readers and insect guides. We supplied magnifying glasses, paper, pencils and modeling clay. Suddenly, Rosa called out, 'I found it! I found it! What does it say in the book? What does it say? I found it!'

And, indeed she had. The pupa was in a book about mealworms, which was promptly read aloud to a very excited class. It is not really surprising that the students then began asking if it would be possible to have mealworms in the classroom.

The research center now became "The Mealworm Research Center." Each student learned what a mealworm would need to survive, and set up small mealworm habitats

Juniper Hill School. Words emerge out of the child's exploration of the mushroom world.

in plastic Petri dishes. . . . The students named their meal-worms, after a few days of caring for, and bonding with, the small creatures under their care. As the mealworms progressed through their life cycle, the students not only made careful observational drawings of them, but also learned yet another substantial group of new words and concepts, including larva, pupa, exoskeleton, grain, beetle, habitat, emerge, Petri dish, and life cycle. (Carroll and Bowman 2006, 20–21)

It's important to connect this investigation with what Sylvia Ashton-Warner referred to as "organic reading" in her New Zealand classroom and the idea of "talking local" introduced earlier. Alicia and Bisse have integrated these two commitments here. They've managed to invest new words like mealworm, larvae, pupa, and hibernation with the same kind of "instinctive" valence that Ashton-Warner felt was important in choosing words for her Maori students. They accomplish this by having the words emerge out of the child's exploration of the natural world, out of discovery, and then the genuine urge to understand and identify.

Rosa's "I found it! I found it! What does it say in the book? What does it say? I found it!" perfectly captures the language development process we aspire to. Genuine interest ("I found it!") is rooted in the natural world and is the sunlight that converts raw materials into the desire to read ("What does it say in the book?"). These children want to write and read—they don't have to be forced to write and read, as is so often the case in the mandated ninety minutes of writing and ninety minutes of reading classrooms. Writing and reading need to be flowers that emerge organically from the soil rather than hothouse plants that are forcibly transplanted and coaxed to grow with unnecessary fertilizer.

Does This Approach Really Work?

Evidence of the success of place-based education when it comes to language development has emerged over the past few years in a variety of evaluation and research studies. (See Smith and Sobel [2010] and a wealth of studies amassed on the website of the Place-Based Education Evaluation Collaborative at www.peecworks.org.) As the nature preschool and forest kindergarten movement is newer, the body of research is not as developed, but certainly promising. Let's take a look at two examples that point to the success of building bridges between the natural world and literacy.

Forest Fridays at the Ottauquechee School in Quechee, Vermont

During the 2013–2014 school year, public school teacher Eliza Minnucci implemented a new Forest Fridays program with her twenty kindergartners, which I and my colleague Riley Hopeman wrote about for the *Community Works Journal* (2014). Each Friday students left the walls of their classroom behind and ventured into the woods, rain or shine, frigid or buggy. To be sure, they also extended their outdoors time on other days of the week as well, but each Friday they tromped into the woods to an outdoor classroom created by the teachers and parents. For Fridays, each child became responsible for dressing themselves and making sure that their backpacks contained a lunch, water, and extra layers. They needed to be prepared for whatever they might encounter. But first, as they filtered into the classroom they chose from one of two options: Forest Plan or Field Guides. A Forest Plan asks students to identify what they would like to do in the woods that day. These plans detail anything from imaginative play scripts they intend to enact, to drawings of local flora and fauna the students hope to see. Each plan is unique and the creator is happy to describe what he wants to pursue in the woods that day.

Students who opt for Field Guides can be found sitting with Minnucci's Forest Friday counterpart, coteacher Meghan Teachout. With Teachout, students peruse New England–focused field guides that have in-depth descriptions and images of local species. *Naturally Curious*, by Vermont-based author Mary Holland, is a favorite

Ottauquechee School Forest Fridays program. Children are "naturally curious" in the winter woods.

resource. The students excitedly flip through this 474-page book and make connections to experiences they've had outdoors or even to texts they've been exposed to in the classroom.

Kindergarten literacy standards are much more demanding than they were ten years ago. Just within the *Reading Informational Texts* section of the Common Core State Standards, there are ten individual standards that students are expected to meet before the end of the Kindergarten year. These expectations range anywhere from

> CCSS.ELA-Literacy.R1.K.1—With prompting and support, (children) ask and answer questions about key details in a text,

to

> CCSS.ELA-Literacy.R1.K.10—(Children) Actively engage in group reading activities with purpose and understanding.

Because the students love being in the woods and figuring out what they're finding, they are compelled to engage with nonfiction texts (field guides) to answer their questions. They are reading with "purpose and understanding."

"Prior to Forest Fridays, finding the right non-fiction texts that were engaging and meaningful to my students was daunting," reflects Minnucci. "Forest Fridays provided real-life connections and inspiration for these students to engage with non-fiction texts. I recently spent a considerable percentage of my classroom budget on more non-fiction books and pamphlets that provide information about the flora and fauna in our woods because of my students' intense interest" (Hopeman and Sobel 2014).

Minnucci's students performed equal to or better than students in the other two kindergarten classes in the school. Even more impressive, there were significant gains for the challenged readers who started the year with lower literacy skills than the other children.

What's significant here is that the literacy success is coming on top of the social-emotional growth in the children, or perhaps because of the social-emotional growth. One parent commented, "This program [Forest Fridays] is probably the best educational thing that could have ever happened to my child. He receives all of the standard kindergarten education, but it is greatly enhanced by all of his experiences

Ottauquechee School Forest Fridays program. Real-life connections inspire students to engage with nonfiction text.

both in the woods and in the preparation for and discussion of their time outdoors." And continuing on this same theme, other parents commented,

> When we go on hikes now as a family, he will point out the deer scat or tell us facts like how beech trees get their buds before any other tree. This year our family tried sugaring for the first time and he knew every part of the process and practically taught his Dad how to do it!

We have noticed that she has become increasingly more responsible at home and is taking it upon herself to do jobs that will help out. She is more confident in knowing she can take initiative to help instead of waiting to be asked to do something. I really, really wish the school would consider adding forest curriculum to upper grades. (Hopeman and Sobel 2014)

Literacy learning can go hand-in-hand with developing initiative and knowledge of worldly skills. We don't have to sacrifice one for the other.

Boston Schools Environmental Initiative in Partnership with Boston Public Schools

The Learning to Read Nature's Book program at Young Achievers Science and Math Pilot School in Boston evolved into the Boston Schools Environmental Initiative (BSEI). This was a collaboration between Massachusetts Audubon's Boston Nature Center, which serves an inner-city population and six Boston Public Schools. The BSEI program placed a Teacher Naturalist (TN) three days per week in each participating school for four or more years and provided ongoing professional development, resources, and project coordination. BSEI naturalists and classroom teachers take advantage of their naturalized school yards, neighborhoods, and nearby natural areas to ground the core curriculum in local studies. Essentially, the program was an elaboration of the Learning to Read Nature's book approach up into the elementary grades. In the most recent evaluation of the BSEI program, PEER Associates, a professional evaluation company, conducted a quantitative evaluation of the Science Journals component of the curriculum. Science journals are a natural evolutionary development of the Mealworm Research Center approach in the Young Achievers Kindergarten classroom. Students choose objects from the natural world that interest them, draw and label these objects, conduct research to identify and understand the objects, and then write summaries of what they have found. Students were given standardized journal prompts before and after the instructional unit on using science journals. The students' responses were scored by objective evaluators to assess whether there was a difference in students' drawing and writing as the result of their instructional journal experience. The evaluators found that using nature journals in the curriculum

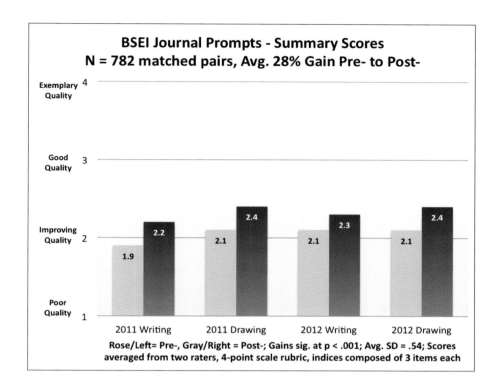

BSEI Journal Prompts - Summary Scores
N = 782 matched pairs, Avg. 28% Gain Pre- to Post-

Exemplary Quality	4		
Good Quality	3		
Improving Quality	2		
Poor Quality	1		

2011 Writing: 1.9 / 2.2
2011 Drawing: 2.1 / 2.4
2012 Writing: 2.1 / 2.3
2012 Drawing: 2.1 / 2.4

Rose/Left= Pre-, Gray/Right = Post-; Gains sig. at p < .001; Avg. SD = .54; Scores averaged from two raters, 4-point scale rubric, indices composed of 3 items each

"Using nature journals in the curriculum led to increases in academic achievement as measured by comparing pre- and post-score of science journals."

leads to "increases in academic achievement as measured by comparing pre- and post-score of science journals" (Duffin et al. 2012).

In other words, when implemented consistently over a number of years in a school setting, the nature/science journaling approach initiated in the Young Achievers Kindergarten class can lead to measureable increases in the literacy skills of young students.

In summary, let's consider that parental question, "Well, I'd like to send my children to a nature preschool or forest kindergarten, but will they be ready for regular kindergarten or first grade the following year?" The answer would appear to be an unreserved yes! First, they are likely to be as competent, if not more competent, than their peers in regard to literacy and math. Moreover, it's distinctly possible that they'll be more independent, more self-motivated, better playmates, and generally more ready to learn. What's not to like?

CHAPTER 7

The Risks and Benefits of Nature Play

KEN FINCH

As I entered the City Museum in Saint Louis, Missouri, the fantastical and playful setting instantly captured my eye and my delight, and thus I nearly missed the sign by the door. But with a last-second glance, the first word drew my attention.

> **Warning!**
> **City Museum is full of Creativity,**
> **Adventure, and Learning . . .**
> **and is fraught with**
> **DANGER.**

The sign goes on to state a few expectations of visitors (such as use care, caution, and common sense—radical thoughts, those!), and advises that the Museum does not take responsibility for accidents or injuries. I was amazed and thrilled. This bold statement promised a unique and wonderful experience, and the City Museum, created from an old shoe factory and warehouse, didn't disappoint.

That museum is truly a one-of-a-kind place, offering the boldest, riskiest, and most offbeat and energizing version of a children's museum I've ever seen. And it really isn't even a children's museum. Nor is it remotely a nature preschool or forest kindergarten, yet in some developmental dimensions they are all kin—sharing DNA that promotes exciting, challenging, and risky play as a cornerstone of healthy and happy childhoods.

In the late summer of 2001, I had a preschool parent's taste of the "ouch" side of that same philosophy. My youngest son, then four years old, was hurt on his very first day at the superlative Dodge Nature Preschool in West Saint Paul, Minnesota. To be exact, he was stung on the neck by a wasp, most likely one of the aggressive yellow jackets that plague our picnics and play. Thankfully, he is not allergic to bee stings. In fact, it scarcely bothered him at all, beyond the unavoidable few minutes of localized pain. His teacher seemed more upset about it than Duncan was, probably because of her duty to call me with the news. She knew a little of my background in environmental education and could guess that I wouldn't be flustered by the incident, but still . . . *the very first day? And on the neck?* Sheesh.

Today that son is aging out of his teens, but he remembers the Great Wasp Sting Incident with a chuckle, except when I embarrass him by talking or writing about it. The lesson here? The degree of injury, angst, and lingering impact caused by that bee sting is about typical for the risks and dangers of nature preschools and forest kindergartens. Which is to say: minimal.

Alas, the danger may be minimal, but parental fears can still be over-the-top about real or imagined threats to their children—in preschool or anywhere else. That's why the City Museum's bold, straightforward approach to the issue of risk *and its benefits* is so fresh and gratifying. It sets an example that nature preschools might do well to emulate, since misplaced and overblown fears about our children's safety are a nearly ubiquitous affliction of US culture, and no free pass is granted to warm-and-fuzzy nature preschools and forest kindergartens.

Nature Play and Risk

To say that today's average American parent is *risk averse* barely does justice to it; *risk paranoid* might be more accurate. So it's not surprising that when promoting kids' reconnection to nature via active outdoor play, perceived risks and dangers are an often passionate topic and an occasional roadblock.

So first, let's be clear: nature play can be dangerous. Children can and do get hurt in nature-based play, as they have throughout human history, and as they always will. Is this valid cause to keep children away from nature play? Is it truly in their best interests to do so?

All of life is dangerous. Our days are full of risk, and we should be grateful for that because risk is a powerful and oftentimes positive force. Without taking risks, no child would ever learn to walk, run, or ride a bike. No adult would ever take up a new sport, or push themselves to do better at a familiar one. No company would ever create new products, or try different approaches to management. Risks pose challenges and the possibility of failure, but they are also an essential part of progress and success. Thus, the goal shouldn't be to eliminate all risks from our children's lives, but to manage them with a wise perspective that considers the full spectrum of dangers to which kids are exposed.

Ahhhh, the challenge of perspective . . . What is the most common cause of accidental death for American children? Give yourself a pat on the back if you know that it is automobile accidents. So, is our society calling out for a ban on carrying kids in cars? Do concerned parents routinely decide *not* to drive the family out for ice cream cones because it's too dangerous? Another example: around ninety thousand US children are injured annually on stairways. In fact, an American child under five is treated for stair-related injuries *every six minutes* (Aleccia 2012)! Perhaps a ban on multistory homes is called for? Or maybe parents should sue homebuilders who knowingly choose to

Juniper Hill School. The benefits of tree-climbing outweigh the risks.

install such dangerous devices where children can encounter them? Need one more? Over twenty-four thousand US children go to emergency rooms each year after accidents involving those most nefarious of devices: shopping carts (Martin et al. 2014). So why aren't CNN and Fox News all over these scandalous tragedies?

These examples illustrate the important concept of "comparative risk." We accept (and even blissfully ignore) legitimate daily dangers to our children that are commonplace and routine. In short, we are used to them. A terrible car accident can still shake us up, as can the rare death caused by a fastball's impact on a young chest. For the most part, though, we tolerate these risks and choose to manage them in order to limit, *but not eliminate*, their dangers. We strap young children in car safety seats, have our fledgling athletes wear protective gear, and put gates at the top of the stairs. Maybe we even keep a close eye on our infants as they roll through the grocery aisles. We accept the dangers of these and many other activities because we subconsciously conduct risk/benefit analyses for them and conclude that the convenience and positive impacts outweigh the inherent dangers.

Family Nature Play. Which is healthier—stream walking or video gaming?

Perversely, given all the mental anguish we devote to the worries, we often do not completely think through a risky situation, considering only the most obvious and immediate perils rather than taking a longer view. For example, when fearful parents forbid their children to enjoy free-range play outside, what are the kids probably going to do instead? Most likely they'll sit in front of an electronic screen, which poses its own set of dangers to a child's healthy development and offers little in the way of value. Any wise caregiver will think through all the play options for their children and look for a healthy balance of risks and benefits.

Frequent and extended nature-based play is a core component of children's experiences in all nature preschools and forest kindergartens. Usually that play is child-driven, allowing them to (at least briefly) engage with most anything they find in the woods, wetlands, or meadows. Therein lies danger, of course, along with discovery, fascination, learning, curiosity, and delight. To gain those powerful benefits, parents, teachers, and organizational leaders must be realistic about the small risks of nature play. The infrequent injuries that do result are almost always minor and familiar to all American adults who grew up playing outside: scrapes, stings, bruises, and perhaps an occasional broken bone. In fact, many of us recall how common wrist and arm casts were in our school classes of the 1950s, '60s, '70s, and '80s, and how they were considered something of a badge of honor, worthy of everyone's autographs! These run-of-the-mill injuries do no more lasting harm today than they did in past generations.

Admittedly, more severe injuries can and do occasionally occur in nature play, but no more often than they do in virtually all aspects of life for any child who is not encased in a protective bubble. For instance, each year more than eight thousand American kids are injured (and some are killed) by falling flat-screen TVs (De Roo, Chounthirath, and Smith 2013). Perhaps it's more dangerous to have children inside watching TV than outside climbing trees!

Undoubtedly, most parents' greatest fear about outdoor play is of other humans: the boogeyman worry. Terrible things *are* occasionally done to playing kids by adult predators, as has long happened and (sadly) probably always will. Yet crimes against children are statistically less common now than they were a generation ago. This knowledge will not squelch all the parental anxiety about outdoor play, though, so it is critical to note that nature preschools and forest kindergartens provide the one most effective protection against stranger danger: attentive and protective adults. Good nature preschool teachers will let their children explore and wander freely in their natural area, but they *never* leave them unsupervised. In addition, other potential dangers in the children's daily outdoor experiences are muted because the teachers know the site: where poison ivy grows, where there's a deep spot in the creek, where dense undergrowth blocks clear supervision, and maybe even where a skunk holes up during the daylight hours.

Just as importantly, the young explorers themselves rapidly become nature experts. Preschoolers love to learn about nature through firsthand play and discovery, and they soak it all up like a sponge! They learn how to identify poison ivy and stinging nettle. They learn their own abilities and limitations for scrambling on boulders, splashing up the creek, and climbing on downed trees. They understand animal habitats and homes, and why a dark, hollow tree trunk merits a bit of caution before sticking your hand or head into it. As a result, it is hard to find any four-year-old who is wiser and more responsible about risks in nature than one who attends a forest kindergarten!

Why Embrace Risk if We Can Avoid It?

The risks of nature play are minor compared to so many other dangers that children routinely face, but what about the benefits? Research has found a remarkable range of positive impacts from frequent, unstructured play in rich, diverse natural settings—exactly the kind of experiences that nature preschools and forest kindergartens provide. These benefits cover the entire realm of holistic child development.

First, though, the bottom line about risk: children need it! It is a powerful catalyst for growth that helps them develop good judgment, persistence, courage, resiliency, and self-confidence. "Can I make it across the stream on that log?" "Should I climb one branch higher than I did yesterday?" "Can I jump from that boulder to the next one?" "Why yes, I can—because I've tried it and succeeded!" Remove risk from children's lives and parts of their growth may stagnate. As adults, we face risks every day—most of them routine, but some bigger. To deal with these risks, we use judgment that we've honed through years of practice, success, and failure. In effect, we go through our days making an enduring series of minor risk/benefit analyses, ranging from whether or not to eat that tempting donut to whether or not to slide through the bothersome yellow light.

However, kids are not born with the gift of informed judgment, nor with awareness of their own abilities and weaknesses. Instead, they must learn their capabilities, their vulnerabilities, and their good decision-making skills through real-life experiences—sometimes happy, sometimes harsh, but always instructive. A child can practice and learn good judgment by climbing trees at age six, or that can wait until they are sixteen and behind the wheel of a car. Either way, that learning must occur if a child is to be well equipped to face the ongoing dangers and challenges of adult life. And risk assessment and good judgment are not abilities that can be developed by sitting at a table coloring.

There is an important distinction to be made, though, between a risk and a hazard. A *risk* is an action chosen by an individual that poses *a chance* of injury. As noted, risks are ubiquitous in nature and in modern life. Crucially, an individual can see a risk and make a judgment about whether or not to accept it and/or attempt to overcome it. An example in nature would be a log lying across a small stream, where a child can clearly see the risk and can decide for herself whether to try crossing it.

Any kind of children's play area that is devoid of all reasonable risks is likely to be boring, and hence not very appealing to children. In fact, research has found that extra-safe, modern playground equipment is often more dangerous than its predecessors because children become bored with it, and then use the equipment in ways it was never intended for (Copeland et al. 2012)! In nature preschools and forest kindergartens, familiar natural settings and well-designed, properly maintained nature play spaces offer the appeal of exciting-but-managed risks for children, with multiple benefits and only minimal danger.

Different from risks, a *hazard* is a condition that poses *a likelihood* of injury. The worst hazards are not clearly visible to the user, so no thoughtful judgment can be made about the degree of danger. Examples in nature preschools might be a dead or broken branch on a tree where climbing is allowed, or the presence of venomous snakes in or near the school's natural area. These are dangers that would not be apparent to most children and could result in significant injury. Needless to say, true hazards are never appropriate for nature play.

Unfortunately, these understandings and distinctions are uncommon in the United States; American culture does not routinely embrace a balanced view of risk. Thus, even amidst the self-selected audiences of nature preschools and forest kindergartens, it is valuable to proactively engage the staff, board members, and parents in commonsense discussions about the risks and benefits of nature play, including comparisons to the array of other dangers that our children routinely face.

Cognitive Benefits

Young children's minds are stimulated by nearly everything around them, so the more diverse, dynamic, and engaging their surroundings, the more the mind learns and grows. Natural areas are the perfect expression of this cognitive richness—far beyond what even the best, most elaborate indoor classrooms can provide. Consider some of the cognitive processes routinely at work in a natural play space: observation, concentration, exploration, collecting, sorting, experimenting, and building. These are not perceived by the kids as "learning," of course; to the children they are just play! Yet they powerfully stimulate the mind and lay the core foundations for academic learning. As a bonus, natural areas change each day, and the more familiar the kids

Juniper Hill School. Deep in observation, concentration, and documentation.

are with the site, the more they will notice those constant changes. So every tomorrow can bring a new array of stimuli!

Creative Benefits

Natural areas also provide endless settings and stimulation for children to make up stories and create elaborate pretend play scenarios—perhaps as explorers, farmers, settlers, or even scientists! Further, nature provides an endless bounty of craft materials, and makes a great subject for painting and drawing—whether with crayons, pencils, watercolors, or simply colored chalk on the sidewalk or patio. Many of these creative, nature-based activities would entail a field trip or a special "outdoor day" at typical early childhood centers, but they are the daily routine at nature preschools and forest kindergartens.

The value of these creative play opportunities can hardly be overstated. Their importance is captured by a long-standing, international, highly validated measure called the Torrance Tests of Creative

Thinking (TTCT). Interestingly, the TTCT is a better predictor of life-time achievement than IQ, high-school grades, or peer expectations of likely future success. Decades of TTCT results reveal that the creativity scores for American children (kindergarten through twelfth grade) have been declining ever since the 1980s, just about when traditional outdoor childhoods started to fade away (Gray 2012).

According to research psychologist Peter Gray (2012), creativity is vital, yet on the decline:

> Well, surprise, surprise. For several decades we as a society have been suppressing children's freedom to ever-greater extents, and now we find that their creativity is declining.
>
> Creativity is nurtured by freedom and stifled by the continuous monitoring, evaluation, adult-direction, and pressure to conform that restrict children's lives today. . . . We are also . . . increasingly depriving children of free time outside of school to play, explore, be bored, overcome bore-dom, fail, overcome failure—that is, to do all that they must do in order to develop their full creative potential.

Juniper Hill School. An endless bounty of craft material.

Physical Benefits

Is it coincidence that we are experiencing an obesity crisis in children at the same time that active, unstructured, outdoor childhood play is vanishing? This problem starts early in life: nearly one in five American four-year-olds is now obese (Anderson and Whitaker 2009). Researchers at the University of South Carolina studied children's activity levels in conventional preschools and found that during the course of a typical day, 89 percent of children's overall activities were sedentary, 8 percent were lightly active, and only 3 percent were moderately to vigorously active. More specifically, 94 percent of their indoor activity was sedentary, compared to only 56 percent of their outdoor activity (Brown et al. 2009). Now think of the sheer physicality of the daily nature play in forest kindergartens and nature preschools: running, jumping, digging, climbing, hiking, balancing, tumbling, skipping, carrying heavy loads, and negotiating uneven surfaces (which improves balance and coordination more than playing on perfectly flat ground).

The advantage is obvious, and importantly, these physical habits learned and practiced in childhood have lasting value. Research from

Natick Organic Community Farm. Balance and coordination are improved in natural play areas.

the Centers for Disease Control and Prevention (1998) indicates that kids who are active at age five end up with less fat at age eight and eleven, and that the greatest contributor to assuring an active adulthood is an active childhood.

As further proof of the physical development advantages of nature-based preschooling, a Scandinavian study compared an outdoor preschool with a conventional day nursery that has a large traditional playground. The study found that the children attending the outdoor school had lower rates of illness, better motor skills (especially balance, agility, and hand strength), and better powers of concentration (Grahn et al. 1997).

As discussed earlier, another interesting health benefit of nature preschools and forest kindergartens is the phenomenon referred to as the "hygiene hypothesis." Its premise is that we are keeping our children too clean! Medical researchers are now finding that regular outdoor experience provides low-level exposure to bacteria that engender the development of antibodies in the immune system. Many Americans have been puzzled by the sharp increase in children's autoimmune diseases such as peanut allergies, Type 1 diabetes, and asthma, which were much rarer (and some virtually unknown) a generation ago. The same increases are occurring in other developed countries, but not nearly so much in undeveloped regions. What is going on?

The human immune system is essentially born partially "programmed." It is designed to protect us from infections and other health threats caused by foreign bodies, but the immune system has to be "educated" during our earliest years in order to discriminate between what is actually dangerous and what isn't. Historically, children were in frequent and extensive contact with many sources of bacteria and germs—soil, plants, animal fur, insects, unfiltered water, etc. Small doses of these strengthened the immune system (much as a flu shot does), and essentially trained it to resist these infections in greater doses, and also to recognize that many common bacteria pose no danger. (In fact, some of them are essential to our health.)

The hygiene hypothesis suggests that the immune systems of children in developed countries are no longer activated by common stimuli because they don't interact with the environment as much by playing outdoors. Instead, they stay in relatively clean indoor settings made even more so by antibacterial soaps, parents who spray disinfecting bleach on every door handle, and the widespread use of commercial hand sanitizers.

Without the early training that used to be normal, maturing immune systems can instead overreact to now-unfamiliar external "threats" that, in reality, pose no danger—such as peanuts. Although there certainly are true allergies that can be present from birth, the hygiene hypothesis suggests that much of the recent explosion in auto-immune disorders is actually caused by overreactions; in essence, the immune system has become the threat, rather than the protector.

Although the hygiene hypothesis is still just that—a hypothesis—the anecdotal evidence is already strong, new research is generating mounting scientific data that supports this premise, and many physicians are already taking it as fact. So what can be done to ensure that young children have ample exposure to soil, plants, bugs, etc., so that their immune systems will develop effectively? Chalk up one more health benefit of nature preschooling!

Finally, another health benefit from time spent outdoors is even more unexpected: improved vision! Since 1970 nearsightedness (myopia) has increased by 65 percent in the United States, with similar changes in other developed countries. Controlled research studies in Denmark have found that exposure to more daylight helps protect children from myopia (Vitale, Sperdato, and Ferris 2009). Spending time outdoors is no challenge for nature preschools and forest kindergartens!

Social and Emotional Benefits

Social and emotional maturity are commonly seen by elementary teachers as the true keys to "kindergarten readiness." These forms of maturity, such as curiosity, a love of learning and discovery, the ability to follow simple instructions, personal initiative, and development of a sense of self have commonly been nourished through play. Equally important are the experiences that can be fostered through *shared* play: taking turns, learning to respect others' opinions, making up rules, working together toward a shared goal, sharing discoveries, and practicing "negotiation skills"—or learning to disagree in a civil and productive way. Collectively, learning these skills nurtures self-regulation, which is a vital prerequisite for future success whether in a classroom or a workplace.

Children can acquire these social and emotional abilities in many settings, but few provide as much stimulation and ever-changing diversity as nature does. While forest kindergartens typically nurture the full range of these experiences throughout their "outdoors all

Boston Nature Center. Learning to respect others' opinions and working together towards a shared goal.

the time" approach, many nature preschools use two complementary strategies to achieve the same goal. One of these is whole-class "hikes," daily group explorations into wild spaces. These hikes foster interactions between the children, with everyone traveling and exploring together even while teachers provide ample opportunity for individual discoveries. The second strategy is daily time in a created and confined natural play space, where each child is free to choose who they want to play with (if anyone), what activities they want to do, and how long they want to stay at any one task or game. These two nature play strategies stress different developmental areas, but combine to provide outstanding holistic growth and school readiness.

Wild Roots Forest School. Time in nature stimulates a child's sense of beauty, wonder, and awe.

Spiritual Benefits

Spiritual development does not refer to religious beliefs, but rather to a child's emerging view of her amazing world. Time in nature, especially quiet, calm times spent patiently observing, daydreaming, and reflecting, can stimulate a child's sense of beauty, appreciation, wonder, and awe. When in nature, young children begin mentally exploring their own place in the larger world, and start to understand that they are but one small piece of a magical existence that extends far beyond their own bodies. Wise nature preschool/forest kindergarten teachers will ensure that their children have dedicated time and special, peaceful places for this quiet side of nature play, which is just as important as the more active aspects of outdoor time.

Unfortunately, today's children are frequently living under a lot of stress generated by media-prompted images of war, an over-programmed daily life, two working parents necessitating multiple transitions during a day, and many other causes. And young children haven't developed a diversity of coping mechanisms. The debilitating physical and mental effects of stress have been well documented, and kids have no innate immunity to them. Multiple forms of "quiet" nature experiences can provide an antidote to children's stress and can simultaneously lay the groundwork for a lifetime of spiritual awareness that is rooted in the natural world. Building children's comfort and love for the outdoors during their early years can guide them toward a lifetime practice of turning to nature for recreation, learning, and respite.

A Different Way of Thinking about Health

The preschool years are a crucial period not only for children's holistic development, but also for the formation of lifelong conservation values. Multiple studies in different countries have searched for the key life influences that foster an adult commitment to conservation. Naturally, many different contributing factors have been found (Chawla 1999) but the overall findings are consistent across very different demographics. The most common influences are rank-ordered (per the research) as:

Frequent unstructured time spent in nature during childhood (also known as nature play)

The influence of mentors who love the outdoors (most often parents, but can be other caregivers)

Participation in outdoor-oriented youth organizations (such as scouting)

Negative environmental experiences (for instance, when a child's "play woods" are bulldozed for new construction)

Formal education

Any one of these factors can ignite a lifelong love of nature, but the single most common influence is frequent childhood play in nature, followed closely by the encouragement of mentors, that is, adults who share their own love of nature with children. Forest kindergartens and nature preschools provide both of these influences daily.

To that end, it is important to remember that great nature play can occur in any place that is wild *in a child's eyes*. Children's worlds are tiny and intimate. While adults may commonly think of "nature" as being places like national parks or wildlife refuges, to a child, "wild nature" can exist in a little vacant lot, an overgrown portion of their schoolyard, or just a few unremarkable acres of woods and wetlands (referred to later as "ratty thickets"). These are exactly the kinds of environments that are commonly and effectively used by forest kindergartens and nature preschools.

So why is this a health issue? Quite simply, all human endeavors ultimately depend upon a healthy, sustainable environment, precisely what conservationists care about and work for. If humanity continues to allow massive doses of toxins to be injected into our soils, waters, and atmosphere; continues to destroy life-giving habitats *en masse*; and continues on an economic development path that is heightening climate extremes, then the holistic benefits of nature-based preschooling may become inconsequential.

Consider this terrible but sadly realistic scenario: coastal cities and countless family lives destroyed by megastorm flooding; rural communities with poisoned water that cannot be drunk; worldwide food supplies diminished by rising temperatures and altered precipitation patterns; and disease vectors increasing as a warmer climate allows unprecedented spread of tropical species. These are likely just a taste of what humanity is facing if conservation practices are not more widely embraced and prioritized.

Today, very few people actually stand "against" nature. However, for a majority of us, protecting nature is not a high priority when considered amidst the full range of societal needs—many of which are perceived as more important or of more immediate concern. Yet environmental health is the crucial umbrella protecting all human activities. Hence, we need to dramatically expand the human commitment to protecting our planet, and as the research cited above indicates, personal bonding with nature is the key to developing conservation values. Learning alone does not sufficiently spur a commitment to the environment. Rather, the crucial first step toward embracing conservation is to "fall in love" with nature—which kids usually do when they play in it, day after day.

With this emotional attachment in place, the child is primed for learning more about nature and for taking care of it. The essence of this understanding is a simple formula: the heart comes first, and the head follows. Nature preschools and forest kindergartens promote this sequence perfectly, with major impacts on children's conservation values and on their cognitive development. Truly, children need nature, and nature needs children. Children need the stimulation, adventure, and wonder of nature to foster their healthy, holistic development, and nature needs children to fall in love with it so they will become the future stewards of the natural world.

Without these future stewards, the conservation movement is facing a slow-motion crisis: the maturation of future generations who may be less likely to feel an interest and commitment to protecting the natural world. Nature-based early childhood education is a powerful antidote to this trend, and is one that can be "scaled up" to enormous size and impact, given wider understanding of its positive impacts and the inexhaustible audience of parents who are searching for excellent early schooling experiences.

Safety

Safety is a concern, a practice, a policy, and a licensing standard for all typical preschools, regardless of their form or emphasis. As such, the vast majority of safety issues for nature preschools are common to all early childhood settings, and don't need particular attention here.

The extensive time that children spend outdoors in nature preschools and forest kindergartens does present unique safety concerns; however, the daily excursions never go deep into a true wilderness where the classes are far from medical help. More typically, the children's activities cover just a few acres, in close proximity to their school building or other structures. Consequently, the essential safety precautions are not extraordinary, but should include the following.

Wild Roots Forest
School. Learning to use
tools safely.

First aid training (including CPR for children). Because distances are rarely great, true wilderness first aid instruction is unnecessary. However, all teaching staff should be competent and confident in treating routine injuries, and in stabilizing any more serious injuries until professional help can arrive.

Comprehensive first aid kits. Comprehensive first aid kits should always be carried on class hikes and excursions, along with health forms for each child. A common inclusion is an EpiPen, an autoinjector device for epinephrine, which can be essential in the event of a child's serious allergic reaction to a bee sting or other unexpected stimulus. Regulations vary in different jurisdictions, but generally staff must be formally trained and certified in the use of EpiPens by a qualified doctor or nurse. If a preschool child is known to have a serious allergy, the ready availability of an EpiPen in the field is potentially lifesaving. But it is good practice, regardless, since any anaphylactic reaction can be very dangerous and fast-acting—faster than outside help may be available—and not all allergies are known to the children and their parents.

Water safety training. Water safety training is a wise precaution if children routinely encounter deep water. In some areas, this may be required by regulatory standards, though licensing treatment of this issue is inconsistent. Usually the dangers of ponds, lakes, and rivers can be sufficiently addressed with specific, formally adopted practices that staff and students are trained in. However, at minimum, basic water safety and rescue training is recommended for the teaching staff. It can also be wise to keep floatation safety devices positioned at water bodies that are routinely visited.

Communication devices. Good communication is absolutely essential between staff in the field and staff in the facility, or directly with local emergency personnel. Today this is most often done by requiring that all staff carry cell phones, but portable radios remain an option.

A third adult. Whenever possible, three adults should accompany student groups who are in the wild, away from their facility. In the event of an injury or other emergency on the trail, one adult can thus go for help (for example, to meet an ambulance crew and lead them to the site), while still leaving two adults with the group—one to tend to the injured child while the other supervises the other children. This "third adult on the trail" role can be filled by an intern or a student teacher if each class only has two regular teachers. Similarly, trained volunteers can fill this role, though they should work regular schedules, assist with other class activities, and go through background checks and first aid training.

Proper dress. Proper dress is a critical safety issue for children and staff alike. All nature preschools and forest kindergartens spend a lot of time outside, usually in all safe weather conditions. With proper outdoor clothing this works very well; with poor clothing it can not only be miserable, but dangerous. The best clothing will vary according to the location, but generally should include the Big Five referred to earlier: rain or snow pants, jackets, good mud boots, quality mittens and hats, and multiple insulating layers if required. These clothes are virtually guaranteed to get dirty and wet, so a second set of clothes should always be kept on hand for each child. When cost is a concern, the school should use donated funds, donated clothing, and/or local sources of used clothes to ensure that every child is well equipped for all weather conditions. The teaching staff need clothing that is every bit as good too, since they not only have to be concerned with their own safety, but with that of the entire class.

Supervision. Children in a nature preschool or a forest kindergarten should never be left unsupervised in the wild (or anywhere else). There can be a fine line here, though. Unstructured, child-initiated play and exploration in a natural area is a core value of nature preschooling; the children benefit from time when they are not being directed or instructed by an adult. This, however, does not mean they can't be supervised. Instead, it is the nature of the supervision that is crucial. It can be likened to the role of a lifeguard at a swimming pool. The guards do not play with the children; instead they only get involved if something dangerous is about to happen or if a child has a specific question or concern. This approach can provide very safe supervision in a nature preschool, as it leaves the teacher free to oversee all the children, rather than focusing their attention on a lesson plan or a particular outcome.

Allaying Parental Fears

The antidotes to parents' unrealistic fears are knowledge and truth, delivered in a competent and convincing manner. Keep in mind that parents can learn and be convinced. Thus, professionals working with nature preschools and forest kindergartens should be conversant about their program's beneficial use of outdoor risks and challenges in nature play, their school's uniquely powerful impacts on children's health, and their standard safety procedures. Nature educators must recognize that parents' intentions are good and their concerns are sincere, but their perspectives are often limited by our culture's overprotective values about childhood. Staff should always be happy, competent, and quick to address concerns, with a good dose of understanding.

Oftentimes the best way to proactively engage a skeptical parent in these issues is simply to ask them about their own favorite memories of outdoor play as a child. More often than not, those memories will be set in "wild" places not too different from your school's setting, and the conversation can then flow from that positive point. With a little guidance, they can come to understand that nature preschooling is good for their children and good for our planet.

CHAPTER 8

The Dollars and Sense of Business Planning and Budgeting

KEN FINCH

If you are starting a nature preschool or forest kindergarten, expect to hear the question, "How do we even know this will succeed?" It may come from your board of directors. It may come from a potential funder. It may come from a prospective parent. And, as likely as not, it will come from your own mind.

It's safe to say that most people who start forest kindergartens or nature preschools aren't doing so with dreams of becoming rich or powerful. These initiatives usually belong to the committed. They belong to individuals and groups who hold a passion for nature, who dream of the best possible futures for our children, and, *especially*, who grasp what a powerful sum these two parts can form when brought together. Typically, these people are driven by mission and are committed to the greater good.

Just as typically, they are not trained in entrepreneurship or business management. Nor are they chomping at the bit to write a business plan, something few of them have done.

Thankfully, there's good news about that. It isn't rocket science. And although your nature preschool may be a first for your community, you won't be plowing new ground with its business model. Ponder the sheer number of preschools and other child care centers that exist, survive, and often thrive. They are large, small, and all sizes in between. They are nonprofit and for profit. They are slick, modern, and high powered, or they are rustic, simple, and warm. Yet amazingly, they all run on the same basic business model. Tuition, other fees, and some fundraising cover the costs of operating. It's really that simple.

Does it always work out? No, of course not. They fail for the same reasons that other seemingly sound business endeavors sometimes fail. Any number of maladies can befall any business, but in the final analysis it most often boils down to one thing—poor performance by the people involved. Good business planning cannot overcome poor performance. But a good business plan will make life a lot easier for good people, and simultaneously demonstrate to others that your nature preschool or forest kindergarten has been well thought out. Potential parents and funders are much more likely to invest in your idea if you've got a delineated path to financial success. Regardless of how warm and fuzzy your mission may seem, people want to know that you know this is a business, and that it will be managed accordingly.

The best demonstration of good planning for a nature preschool or forest kindergarten is the creation of a written business plan. There is no single model that you must follow. There are, though, primary categories of research, planning, and calculations that should be included, and this chapter touches on all of those. Do not fear the creation of a business plan! Instead, make it your friend, welcome it into your home. Not only will it make your program's development easier, it will be an excellent selling point for anyone who may choose to support you. Remember: thousands upon thousands of preschools are *for-profit* operations! Their managers are not in business to save the world; they are in business to make money for themselves and their stockholders. The most prominent example is Knowledge Learning Corporation, the organization behind several major early childhood education brands including KinderCare, Knowledge Beginnings, and the Cambridge Schools. They operate over 1,700 child care and early learning centers in the United States, and their annual revenues are approximately $1.5 *billion.*

Your program will use the same core financial approach they do, even though your educational strategies and values may differ dramatically. You may need significant contributed or loaned funds to buy and/or build your facilities and also for start-up operational funding. But after that, if you run a good operation, your program will not need to exist on an eternal fundraising treadmill like so many nonprofit groups do. Nature preschools and forest kindergartens can and should make money, plain and simple, and do so without compromising their mission. Good business planning will help you reach that happy circumstance.

Many people have the false notion that nonprofits are not allowed to make a profit. Actually, they can legally make as much money as they choose. The key is that all the profit must be used to further the organization's nonprofit mission; it cannot be used to enrich shareholders or other supporters.

Planning for a Nature Preschool
at the Hartley Nature Center

*A Report and Business Plan
on the Potential Development of a Nature Preschool
in the Existing Hartley Nature Center Building
or on the Zamzow Property Addition.*

HARTLEY
NATURE CENTER

**Prepared for Hartley Nature Center by Ken Finch
of Green Hearts Institute for Nature in Childhood
www.greenheartsinc.org**

**Green
Hearts**
Institute for Nature in Childhood

Audience and Other Feasibility Concerns

Who will enroll their children in your program? That should be one of the first questions you ask when you begin planning. Note that for the purpose of business planning, your audience is not the children who will attend; it's their parents and other caregivers. They are the decision makers; they are the payers. Having a program and reputation that makes kids want to attend is a great thing and certainly exerts some sway over parents. But three-year-olds never sign tuition checks; four-year-olds don't pay for lunch out of their allowances.

If you are an environmental educator, you may be in for a pleasant surprise regarding the audience for nature preschools. Most environmental education (EE) centers are constantly trying to "sell" schools, youth groups, and parents on the value of environmental education. That is, not just why these potential clients should choose *their* environmental education offerings, but why they should bother with EE *at all*. To many would-be clients, EE seems like an unnecessary luxury. Many EE customers start off needing to be convinced that environmental education is something they should commit to and pay for, amidst the plethora of other demands on their time and money.

Early childhood education (ECE) is different. Parents and other caregivers already know they need child care services and that they will have to pay for them; they do not need to be convinced of its value. Instead, the existing ECE audience mostly needs help in choosing among the many, many options they may find—different philosophies, program designs, price points, schedules, quality standards, and locations. In any US community, there is already an audience for early childhood education. Your job will be to reach out to that existing audience and explain, convincingly, why your nature preschool or forest kindergarten is the best option for them.

Location, Location, Location

That being said, there are still essential planning steps to take in answering that initial question of who will attend your program. One of the key factors is location. Some nature preschools have enrolled children whose parents drive nearly an hour each way to and from the center, day after day, but that is the exception. Most parents and caregivers want to find preschool options that are within a much more reasonable driving (or walking or biking) distance, perhaps twenty minutes or so. After all, they will be taking their kids back and forth for two to five days per week, for many months, and time is always a precious commodity.

So you need to know where families with young children are living in the surrounding community. It is easy to do an Internet search for US census data (census.gov) that will help tell you this; US census data includes multiple age categories, and you can search by zip code. The Census Bureau's website is easy to navigate, and there are effective titles to guide you to your specific location. Although the age categories may not perfectly match what you need, they will provide a comparative idea of how many young children live in various neighborhoods (or towns) that are reasonably close to your intended location. You can also get census data on income levels within zip codes, and even average commuting times for different zip codes.

This data must then be combined with thought about road access, since the key variable is not so much distance as time. You may be able to successfully operate at a relatively remote location if the drive is fast and easy. Conversely, a closer but more urban site may be problematic if parents must negotiate spaghetti-like mazes of roads, rush-hour traffic, stoplights, and stop signs to get there. Most nature preschool/ forest kindergarten founders will already know the area where they intend to operate, including which neighborhoods have lots of young families. They also will know the local road systems. Nevertheless, these factors should be clearly stated in a business plan because your board members and possible benefactors may not be so well informed.

Other possible audience concerns would be the perceived safety of the area around the program, and whether the location offers other nearby resources that parents can make use of during the school day, such as grocery stores, other shopping, or even volunteer opportunities. The latter can apply to your program as well: parents who have a relatively long drive to your nature preschool or forest kindergarten might be delighted to hang around and help out as volunteers while their child is in class rather than driving back and forth.

Daily and Annual Schedules

This chapter is primarily oriented toward half-day, school-year nature preschools and forest kindergartens, the model used by the vast majority of existing programs. Logistically, it is an easier approach than offering a full-day, year-round program. It does not require food service, naptime (and the related accoutrements), long days that may necessitate double shifts of staff, summertime staffing (which is difficult for some preschool teachers who have school-age children of their own), and (in some states) more restrictive licensing standards. It also allows nature preschool facilities to be used for different purposes during the summertime—most often to host summer nature day camps for young children, which can be very lucrative while also attracting new families into the fold. These day camps can use summer-only teaching staff or can give your school-year preschool teachers a summer employment option.

However, the half-day schedule does significantly limit the potential audience, since it requires a caregiver to either pick up or drop off a child in midday—something most working parents cannot do. This often means that single-parent families and two-earner families cannot use half-day programs; they need an ECE center where they can drop their children in the morning and pick them up after work. Hence, your chosen schedule will likely have a correlation (albeit imperfect) to income, since families with a stay-at-home parent (or nanny, perhaps) who are able to do the midday shuttle are usually in a relatively higher income bracket.

An unintended result of half-day, school-year programs is that they tend to serve wealthier families and may not attract a degree of economic diversity that represents their community at large. From a hard-edged business point of view, this probably does not matter. In fact, the middle-income families who use half-day care are likely able to make a program fiscally stronger. However, many people and organizations operating nature preschools have a socially conscious mission orientation, and they may be uncomfortable serving only a wealthier clientele. With this in mind, several efforts are underway (and some already operating) that use a true nature-based model in full-day, year-round programs. Hence, when planning your new program you will need to carefully consider what schedule you will offer, and all the implications inherent in that decision.

Reaching out to an economically diverse audience is both commendable and possible, despite the challenges. However, there is no shame in serving a well-off audience either. For one, rich kids are also losing contact with nature; nature deficit disorder (Louv 2008) is a nearly universal affliction. Although wealthier families may be more able to live near or visit great natural areas, that benefit may be negated by their ability (and often, inclination) to provide their children with every indoor technological toy! In addition, your new program may be located in an area that is easily accessible only for middle-income or high-income families, so that would be your strongest geographic audience. Ultimately, the creation of a culture of conservation in the United States will be best served by reconnecting *all* children with nature, regardless of their economic status, ethnicity, creed, or location. Do your part, as best as your resources and circumstances allow.

Scholarships for Audience Diversity

No matter what schedule a nature preschool or forest kindergarten chooses, it can and should commit to developing a significant scholarship fund to ensure that its program is affordable for families who might not otherwise be able to enroll. Some extant nature preschools host elaborate annual events to generate scholarship funds, but many others simply include this as an option in their ongoing fundraising efforts. It is, in fact, an appealing choice for many donors since nature preschools and forest kindergartens are concrete programs that they can see (and even visit), they work equally well as a conservation strategy and as an early education strategy, and they have the nostalgic, "warm and fuzzy" appeal of engaging young children with the outdoors.

Typically, nature preschool scholarship funds are held as a restricted account. Money is set aside solely for that purpose and is tracked as a separate fund (even if the actual dollars are comingled in the bank account). In practice, families with need are allotted dollars from this account. Often a family is expected to contribute at least 50 percent of the full tuition to ensure that they are invested in the program. Some nature preschools actually review the incomes of scholarship applicants, with a goal that no family should pay more than (for instance) 5 percent of their total income for preschool tuition. Other organizations keep the process simple, asking the applicants only to submit a serious statement of their need and then moving ahead on an honor system. Either way, a scholarship program can increase a program's student diversity and can be vital to families in need.

Note, by the way, that awarding scholarship funds does not necessarily reduce a preschool's actual gross income. That could be the case if families are just given outright discounts without compensatory scholarship funds being available. But usually a scholarship amount is awarded and then that amount of the scholarship is transferred from the restricted scholarship account into the general tuition income account, hence accounting for the full tuition fee.

Appealing to the Right Families

Competition is a routine consideration in business planning, often one of the largest considerations. But in the case of nature preschools and forest kindergartens, competition may not be a pressing concern.

Early childhood education is a business (in fact, a very large one), and it can be cutthroat in its competition. ECE centers strive to outdo each other with nicer facilities, fancier technology, slicker advertising, better staff qualifications, and more. But this competition usually occurs among programs that are more similar than dissimilar.

This points to a serious question about nature preschools and forest kindergartens: Do they have any *real* competition? At first glance that may appear an absurd query, since many communities seem to have ECE providers on nearly every other block. "Of course, they must all be competition for our new program," you may think! But how many of these centers use nature as the core concept for their teaching, their facilities, and their grounds? Nature is the very visible and appealing hallmark of nature preschools and forest kindergartens; nature is their assurance of quality learning experiences; nature is their distinction from virtually all other ECE centers. This does not mean that forest kindergartens and nature preschools should ignore what other local ECE centers offer or how much they charge, but they don't need to feel constrained to equal them tit for tat because they have a defining essence that few "typical" ECE centers can begin to match.

Hopefully every community will one day have multiple nature-based preschools. Then there really will be competition, and (as usually happens in business) it will ultimately make most of them stronger and put a few out of business. Until then, this class of ECE provider is *truly* unique; there are currently not many locations in the United States where they are close enough to truly compete.

Inevitably, nature preschools and forest kindergartens will never appeal to all people, but they will draw the interest of many families who recognize their very special approach to childhood. Nature preschools and forest kindergartens have a strong emotional appeal for parents, many of whom fondly remember playing outdoors in their own childhood and also see the value of daily fitness experiences in the fresh air, safe physical challenges, and inexhaustible outdoor learning resources. And, as any good advertising executive can attest, emotion is the strongest driver in purchasing decisions!

That said, nature is not the only thing drawing on parents' emotions. Today there is huge pressure on parents to prepare their children for school—and not just for kindergarten, since some obsessed parents act as though it is never too early to begin laying the groundwork for admission to the Ivy League. This is a powerful societal trend that is also driven by emotion—namely, parents' love for their children and understandable hopes that their children will have successful lives. There is nothing wrong with these emotions, of course. But a serious breakdown occurs in how to effect those desires. Today's burgeoning push is for more and earlier academics.

Sadly, there is little evidence that this push for early academics is based on sound research or that it is good for children in the long run. But anyone opening a nature preschool or forest kindergarten will quickly hear the question from prospective parents: "Will this prepare my child for school?" The truth is yes, it will. To "sell" a nature preschool to today's parents you must be well informed about this research, absolutely convincing in your arguments, and facile with your command of facts. Besides this book, research reports on the website of the Children and Nature Network (childrenandnature.org) are a great resource. A simple web search will turn up even more.

Realize that the central challenge is convincing parents of the benefits and getting them to think beyond the knee-jerk advice they are hearing about the "need" to turn their three-year-olds into pint-sized scholars who bring home an hour's worth of worksheets each night. You will not win all of these discussions, and that's okay. You want to weed out those parents (and sadly, their children) before they enroll, as they will likely be difficult and dissonant voices in your program should they decide to register despite their strong concerns. It is much easier to turn them away early, with kind and gentle statements that your program may not be the best fit for their interests and priorities. Be ready to stand your ground for the greater good of your program. Your program cannot be all things to all people.

Competition with Fees and Facilities

The question of competition cannot be considered without a brief discussion of fees and facilities. How much you should charge for tuition is a complex decision with many ramifications. To determine your rates, it is important to know the typical preschool tuitions in your area. Thankfully, the Internet makes this easy as more and more ECE programs post their rates on their websites. Inevitably you will find a wide range of tuitions, and it will be hard to get "apples to apples" comparisons due to different day lengths, varying seasonal schedules, and different degrees of quality. Nevertheless, it is crucial that you be familiar with the range of tuition rates in your area/community and decide where you will want your own fees to fall within the spectrum.

You will usually find that the highest-quality preschool programs have the highest tuitions rates (surprise, surprise!), though there are certainly gems that cost less. Your nature-based program will be a unique offering, and (if you do your job well) will quickly become known as a high-quality program itself. Your pricing should reflect this. Hence, for initial planning purposes, set your fees at or above the local average, but not at the very top of the tuition range. When a product is too inexpensive, people are suspicious about its value.

Remember, the effect of somewhat-high tuition rates can be mollified with a robust scholarship program.

Competition also comes among facilities. Parents are often impressed by nice buildings, well-equipped classrooms, and new and extensive playgrounds. Indeed, today's most elite preschools have facilities that might fit well in an Ivy League campus. You do not need to aspire to these levels, but you do want your facilities to be perceived by parents as decent; as "good enough" that they can focus their greater interest on your actual program and teaching. Also keep in mind that, in most cases, a nature preschool or forest kindergarten will also have a huge advantage with its natural land. Even just an acre or two will far eclipse the outdoor environment of any typical commercial preschool. Ten acres or more will be dazzling in their beauty as well as their richness as a site for learning and playing (which, for preschoolers, are actually one and the same).

Forest kindergartens have a particular challenge regarding facilities since sometimes they have no traditional building at all, using only (for example) an open-air outdoor shelter and latrines. They can work very effectively with this model; however, the appearance of a typical forest kindergarten does not fit the image that most parents have of a preschool. If parents are really concerned about having a nice building, and there are legitimate reasons to want that, then they likely will not give much consideration to a rustic forest kindergarten. Instead, forest kindergartens will commonly draw a self-selecting group of parents who see the beauty and wonder of their program and understand how much more vital this is than having a building that resembles the KinderCare down the street.

Other Feasibility Issues

When deciding on a location for a nature preschool or forest kindergarten, there are many subjective questions about the size and quality of the land and building you choose to use. However, there are a few more finite issues that must be explored:

Zoning. In most communities, you will need to locate your program in an area that is zoned for use as a school or child care center. Alternatively, you will need to work with your local planning agency to request an exemption or special use permit.

Utilities. Access to municipal drinking water, sewer, electricity, gas, phone service, and Internet service are all very desirable. Usually all of these can be installed if necessary, but that will likely increase your costs significantly. In more rural locations, alternatives are certainly possible: well water, septic systems, propane tanks, alternative sources of energy, and cell phone service only. Again, there will be costs involved and you should especially be certain that you can provide drinking water and septic service that will meet licensing standards.

Environmental audit. If you are not certain about past uses of the land you are considering, then it is wise to contract for a Level One environmental audit. This study will research the site's history and check for toxins, old waste dumps, and other hazardous materials that may not be readily visible.

Flood zoning. Flood ratings affect the feasibility of a site; these are available from your local planning agency (often online too). A "flood zone" cannot be built in; a "floodplain" can be built in, but only with specific design accommodations that will add cost and may limit usage.

Older buildings. If you hope to renovate and use an old building, be sure to have it professionally checked for rotting wood, structural integrity, roof condition, radon, asbestos, mold, safe electrical and plumbing systems, and vermin infestations. Any of these can sometimes be cost prohibitive to resolve.

Telling Your Story

Any product or service, no matter how exceptional, can fail financially if its potential users don't understand it. Nature preschools and forest kindergartens are new and unfamiliar to American parents, educators, and philanthropists. Don't be fooled by the excitement and understanding of your immediate colleagues and friends. If you are seriously thinking about starting a nature preschool or forest kindergarten, you are a rebel and an outlier, and you must think from that perspective. Most people do not know what you are talking about when you say nature preschool or forest kindergarten, and it is your essential task to change that.

Therefore, laying out your strategies for communications and promotion is an especially important part of your business planning. You might begin by creating short statements of your new program's core values and understandings—beliefs that will underlie all you do. These can be included (in concise form) in a business plan, or you can just use them to build internal clarity about your mission and methods.

A formal business plan should mention each major communication strategy you intend to use and provide a synopsis of what each will include. Here are basic recommendations.

Prepare the Essential General Presentation

The first task should be to prepare a comprehensive presentation about your nature preschool or forest kindergarten and have it be flexible enough to be adapted to diverse audiences and different lengths. PowerPoint remains effective if used wisely, but *do not* use it to project "books on the wall"! Instead, keep the words brief and the images compelling. Remember, you are aiming at an emotional connection as well as an intellectual one. A short video presentation can also serve well, though for most people a video will be harder to create and harder to modify than a PowerPoint presentation.

What should be covered in your general presentation? The following generic outline can get you started. This is primarily intended for spoken presentations, but it can be readily adapted to written materials.

1. Engage the audience immediately with humor, a human-interest story, "wow" images, and/or something for them to personally ponder. I always ask audiences to "think about their favorite memory of outdoor play as a child," which both stimulates their focused thinking and usually generates a few great stories for sharing.
2. Briefly introduce yourself: a few professional highlights along with your program's origin, intended mission, service location, and audience.
3. Succinctly explain the problem/need underlying your efforts (such as nature deficit disorder), your approach/solution to it, and why you have chosen this methodology.
4. Describe your program's uniqueness, how you will gain the public's attention, and how you will succeed in the marketplace.

5. Set out the quality standards you will uphold, along with the strengths of your program model and your organization.
6. Share what you need to move forward and how they can be personally involved.
7. Provide your contact information: a website, along with handouts (at least business cards), and allow time for a few questions and answers.

Your "long" version of this should be designed as about a forty-five-minute presentation and should be written out both as speaking notes and as a stand-alone document. Creating this presentation will help you to gather your own thoughts and refine your rationale. Then you must edit it for clarity and brevity.

If you prepare this as a written document to be publicly distributed, have friends and colleagues review it and insist that they be frank with their reactions and suggestions. Before delivering it as a talk, practice repeatedly and use only an outline to guide you. Become familiar enough with your content that you can direct most of your attention to the audience and their reactions, rather than to your notes.

Once you are satisfied with the core presentation, plan for variations of it. Different groups should hear the same core message and values, but with varying highlights and structure. Here are a few types of audiences and ideas about their particular interests.

Civic groups and service clubs typically need short (fifteen- to twenty-minute) talks that connect with a business mentality and offer points of pride for their community. Sometimes they will want to know how their group can directly help.

Parents need to hear how and why your program is good for their children, what it will cost, and what the logistics will be.

Educators will need to clearly see the child development strengths of the model nature preschools and forest kindergartens use, how it can help achieve kindergarten readiness, and how they might adapt the core concepts to their own schools.

Funders will want to know your audience, the numbers to be served, how you will measure impact, how you will serve disadvantaged children, what fiscal resources you will need, and how you will financially sustain the effort.

Conservationists will want to understand how nature preschools and forest kindergartens work as an environmental strategy, and perhaps why resources should be targeted to such a long-range approach when there are so many immediate needs.

With this core piece done, you are now ready to expand your menu of communication elements.

Develop an Engaging "Elevator Speech"

This important verbal tool is for use in short-contact situations like business networking or introductions to potential supporters; it should be no more than thirty to sixty seconds long. It must capture the essence of what you're doing in a way that engages the listener's own thinking. Hopefully it leads to questions and a longer conversation. You will need to memorize this and then be able to deliver it without it sounding memorized! Try to use words and phrases that will create positive mental images in your listener's mind. (This should be easy when speaking of nature preschools and forest kindergartens.)

Create a Website

A good website is essential, even if it is relatively sparse to begin with. Modern website creation tools are user-friendly enough to do this yourself if you have basic computer skills and a lot of time. However, you will almost certainly get a better product by using a professional, which will likely cost anywhere from $2,500 to $10,000, depending on what you ask for. College interns can be a dollar-friendly option, and some university advertising classes might even take on your website creation as a demonstration project.

Websites need the same clarity, compelling images, and effective design as any good document. They set a powerful image for your program, so be sure your website conveys the image you desire. Thankfully, websites are perfectly suited for hierarchical information sharing. That is, basic concepts, core components, and "teasers" can be briefly highlighted on a home page, each of which can link to more details. Design your website for this kind of hierarchical exploration and avoid making the home page too dense and difficult to visually navigate.

When your prototype website is ready, test it on multiple computers and devices, using different operating platforms, and have friends and colleagues evaluate it for you. Do not go live with your website until the bugs are worked out and you are comfortable with the information it offers. It is better not to have a website up at all than to publish a broken and frustrating version of it. Remember, though, that your website content need not be all-inclusive to start; it can easily be augmented in the future.

Create a Facebook Page

Regardless of what you may personally feel about Facebook, it has become the communication tool of choice for many people. It is secondary to your website, but is still a nearly essential promotional component. Facebook pages are reasonably easy to create and modify and are excellent for using numerous and frequently changing photos. They lend themselves to reader input and dissemination of current news and are most effective when updated regularly. Do not put too

Boston Nature Center. Marketing brochure for the Pathways to Nature Preschool.

much "hard" information on a Facebook page, though; instead, use it to send interested visitors to your website.

Explore Other Communication Strategies

These can include blogs, Twitter, paid advertising, invited media coverage, and participation in parenting fairs and educational expos. For these in-person promotional appearances, be sure to have paper pieces that you can hand out in large quantities: a basic brochure, small "bookmarks" of concise information, perhaps newsletters, enrollment materials (if ready), and (essentially!) business cards, with the reverse side used to add more compelling information about your program.

Note that nature-focused preschools and forest kindergartens are unique and interesting enough that they are often seen as newsworthy by both print and electronic media. So be prepared with a concise fact sheet about your program and its rationale, and also have high-quality human-interest photos available in digital form. (Be sure to have signed photo releases for pictures of people.)

Finances: Where Will the Money Come From?

Within the nonprofit world, nature preschools and forest kindergartens are delightfully unusual in that their ongoing operations can be completely supported by mission-focused earned income—namely, tuition and other program fees. Their emergent popularity is due to the fact that many nature centers have found them to be profit centers that generate revenue to support other needs of the center. You will likely still need to do some ongoing fundraising, but the relative fiscal self-sufficiency makes a compelling point for many philanthropists. Many foundations are especially loath to give grants to a new initiative that they fear will become dependent on their dollars. They are much more inclined to help a program get off the ground if they can see a well-planned-out funding model that will not require their foundation's long-term support.

Start-Up Funding

For many new nature preschools and forest kindergartens, how to reach that self-sustaining state is a challenge; start-up cash is essential. It is impossible to state how much is needed, since circumstances vary so widely. The creation of a brand new nature preschool—complete with building, land, utilities, equipment, supplies, and a year's worth of initial salaries—could easily run to $2 million or more. On the other hand, a new forest kindergarten might be able to open with only a few thousand dollars if land is available and the founder is willing to donate her time for the first year.

An incomplete list of start-up needs would include the following, with the caveat that not all of them will apply in any single situation:

- an appropriate building with classrooms and support spaces, such as offices, a reception area, bathrooms, a lobby, and lots of storage
- an entry road, parking lot, and walkways
- utilities: electric, water, sewer/septic, gas, Internet, telephone
- entry and site signage
- classroom furnishings, equipment, and supplies
- support space furnishings, equipment, and supplies
- promotional expenses: website, advertising, brochures, and more
- licensing and inspection fees
- consultant fees
- registration and enrollment materials
- salary for six to twelve months of a director's time (that is, before registration and tuition fees start coming in)
- a play space with fencing
- other outdoor improvements: trails, trail bridges, trail signage, picnic pavilion, gardens, latrines, storage shed, plantings, and lighting

Following are possible funding sources for these initial needs:

- the founder's own resources (cash, land, house, and such) (Being independently wealthy is definitely an advantage!)
- a partner organization (such as a park district, college, nature center, or corporation with a suitable campus)
- a fiscal sponsor (such as a committed foundation, one or more wealthy individuals, a governmental entity)
- a Kickstarter campaign to raise many small contributions
- a major community fundraising campaign
- a small business loan from a bank or governmental agency

Business loans are usually only available to for-profit operations. Note, though, that a nature preschool or forest kindergarten may choose this fiscal structure and still remain true to their public service mission and nature focus, and a for-profit will usually be easier to establish and govern than a nonprofit organization.

Conversely, nonprofits are more difficult to create. They require state incorporation just like a for-profit does (a fairly simple process), but also need federal certification through the Internal Revenue Service (IRS). This requires a lengthy application that is challenging to complete but has the benefit of forcing much good thought and planning. It is a sizable task for a novice, so often an attorney is asked to volunteer his or her time to write up standard documents for a new nonprofit (such as articles of incorporation and bylaws), and to complete and file the IRS application for 501(c)(3) nonprofit status. This is a lot to ask, so start cultivating a strong relationship with a corporate attorney! Even if the IRS work is donated, the initiative's founder/manager will still need to recruit board members, create a budget (three years are needed for the IRS application), establish policies, and plan for a host of other operational needs.

Once you submit your nonprofit application, the IRS review process can commonly take from three to twelve months, and they may even return your application without a decision for modifications or additional information. (And in some cases longer. Juniper Hill School waited almost two years to get approved by the IRS.) You may begin operations while your application is pending, and you can even accept donations during that period, but donors should be informed that their contributions will be retroactively tax-exempt only if IRS approval is ultimately granted.

Difficult as it can be to establish a nonprofit, the financial benefits of doing so are momentous. It will allow you to attract donations from individuals, foundations, corporations, and other organizations, since for most of these entities it is crucial that their gifts be tax-exempt. This is only allowed when the recipient is a nonprofit, charitable organization.

Fundraising: How Hard Can It Be?

Very.

The United States is awash in wonderful fundraising stories wherein a worthy nonprofit initiative is funded rapidly and generously by major donors. This happens; it may happen for you, especially if you have diligently lined up your support before launching any public efforts. But new nature preschools and forest kindergartens should be realistic about the fundraising challenge. Virtually all possible funding sources are bombarded with requests, and most of these "asks" are legitimate, commendable, and sophisticated. It is not easy for funders to decide what to support and what to turn down. In short, competition for donated funds is intense.

Further, donated funding most often arises from well-established personal relationships, which take time to cultivate. You may be able to get a foundation grant without anyone ever having heard of you before, but that is a challenge. Note that the majority of contributed dollars in the United States come from individuals; foundations and corporations are both comparatively tiny in their total giving.

Besides the requisite 501(c)(3) IRS status, fundraising requires excellent communication skills, along with a good dose of "moxie." Many people find it very intimidating to ask another person for money, and many are hesitant to experience the sense of rejection that comes with having your request turned down. Yet most philanthropic sources are eager to have good projects to support; the challenge is one of matching.

The Good News

Nature preschools and forest kindergartens have numerous persuasive characteristics for fundraising:

- their dual impact on healthy, holistic child development as well as on personal conservation values
- the emotional and often nostalgic appeal of facilitating children's explorations, play, and learning in natural settings
- the long-term relationships they form with students and families, which can result in deep and lasting impacts
- their use of a well-proven business model that offers a realistic expectation of being self-funding once established
- their status as a conservation strategy that is completely apolitical, and thus can be supported by a diversity of people and organizations
- their typical novelty as a locally unique and emotionally appealing program

The Not-so-Good News

Unfortunately, nature preschools and forest kindergartens also have some problematic characteristics for contributors:

◆ New organizations with no track record are usually considered risky investments. This concern is lessened if the founder is well known and highly regarded in the community, or if well-known, respected individuals have joined the new organization as board members.

◆ Nature preschools and forest kindergartens serve very small numbers of children. Most donors are used to funding outdoor organizations that serve thousands or tens of thousands of children annually, such as zoos, nature centers, scouting groups, etc. A nature preschool with ninety children enrolled can seem very small by comparison. The key is depth, as measured by contact hours. Nature preschools and forest kindergartens give children hundreds of hours of direct contact with nature—the kind of experiences that really can change lives. Zoos, museums, and their ilk more often provide only a few hours of contact per child. This comparison is legitimate and essential to advance, but realize that many donors like to feel good about serving large numbers of people, without engaging in any deeper analysis.

◆ Donors may be concerned with the ability of nature preschools and forest kindergartens to serve disadvantaged children. This can especially be the case with half-day, school-year programs, and some geographic locations can aggravate the issue. This concern can be lessened by the proactive provision of scholarship funds, but it must be realized that this is an incomplete solution.

◆ Relationships are often central to major donations. New initiatives (of any kind) often lack such meaningful relationships; even interested donors may give only token funds until they become more familiar with your operation and sure of its future success.

Budget Planning

The heart of a formal business plan is its financial blueprint. Any organizational budget is a series of educated, well-informed guesses, and is always subject to countless variables that can affect actual fiscal performance. However, there is no more difficult budget to prepare than one for a brand-new organization with no prior operating history to draw on. The guesses will (hopefully) still be educated ones, but they can't be as well informed as those of an existing organization.

Nevertheless, a detailed business plan is your vehicle for preparing as thoughtful and realistic a budget as possible. For starting a nature preschool or forest kindergarten, there are three categories of budgeting.

Capital Budgets

Capital budgets are the projected expenses for all physical needs, such as purchasing land, designing and constructing facilities, installing a road and parking, making improvements to the site, acquiring all necessary equipment, and creating a play space. As mentioned earlier, these initial costs might range from a few thousand dollars for a forest kindergarten to seven figures for a complete preschool building and site.

To prepare a realistic capital budget you must depend upon your architect, engineer, and landscape architect. They are experienced with estimating these items, but often even they will contract with a specialized cost estimator. If you are not already familiar and experienced with building projects, you should consider hiring a Project Manager (sometimes known as an Owner's Representative) to assist you. These are independent, highly experienced individuals who can guide you through the many decisions involved in capital budgets and the construction process and can give you unbiased advice. Oftentimes Owner's Reps can save you much more money in the long run than their fees. Since capital budgets depend on the specific circumstances of any given nature preschool or forest kindergarten, no realistic attempt can be made here to detail these expenses.

Start-Up Budgets

A *start-up budget* covers the noncapital costs of preparing to open your nature preschool or forest kindergarten, such as promotional and registration materials, inspection and licensing fees, hiring expenses, new staff training, and curriculum design. However, the biggest part of a start-up budget is usually the salary and benefit costs of hiring a preschool director at least six months ahead of the scheduled opening, and ideally twelve months. This person will be responsible for all of the other start-up needs, and probably will also work with the construction team (when applicable) on final finishes for the building and site.

Timing is crucial for hiring the director, and to guide this, it is helpful to consider a backward timeline. Most families looking for an early childhood education center (on a school-year schedule, with entry at age three) will begin their search during the fall and early winter when their child is two. Most preschools begin taking actual registrations in January to March for classes that begin in September—and hence the most-desired preschools may be full before spring officially arrives. If a new preschool or forest kindergarten is not ready to meet these common search-and-enrollment schedules, they may struggle to fill their enrollment. Many parents will not wait too late to secure a preschool spot for their children, lest they be shut out.

So ideally the new program will be ready to begin promotional activities by the November or December before it intends to open for the next school year. Having the physical site ready by then is advantageous, but not essential. What is crucial, though, is to have a director on board who can host open houses, meet with prospective parents, provide a thorough picture of the program and its strengths, answer any questions, and consistently represent the program well. The single largest factor in the success of your preschool/kindergarten will be the quality of the staff, and no one more so then the director— so the sooner you have one on the job, the better! In most cases, it is possible to hire a director on a part-time basis at first, but the position will need to change to full-time for at least the last two or three months before opening.

Following are examples of typical start-up budget expense categories for a new program with a separate capital budget:

◆ director/lead teacher salary and benefits
◆ initial classroom and office supplies
◆ promotion and advertising
◆ signage
◆ postage and mailing expenses
◆ local travel reimbursement
◆ consultants' fees (as needed)
◆ initial utility fees (often security deposits and a month's advance charge are required of new users)
◆ licensing and inspection fees

If the new program does not have a capital budget (for example, it is using existing facilities), then start-up expenses might also include landscape improvements, play space design and creation, furniture, equipment, and some classroom and office supplies.

Operating Budgets

The *operating budget* is the crucial predictor of fiscal success. It is where all the projected annual income items and expenses are listed and tallied—hopefully with the former exceeding the latter! The calculations can be quite complicated if there will be multiple classrooms and varying enrollment schedules, and again, the operating budget for a *new* program is especially volatile. You will need to choose an appropriate tuition structure, make reasonable estimates for enrollment numbers, gauge how many staff you will need and at what pay rates, allow for all employment taxes and perhaps for additional benefits, consider training costs (both initial and ongoing), and so on.

Each nature preschool or forest kindergarten will need to choose a fiscal year. Most nonprofits match their fiscal year to the calendar year, though a July 1–June 30 fiscal year is also common. You can actually start your fiscal year at any month, and it might seem logical to start your fiscal year on September 1 in order to match the school year. But you will be receiving registration fees and tuition payments months before that; no matter what date you choose, there will inevitably be income and expenses that carry over into other fiscal years. This must be appropriately accounted for in your bookkeeping.

To create a business plan for a new nature preschool or forest kindergarten, it is strongly recommended that you plan out your first three years of operating budgets. This is the greatest period of both uncertainty and growth, and your sequential budgets should reflect this. For instance, most quality preschools do not immediately fill to capacity after their initial opening, but instead see their enrollment rise as their reputation grows. You'll want to reflect this in your operating budgets' tuition estimates—for example, perhaps budgeting for 75 percent enrollment in year one, 85 percent in year two, and 90 percent in year three. Other budget items will also need to be adjusted for each year, such as registration fees, salaries, supply costs, and perhaps even number of teachers hired.

Salaries and benefits will always make up the largest portion of the expense budget—perhaps as much as 80 to 90 percent if you're not paying a mortgage or an expensive lease. As a rule of thumb, it is good to plan for annual pay rate increases of 2 to 4 percent, though these can be determined through performance evaluations rather than being automatic.

Nearly all other expense categories should also be expected to increase yearly, but most of these will only be by a couple of percentage points annually. Their cumulative effect on your budget will likely be small, since personnel costs make up such a large proportion of your total expenses.

On page 183 is an example of an initial three-year operating budget created as part of a business plan for a nature preschool to be operated by an existing nonprofit nature center. It will have a separate capital budget which will cover portions of some first-year operating expenses, such as classroom materials and advertising. Of course, the actual numbers are meaningless for your specific needs, but take note of the categories and yearly progressions, as well as the two explanatory paragraphs that follow (as written in the business plan). The first-year deficit is not unusual and should not be feared so long as the future-year projections seem sound. It inevitably takes time to build your enrollment and support.

As the budget figures on the next page show, during their first year of operation the preschool is projected to lose $21,457. In subsequent years, the expense increases are outweighed by income growth, driven both by higher tuition fees (roughly 5 percent increases annually) plus higher attendance numbers. Year two projects a surplus of $2,990, and year three projects a surplus of $16,206. There is a great deal of variability in these computations, but the key point is that as the nature preschool gets established, it can be expected to work very effectively both as a new and powerful addition to the (nature center's) mission-driven programming and as a sound financial strategy.

Tuition Computation

On page 184 is the detailed tuition computation sheet for the first year shown on the next page. Note that each class was calculated at three different tuition rates, reflecting average, above-average, and high rates for the local area. Each class's total tuition was also calculated at two enrollment levels, representing full (maximum) enrollment and 75 percent of maximum. The nature center's Board and Director were consulted to determine which of these options would be reflected in the projected three-year budget shown in the plan. This level of detail

Summary Operating Budget: First Three Years

Operating income	Year 1	Year 2	Year 3
Preschool tuition	80,100	124,520	142,350
Application fees	3,750	6,050	7,200
Memberships	2,450	3,360	3,640
Donations (cash, not scholarship)	1,000	1,500	2,000
Preschool fundraising event	750	1,200	2,500
Total	**$88,050**	**$136,630**	**$157,690**

Operating expenses	Year 1	Year 2	Year 3
Personnel (including benefits and payroll taxes)	98,857	111,190	115,784
Health consultant	1,000	1,000	1,200
Staff training/development	2,500	4,000	5,000
Classroom materials and supplies	1,500	6,000	7,000
Advertising and promotion	1,000	4,000	4,500
Office and general supplies	1,000	1,400	1,500
Printing and copying	1,500	2,500	2,500
Postage and mailing	800	1,000	1,000
Miscellaneous	500	1,000	1,000
Licensing and other fees	600	500	600
Equipment and furnishings (replacement)	0	750	1,000
Travel (local mileage)	250	300	400
Total	**$109,507**	**$133,640**	**$141,484**

Net	($21,457)	$2,990	$16,206

Tuition Computation Year 1: Two classrooms; 5 mornings of double classes; 4 afternoons of single classes.				
Friday afternoons left open for teacher meetings and training.				
Tues/Thurs mornings, maximum of 32 children			32 Kids	24 Kids
Tuition options:		$ 990 per child	31,680	23,760
		$1,125 per child	36,000	27,000
		$1,260 per child	40,320	30,240
Mon/Wed/Fri mornings, maximum of 32 children			32 Kids	24 Kids
Tuition options:		$1,440 per child	46,080	34,560
		$1,620 per child	51,840	38,880
		$1,845 per child	59,040	44,280
Mon/Wed afternoons, maximum of 16 children			16 Kids	11 Kids
Tuition options:		$ 990 per child	15,840	10,890
		$1,125 per child	18,000	12,375
		$1,260 per child	20,160	13,860
Tues/Thurs afternoons, maximum of 16 children			16 Kids	11 Kids
Tuition options:		$ 990 per child	15,840	10,890
		$1,125 per child	18,000	12,375
		$1,260 per child	20,160	13,860

Year 1 totals, all classes combined

At lowest tuition rates:
    With maximum enrollment = $109,440
    At 24/22 kids enrollment   = $80,100

At medium tuition rates:
    With maximum enrollment = $123,840
    At 24/22 kids enrollment   = $90,630

was prepared for each of the three years, with tuition increases each year (as noted, about 5 percent, albeit rounded off), and with annual enrollment increases (roughly 85 percent in year two; roughly 95 percent in year three).

Also, in this case there were two classrooms and all sessions were half-day, but in year one, only one classroom was projected to be used in the afternoon. This is because afternoon classes are typically the most difficult ones to fill. In year two, the second classroom was added for the afternoon sessions, and the projected budget reflects this added tuition—as well as the correlating increase in teacher staffing.

However, afternoon enrollment rates were kept at a lower projected percentage than the morning sessions.

Salary Computations

Just as tuition fees make up the huge majority of income, salary expenses comprise the bulk of expenses. To set your salaries, you will need to survey what other nearby, comparable early childhood centers are paying. Some centers will share this information with you directly, but most are hesitant to do so. Instead, search the Internet for employment categories and average pay rates in your state.

Another helpful source for salary information will be local ECE professional groups, such as your state or regional affiliate of the National Association for the Education of Young Children. They often have pay rate survey information available. You might also contact any local university or community college that has a degree program in early childhood education. They are likely to have a good idea of local pay rates, and/or can refer you to other sources. Your state's child care licensing agency may also be a good source of information and guidance.

Calculating your own personnel needs and salary costs can be very complicated if you will have a substantial operation. First, you'll have to determine the exact schedule and structure you intend to use: how many classes and what daily length they are, whether you'll offer half-day or full-day sessions, whether school year or year-round, what daily enrollment options you'll offer (such as Tuesday and Thursday; Monday, Wednesday, Friday; Monday through Friday) how many children you'll accept in each class, how many teachers you'll use for each class, what mix of lead teachers/teachers/assistant teachers you'll use (these designations vary from state to state), and how much paid time you'll allocate for training.

The preschool must have a director, and although she will likely have some teaching duties, she must also have reasonable time available for the many administrative, supervisory, and promotional tasks that are essential for any ECE center. An administrative assistant can assist here and might also serve as a receptionist. You will need at least two teachers per classroom; three can be very helpful—especially with the extended outdoor excursions of a nature preschool or forest kindergarten—but an additional teacher is a significant cost factor. Funds must also be allotted for cleaning and maintenance services.

In the example shared above and below, each class is to have two teachers—one a head (or lead) teacher, and the other an assistant teacher. These are formal state designations with required minimum qualifications. These can vary from state to state, but most states require at least one qualified lead (or head) teacher in each classroom. In our example, calculations are made with the director serving as the lead teacher in some classes, and with a separate lead teacher hired for each other class. Here is the detailed salary calculation information for the first year of operation of the three-year budget example shown above:

> Two classrooms, each being used five mornings per week, and one classroom being used four afternoons per week. The director/lead teacher will teach three mornings and two afternoons, and will also handle all supervisory duties and some administrative and promotional tasks, with help from the administrative assistant. In order to handle the nonteaching duties, the director/lead teacher will work a forty-hour week starting two weeks before the beginning of the school year and extending two weeks past the end of the school year. That person will be paid regularly for the winter and spring break weeks, will have two unpaid weeks during the summer, and will work the other summer weeks at twenty hours per week.

> The director/lead teacher will be assisted by a lead teacher for each class where the director is not teaching, plus one assistant teacher for each class. (The tuition projections are for eleven to twelve kids per class—the lower number being for afternoons.) All teachers will be paid for thirty minutes before and after class times, for prep and cleanup duties. They will also be paid for working one week before school begins (at twenty hours) and one week after school ends (also twenty hours). They will not be paid for three weeks of school vacation during the school year.

> There will be no classes on Friday afternoons (teacher meetings and training time).

> A janitorial service will be paid for three hours of cleaning each afternoon. Any additional janitorial work or heavy maintenance will be unbudgeted assistance from (the nature center's) regular staff.

An administrative assistant will work twenty hours per week.

Only the director/lead teacher will meet (the nature center's) threshold for full benefits (twenty-four hours per week, averaged year-round).

As you can see, there are numerous details to consider such as vacation pay (or not), daily paid time for cleanup and prep work, paid time for training and staff meetings, summertime employment, etc. The more of these you can identify and specify, the better your budget will be.

Related to salaries are the mandatory Social Security, Medicare, and workers' compensation expenses. Social Security and Medicare, taken together, are calculated (as of 2014) at 7.65 percent of pay. This rate has only rarely changed in recent years, but note that the actual budgeted amounts must rise as salaries increase. Workers' compensation expenses vary by location and are sold to you much as other insurance coverage is.

The other major component of personnel expenses are benefits packages—typically covering things such as sick leave, annual leave, health insurance, dental insurance, and retirement plans. None of these is currently required by law, though obviously they are highly valued by employees. If your program will be part of an existing organization—for instance, a nature preschool being started by a parks district—then your benefits package will be determined by the parent organization's existing policies and they will be able to provide you with estimated benefit costs once you have determined your staff structure. If your program will be an independent entity, then you (and your board, if a nonprofit) will need to determine your benefits policies. This can be a tricky area due to the potential magnitude of the costs involved.

Very commonly, a complete benefits package is given only to full-time employees—though sometimes this is defined as only twenty-eight or thirty hours per week. Employees working less than full time may be given no benefits (other than the mandated ones of Social Security, Medicare, and workers' compensation); they may be given some benefits but not others; or they may be given prorated benefits—for instance, sick days calculated as a percentage of a full-time employee's number. Of course, health insurance is the "elephant in the room" due to its expense and volatility. In order to minimize these costs, many nature preschool programs have only one or two full-time employees,

Salary Computations: Year 1

Director/lead teacher: FTE salary: $36,000 per year

This year: 40 hours per week for 42 weeks; plus 20 hours per week for

8 weeks; 2 weeks unpaid	=	$30,462
Social Security + Medicare (.0765)	=	$ 2,330
Vacation: 10 days X $138.5 per day	=	$ 1,385
Retirement: max. contribution match of 3%	=	$ 914
Health insurance: estimate $400 per month	=	$ 4,800

Total: $39,891

Lead teachers: $14.00 per hour

This year 1 lead teacher position will work two mornings per week, for 4.0 hours per day (including prep and cleanup) for the 35 weeks when school is in session, plus 40 additional hours on the before/after school weeks.

320 hours total	=	$ 4,480
Social Security + Medicare	=	$ 343

Total: $4,823

One other lead teacher position will work five mornings per week, for 4.0 hours per day (including prep and cleanup) for the 35 weeks when school is in session, plus 40 additional hours on the before/after school weeks.

740 hours total	=	$10,360
Social Security + Medicare	=	$ 793

Total: $11,153

One other lead teacher position will work two afternoons per week, for 4.0 hours per day (including prep and cleanup) for the 35 weeks when school is in session, plus 40 additional hours on the before/after school weeks.

320 hours total	=	$ 4,480
Social Security + Medicare	=	$ 343

Total: $4,823

Assistant teachers: $10.00 per hour

Two assistant teacher positions will each work five mornings per week for 4.0 hours per day for 35 weeks, plus 40 additional hours for the before/after weeks. These positions could be shared between 4 people.

1,480 hours total	=	$14,800
Social Security + Medicare	=	$ 1,132

Total: $15,932

One other assistant teacher position will work four afternoons per week for 4 hours per day for 35 weeks, plus 40 additional hours for the before/after school weeks. This position could be shared between 2 people.

600 hours total	=	$ 6,000
Social Security + Medicare	=	$ 459

Total: $6,459

Salary Computations: Year 1, continued		
Administrative assistant: $12.00 per hour		
The administrative assistant will work 20 hours per week for 35 weeks, plus 40 additional hours for the before/after school weeks.		
740 hours total	=	$ 8,880
Social Security + Medicare	=	$ 679
		Total: $9,559
Janitorial service: $11.00 per hour		
The person providing janitorial service will work 15 hours per week for 35 weeks.		
525 hours total	=	$ 5,775
Social Security + Medicare	=	$ 442
		Total: $6,217
Total salaries, year 1 of operation		
Director/lead teacher		$39,891
Lead teachers (all)		$20,799
Assistant teachers (all)		$22,391
Administrative assistant		$ 9,559
Janitorial service		$ 6,217
		Total: $98,857

with most teachers being half-time or less. This is a fiscal policy decision that has ethical and promotional implications, but each organization must determine its policies based on its resources and values.

There are scores of other expenses involved in any ECE operation, as well as other sources of income. But these are generally quite minor in comparison to the personnel expenses and tuition income; if you get these "biggies" right, the budget planning is likely to be effective.

Now Make It Happen

The educational concept of nature preschools and forest kindergartens is simple and appealing. The business planning is not so simple and for many people is certainly not so appealing. Keep in mind, though, how many thousands of ECE entities have successfully worked through this business model—with many of them led by people far less qualified or dedicated than you are.

Careful planning will make your initial years of operation much smoother and easier; by preparing a detailed business plan, you will essentially be "paying in advance" for this increased effectiveness. Keep in mind, though, that ultimately the single most crucial factor toward success of the nature preschool will be the quality and experience of the program staff. Early childhood education is very much a "people business." Excellent staff can make any program succeed, almost regardless of the quality of the facilities. Conversely, no preschool is likely to succeed if the staff members are not capable—both in their work with children and in their relationships with parents. Your nature preschool or forest kindergarten will have huge advantages in its unique focus and exceptional grounds, but it is imperative that you hire the best possible staff. Good luck in your initiative.

CHAPTER 9

Finding the Right Place to Put Down Roots: Facilities and Infrastructure

We all know what to look for in optimal indoors early childhood settings. I described one version of it at the Dodge Nature Preschool in chapter 2. The classroom is brightly lit with easy access between indoors and outdoors. There is a diversity of areas that support distinctive kinds of play/work. There's a big collection of hardwood blocks for building, an arts area with easels and tables, a dress-up corner for dramatic play. And something serendipitous you've never seen before—maybe a mattress on a box spring that serves as a gentle indoors trampoline or a collection of leashes so children can take the stuffed animals for walks. In Waldorf early childhood classrooms, there are moss gardens that serve as miniature worlds for fairy play. In Montessori classrooms, there are the carefully designed materials so children can practice household tasks, like food preparation and sorting.

But when it comes to the outdoors, we're much more unsure and ambivalent. Outdoors is dangerous and needs to be closely controlled. That's why many early childhood facilities only have a clearly fenced, closely guarded playground with a sandbox, a balance beam, some low climbing structures, and a few big wheel trikes. Nature preschools and forest kindergartens aspire to naturalize what's inside the fence, make it more like the forest, *and* move beyond the fence into the natural world and community beyond. Granted, at some urban sites there isn't a safe natural world to easily explore. Let's look at how different programs solve this problem.

The focus here will be on finding and creating useable spaces for natural world exploration. As suggested above, we know what the National Association for the Education of Young Children's (NAEYC) best practices for indoor classrooms look like. There are also a variety of new books describing how to transform play yards. (I recommend *Cultivating Outdoor Classrooms* by Eric Nelson, the work of Robin Moore's Natural Learning Initiative at North Carolina State

University, and Ginny Sullivan's Learning by the Yard website for examples of what's possible.)

Here my goal is to look at various ways of accessing, evaluating, and using outdoor natural spaces (as different from designed outdoor spaces) as a setting for a substantial proportion of early childhood programming. Earlier we've suggested that there's a range in nature-based programs from having the children outside 50–90 percent of the time. In truth, in midwinter weather in northern New England, it probably goes down to 20–25 percent of the time at many sites (although the Juniper Hill teachers, children, and parents are real troopers when it comes to frigid weather, as illustrated in chapter 1). The Cedarsong program described in chapter 11, in the milder but drizzlier Pacific Northwest, has a shelter, but no indoor facility at all. Regardless, from rural to urban, early childhood programs are moving out into the wild woods and semiwild parklands and cemeteries to give children the freedom to roam, play, and explore.

The Garden of Eden

What we're all after, deep in our hearts, when we create a nature preschool or forest kindergarten, is the re-creation of the classic image of Eden. Birds flit merrily in the trees, the lion lies down with the lamb, the grass is lush and free of biting insects, a shallow stream of crystal clear water babbles and burbles nearby. The children and teachers gather in the shade of a mature apple tree; there are no snakes when children want to eat of the fruit of knowledge. And, as Regina Wolf Fritz of the Forest Gnomes program in Natick, Massachusetts, says, it's always October when parents visualize forest kindergarten.

I've actually been to this place, or a close facsimile. It's the morning gathering site for the Wild Roots Nature School at Stonewall Farm in Keene, New Hampshire, directed by Liza Lowe. Wild Roots was started in 2013 at Stonewall Farm, an agricultural education center on the outskirts of Keene. They have a milking herd of about thirty cows, large market gardens, a community-supported agriculture program (CSA), a well-tended sugarbush and maple sugaring operation, a cider press, a big pumpkin crop, and a wide array of domestic fowl and fauna.

To get to the morning circle, families walk a short distance along an untrafficked farm road, cross the babbling and burbling stream on a *Who's-That-Trip-Trapping-Over-My-Bridge* wooden bridge, and then the children scamper over to the log stump circle in the shade of the aforementioned fruit tree. The September sun gently dapples the children's faces—just the right balance of protective shade and playful glisten. Before coming to the circle, some children divert to the wooden play structure complete with a few slides, hiding nooks, and a climbing net. Beyond the circle to the west are raised garden beds planted by the children last spring and maintained by the summer camp kids and staff over the summer. To the north, a stone wall (suitable for balance walking) separates the morning circle from the extensive market gardens. To the east is the goat pen with three frisky kids anxiously awaiting the children to come feed them. On the south, that susurrating stream, easily wadeable in rubber boots, no more than six inches deep. The comfortable lawn, no tripping problems here, slopes gently down to the edge of the water. It's a vision of loveliness.

After the circle, it gets even lovelier as Fridays are animal feeding day. One group of boys feeds and gambols with the goats, other children scatter chicken feed and put down fresh bedding hay, some cuddle rabbits as the water bottles are refilled.

Later they'll trundle off to their forest classroom, a five-minute walk into the woods with a circle around a fire pit, log seating, mossy

Juniper Hill School. Outdoor story reading in an idyllic meadow.

nooks at the base of trees, a little shelter for backpacks and equipment storage. It's the perfect blend of wild and cultivated, healthy risk and safety, and when necessary, indoors and outdoors.

Ratty Little Thickets

What if you don't have access to a little piece of paradise? Don't fret. I want to encourage urban early childhood educators, and those with only limited natural areas, to consider the virtue of oft-neglected spaces around your sites. In the mid-1980s, I researched children's landscapes with five- to thirteen-year-olds in Devon, England. I collected children-drawn neighborhood maps from all 110 children at the Denbury Primary School in Denbury, Devon. Then, with groups of children from the same neighborhoods, I had children take me on walking field trips to see their favorite places, dens, mud kitchens, and climbing trees. Much of Denbury had quickly suburbanized over the previous decade. Some children had easy access to open meadows and conservation land, while others had access only to little slivers of undeveloped space in between housing developments.

One of the most intriguing areas was a bit of neglected shrubs bordered by roads and suburban houses on three sides and a pig farm on the far side. This shrub and sapling area was by far the most popular and private getaway for the half dozen seven- to eleven-year-old children in this neighborhood. It sloped down from one road to another and was littered with old shopping carts, discarded gallon paint cans, beheaded dolls, some scrap lumber, and plastic shopping bags. But once you got past the trash zone, you entered into a labyrinth of narrow trails, secret dens, lookout trees, group dens, treehouses, and fire pits. It was only about 250 feet by 150 feet, barely an acre, but it was a world unto itself. The grapevines and brambles turned many of the trails into tunnels. I could barely stoop low enough to wend my way through, and it was evident that few adults ever entered this children's domain. I came to refer to it as a "ratty little thicket."

For most adults, it was just a wasteland, a place waiting to be turned into housing lots. It was full of trash, impenetrable, dank, unappealing.

Family Nature Play. Abandoned urban lots provide access to nature for inner city programs.

But for these children, it was the kind of place Edith Cobb (1959, 537) described when she claimed that children want "to make a world in which to find a place to discover a self." Noted ornithologist Bob Pyle's "ratty little thicket" was the High Line Canal on the east side of Denver. He refers to it as his "ditch," similarly neglected by most adults and surrounded by commercial, industrial, and residential cityscapes (Pyle 1998). But it was his private world and the source of his eventual environmental commitments. Educators in urban settings need to creatively take advantage of ratty little thickets and ditches to provide children with natural play opportunities.

Boston Nature Center, a sanctuary of Massachusetts Audubon, started their Pathways to Nature preschool program in 2011. Located on the grounds of the old Boston State Hospital, the nature center shares the sixty-acre site with biotech firms and other small businesses. It's an inner-city oasis of meadows, marshes, gardens, and small patches of forest. Two of the old staff houses have been repurposed for the preschool. The small kitchens, dining rooms, and living rooms provide comfortable, homey classroom spaces for the young children. Outside, on the grounds of the nature center, the teachers and children have access to a boardwalk through a marshy area, the meadows, some urban vegetable gardens, a newly designed natural play area, and right behind the classrooms, a "ratty little thicket."

Head out the back door of the preschool classrooms at Pathways to Nature and there are small, grassy backyards. These tip down and transition into the thicket of sumacs, red maples, and alders that borders the marsh. The thicket is barely twenty to thirty feet wide, but it's filled with short, stout, climbable trees; broken branches; and patches of mud and gravel. It's a natural playground of climbing structures, loose parts, and minichallenges, without the staff having had to do much more than reduce unnecessary hazards.

The boardwalk, gardens, and designed natural play area all see frequent use, but this area is the home ground. To most adults, objectively, there's really nothing very special about it. It's messy and a bit unattractive. But, subjectively, for the children, it's their world. The point is that some outdoor natural areas don't need to be spectacular, or glamorous, or pristinely tended. Instead, as Bob Pyle said, "For special places to work their magic on kids, they need to be able to do some clamber and damage. The need to be free to climb trees, muck about, catch things, and get wet—above all, to leave the trail" (Pyle 2002, 319). This is happening at Boston Nature Center, and you can find places for this to happen near your program as well.

Boston Nature Center. The thicket just outside the back door serves as a suitably challenging nearby play area.

Taking Advantage of What You've Got

Let's take a look at how other programs take advantage of nearby nature to provide natural world experiences for children. It's important to recognize that for young feet and minds, the patches of natural world don't need to be that big or beautiful to offer months of compelling adventures. Maybe it's not William Blake's "world in a grain of sand," but there can be an explorable world in an acre or two. Here are some examples of the interesting diverse settings:

San Francisco Waldorf School. The preschool at SFWS is located on a densely residential and commercial street. Hardly a tree in sight. During the 2013–2014 school year, the school and play yard were under renovation, so they relocated to the upper corner of the Presidio, a city/national park a few blocks from the school. This large diverse park provides lots of room to roam, but they spent most of their time in an acre of meadow and scattered eucalyptus trees in the little upper corner. Even here, I heard one of the children imagining, "We're in Neverland. No one ever gets old, no one ever dies. We'll always be children."

Brooklyn Forest, Brooklyn, New York. On the other coast, Brooklyn Forest started running forest kindergarten parent/child programs in Brooklyn's Prospect Park. More in tune with the European model, they didn't start with a facility and then move outside, they just started outside. There are no indoor facilities. Their popularity with parents led them to expanding to programs in Central Park and other sites around the city.

Live and Learn Early Learning Center, Lee, New Hampshire. This program, located on an old farm near the university town of Durham, has one of the most novel outdoor playscapes I've come across. The enterprising owners run a paintball business on weekends and some evenings and a forest kindergarten program during the day. Both programs use some of the same terrain. The paintball arena is located in an open stand of white pines and is filled with old sheds, log barricades, tree stands, and other scrappy structures to provide cover and hideouts for paintball assaults. There's a separate little corner developed for the children with a yard boat, tepees, and tables for artwork, but the paintball arena and structures turn out to be a great play area for young children as well! How ingenious!

Mariposa, Providence, Rhode Island. Mariposa shares its space with a Boys and Girls Club in Providence. The building is surrounded by parking lots and then there's an almost impenetrable thicket sloping into wetlands beyond that, problematically suitable for play. Other than field trips to the zoo and other urban parks and cemeteries, the teachers and children are limited to two tiny play yards, one with conventional playground equipment, the other mildly naturalized and framed by about a dozen white pines. The children spend most of their time in the naturalized play yard, and even though it's barely an eighth of an acre, it serves them well—a great example of making the most of what you've got.

The Forest as Piazza

Of course, if it's possible, it's great to have access to expanses of open space. One of the core aspirations of nature-based early childhood programs is to have children feel at home in the forest, or in the meadows, or along the beach. In the Reggio Emilia early childhood programs in Italy, the teachers create a piazza, a central gathering space that becomes a shared home ground for the school community as a whole. In a wonderful article called "Exploring the Forest: Wild Places in Childhood," Anna Golden (2010) describes an evolution in thinking that emerged at her school. Anna is the *atelierista*, or art studio teacher, at the Sabot at Stony Point School, a progressive school in Richmond, Virginia, that is influenced by the philosophy of the schools in Reggio Emilia, Italy. Located on the outskirts of Richmond, the school abuts a large tract of forestland, which provides an attractive backdrop for the school. Up until a few years ago, the teachers neglected the forest,

Cedarsong Nature School. The forest as the piazza—the heart of the school/community.

with numerous downed trees and a creek, as a resource or affordance for the curriculum. Then Anna Golden started to wonder about the role of the forest in shaping the culture of the school in relation to the concept of the piazza.

Many Italian towns are built around a central square called a piazza. It's a place for open-air markets, socialization, celebrations, animated conversation, and it serves as the heart of the community. Similarly, the preschools of Reggio Emilia are built around a central piazza, a common area where children of different ages play and learn, families gather for events, and school meetings convene.

At the Sabot School, the teachers wondered about what could serve as their piazza, a place to bring the children, their parents, and all the teachers together. And because the school's families came from the city, the suburbs, and outlying countryside, they realized that the school grounds were the only place that they all shared in common, and then they realized that perhaps the forest could serve as their community gathering space.

> As we thought more about the woods, many questions
> came to mind. How could we use the forest as a space for
> young children? What could the school community gain
> from moving out into this space? Would families use the
> space? Could expanding into the woods bring our school
> community together? Could the forest become the Sabot
> School's piazza? (Golden 2010, 8)

In other words, could the forest (meadows, rocky ledges, salt marsh, coast, essentially the natural world) be the piazza for a school community?

I'd seen this emerging as a board member at the Juniper Hill School in Maine, but I didn't have words for it until I read Golden's article. I was intrigued by Anne Stires's intuition to build school events around seasonal rituals—solstices, equinoxes, full moons, phenological events like the first flowers in spring or the height of the autumn foliage. These celebrations of the seasons occurred in the curriculum, but also shaped family and community gatherings—songfests, contra dances, sledding parties. It was the glory and richness of living a life shaped by the seasons that was the shared fabric for children, teachers and parents. The forest (natural world) truly was the piazza, "the heart of the community."

The Frontier Hypothesis

Perhaps there's something deeper at work here in this commitment to the forest, immersing children in this changing and challenging outside world? Join me for a historical and philosophical interlude.

In 1893 Frederick Jackson Turner delivered a paper at the American Historical Association in Chicago entitled "The Significance of the Frontier in American History." Simply, Turner contended that the existence of the frontier, the provocative edge between civilization and the wilderness, had shaped the nature of American consciousness. There's a parallel conversation about the frontier in Canada, but whereas in the United States the frontier is always the West, in Canada the frontier is always the North. Turner (1921, 1) said, "The existence of an area of free land, its continuous recession, and the advance of American settlement westward, explains American development." In other words, the unique character of American consciousness was shaped by the fact that a significant portion of the population was always making life anew, facing the challenges of living life in the wilderness.

In the 1600s, American colonial civilization was a narrow band of colonies along the Atlantic coast. (Of course, there were the Native Americans who were here first and were at one with the wilderness that colonists were soon to expand into.) The frontier for Boston was the Connecticut River. The frontier in Virginia was the Appalachian Mountains. By the early 1800s, the frontier was the Mississippi River, and Thomas Jefferson funded Lewis and Clark to survey the wilderness between Saint Louis and the Pacific Ocean. Think of Davy Crockett, John Wesley Powell, John Muir, and Sacagawea and how their forays into the wilderness have captured our imaginations, shaped our consciousness. By 1893 Turner claimed that the frontier was closed, signifying a major shift in American history, but in the twentieth century, Alaska became the new frontier. Turner (1921, 2–3) claimed, "This perennial rebirth, this fluidity of American life, this expansion westward with its new opportunities, its continuous touch with the simplicity of primitive society, furnish the forces dominating American character."

What were the effects on American consciousness of continually confronting the "simplicity of primitive society," the challenges of the wilderness? Here's the crux of Turner's argument:

> The wilderness masters the colonist. . . . It takes him from
> the railroad car and puts him in the birch canoe. It strips off
> the garments of civilization and arrays him in the hunting

shirt and the moccasin. . . . At the frontier the environment is at first too strong for the man. He must accept the conditions which it furnishes, or perish, and so he fits himself into the Indian clearings and follows the Indian trails. Little by little he transforms the wilderness, but the outcome is not the old Europe. . . . The fact is, that here is a new product that is American. . . .

The result is that to the frontier the American intellect owes its striking characteristics. That coarseness and strength combined with acuteness and inquisitiveness; that practical, inventive turn of mind, quick to find expedients . . . that dominant individualism, working for good and for evil, and withal that buoyancy and exuberance which comes with freedom—these are traits of the frontier, or traits called out elsewhere because of the existence of the frontier. (Turner 1921, 4, 37)

Look at the attributes that Turner claims are brought forth by the frontier—"strength combined with acuteness and inquisitiveness," an

Family Nature Play. The forest encourages "acuteness and inquisitiveness."

"inventive turn of mind," "individualism," and "buoyancy and exuberance." Are these traits we want to cultivate in children? Does moving into the "forest" in forest kindergartens replicate the American encounter with the frontier and wilderness?

Consider this description from John Muir's autobiography of arriving at his family's first homestead in Fountain Lake, Wisconsin, in the 1850s, on the edge of the frontier:

> Just as we arrived at the shanty, before we had time to look at it or the scenery about it, David and I jumped down in a hurry off the load of household goods, for we had discovered a bluejay's nest and in a minute or so we were up in the tree beside it, feasting our eyes on the beautiful green eggs and beautiful birds,—our first memorable discovery . . .
>
> The sudden plash into pure wildness—baptism in Nature's warm heart—how utterly happy it made us! Nature streaming into us, wooingly teaching her wonderful glowing lessons, so unlike the dismal grammar ashes and cinders so long thrashed into us. . . . Young hearts, young leaves, flowers, animals, the winds and the streams and the sparkling lake all wildly, gladly rejoicing together! (Teale 1954, 31–32)

Muir's accounts of his childhood are full of the "acuteness and inquisitiveness" the "buoyancy and exuberance," that Turner claims is an integral part of the American consciousness.

Therefore, let's weave these ideas back into the ongoing narrative. Here's the *something deeper* about forest kindergarten. Whereas the piazza shapes the Italian consciousness, the forest/frontier shapes American consciousness. Bringing young children into the forest re-creates the historical American experience. Having to find your way, encounter the elements, negotiate rough ground, face moderate risks and dangers, and live with the animals is a reliving of the American expansion westward. Children are brought back to their original hunting and gathering selves, and they learn to live off the land.

Though the forest kindergarten idea emerged in Europe, it's serving a unique purpose in North America. It reconnects us with our roots; it revives the American and the Canadian spirit. It allows children, teachers, and parents to relive our history, to reconnect with letting the land shape our character. Think of John Muir's description of Fountain Lake as a basic principle for curriculum design.

Young hearts, young leaves, flowers, animals, the winds and the streams and the sparkling lake, all wildly, gladly rejoicing together! (32)

Site Selection: Learning from Scotland

Choosing a good site for a nature-based program is a crucial first step. In some cases, you don't have a choice. The early childhood program owns the building and there's no option of moving. In these cases, two strategies prevail. First, you can work to naturalize the limited play space you have available. In New England, play yards at Brown/Fox Point Early Childhood Education Center in Providence and Leila Day Nurseries in New Haven have evolved significantly. Both organizations have raised money to redesign their outdoor play areas, incorporate more loose parts, and differentiate the natural play opportunities on their small urban sites.

The second strategy for centers with limited outdoor play space is to find the nearby local places that, even in the inner city, provide natural world exploration opportunities. In "Learning from Nature in the Urban Wilds," two parents, Margaret Connors and Bill Perkins (2005), leaders of the after-school Young Naturalists Project at Young Achievers Science and Math Pilot School in Boston, describe how they solved this problem. They visit the unkempt section of the Arnold Arboretum and Forest Hills Cemetery to take advantage of meadows, pristine pine-covered knolls, and ponds:

> Now into our third year, our students in the Young
> Naturalist Project have had the opportunity to meet the red
> fox of Bussey Brook Meadow, observe the tracks of coyotes,
> raccoons and opossums, and catch sight of the enormous
> wingspan of a red-tailed hawk flying just a few feet above
> us. . . . They have dug down into a virtual mountain of com-
> posting leaves to discover its steaming temperature of 140
> degrees in the dead of last winter's record cold—easily hot
> enough to cook an egg, so we did! (30)

All these urban explorations were just a short walk from the school at that time in a congested part of the Jamaica Plain neighborhood of Boston. As well as redesigning the play yard, the teachers at Brown/Fox Point in Providence have also been walking their urban Providence neighborhood to find opportunties for nature play and exploration.

But what if you're starting a new program and you've got some choice about location? Educators in Scotland, home to many forest kindergartens, have thoughtfully considered how to select the best outdoor sites for program use. Here's a useful set of parameters inspired by a document created by Juliet Robertson and her coauthors (2009) of Creative STAR Learning for the Forestry Commission of Scotland. I've translated her ideas to be applicable to North America.

Essential Parameters for Choosing a Suitable Forest Kindergarten Site

Minimum Requirements

Outdoor site with diverse natural features. This includes meadows, rocky areas, and small water features, as well as some trees and shelter.

Good cell phone reception. In case of emergencies. (Yes, cell phones can be a curse, but in this case they're a blessing. They provide the opportunity to be away but connected.)

Within easily walkable distance from drop-off area. For young children, certainly no more than one-quarter mile.

Openness within the wooded area. In other words, it's easy to move from place to place without too much thickety underbrush. (But look at Cedarsong videos to see that this is sometimes not the case.)

Bathroom facilities provided. Outhouses suitable if necessary. This is crucial. There was almost a parent rebellion the first year at Juniper Hill School because the toileting arrangements were insufficient.

Little or no dog waste. Sometimes little children and dogs just don't mix.

Little or no dead wood in upper canopy. See the hazard versus risk discussion in chapter 7. It's important to remove hazards but accept some risk.

Permission granted by landowner or city officials. In many North American cases, some programs are using city parks and conservation land and don't own any actual facilities.

Additional Desirable, but Not Essential, Parameters

Diversity of habitat. It's useful to have conifers and hardwoods, flat areas and slopes, pickable berries and raw materials for crafts—vines, pebbles, mud.

Clear boundaries. If these don't exist, then it's important to visually mark the edges beyond which children cannot travel.

Little or no dangerous plants. And when you can't completely eradicate poison ivy or oak, you need to be conscientious about teaching children to recognize and avoid it. This is also somewhat a function of your knowledge/comfort level. Many schoolyards contain strongly hallucinogenic/poisonous species of mushrooms and they rarely present any problems. And nettles provide a mildly painful but useful learning opportunity.

Little or no busy public access.

Permission for use of fires. Europeans are staunch about their conviction that fire is essential for warmth and for training children in fire safety. I concur. Work with the local fire department to get permission for small, well-contained outdoor fires.

An Example of a Great Site: The Forest Kindergarten at Waldorf School of Saratoga Springs (WSSS)

The WSSS has two kindergarten programs, one somewhat more indoorsy at their main site in downtown Sarasota Springs, New York, and the other located at a mostly undeveloped piece of state forestland located on the edge of the city. Until the school approached the park administrator, the site sat mostly unused. There's a historic brick building for indoors time (previously neglected and wonderfully homey as a school facility), and then two hundred acres of explorable woods. It's significant that the woods are particularly un-intriguing—mostly flat, no significant features, lots of old stone walls and marshy streams. Not terribly appealing from a "park" perspective, but great for young children. Teachers and children spend most of their time in either the Baby Bear woods (nearby), the Momma Bear woods (a medium walk), or the Poppa Bear woods (a long walk) on the property.

I spend an April morning at the school. As children arrive, they head to the backyard for about a half hour of play in the meadow, with an array of natural play features—swings, balance beams, natural climbing elements, a tiny little stream. This is followed by an indoors circle of songs and chants and a quick birthday party. The rest of the morning, almost two hours, is spent on a long walk, perhaps half a mile, back to Momma Bear woods—a bit of a grassy opening on a slight rise surrounded by forest.

When we get to the Momma Bear woods, many of the children start to plead, "Can we go to Greenland? Please, can we go to Greenland?" Off in the distance a bit, where the children were pointing, I could see flecks of darker green through the trees. The teachers consent. Greenland, it turns out, is a network of tiny marshy streams about three feet wide and a foot deep, harboring a crop of emergent, vivid green Indian poke. The emeraldness of the Indian poke against the drabness of the April woods made this a vibrantly "Green" land.

For the next hour, a quiet spell settles over the children as they sink into self-directed play. One child sculpts herself in between two root

Cedarsong Nature School. A quiet spell settles over the children as they sink into self-directed play.

lobes of a hemlock tree and harvests Indian poke leaves. Three other girls unfurl some of the leaves, poke a vertical twig into the surface, add some violet leaves, and then float these fairy boats down the gentle current. I watch another child perched on the middle of a fallen log bridge that straddles a stream. She collects beech leaves off the bottom of the stream and then uncurls and flattens them on the log. Then she scoops up fine sand and creates leaf and sand sandwiches, of which she is very proud. There is very little teacher intervention, very few "be carefuls" or "no, you can't get wets" or "please don't pick the fragile plants." Similarly, there is very little teacher direction or suggestion like "let's see how many different leaves we can find." Instead, the children are self-directed, enthralled, immersed in this green land.

On the walk back, I commented to director Sigrid d'Aleo, "You know, lots of places spend $100,000 to build play areas that simulate these kinds of opportunities. How wonderful to have access to this place *and* to allow the children to take advantage of it." Herein lies my point. Tune your sensibilities to seeing the affordances and opportunities in the niches and interstices of urban parks, suburban backyards, plain old marshy woods, cemetery edges. Often we don't need to spend lots of money to find suitably wonderful natural areas that allow children to spend a bit more time in Neverland.

Site Enhancement: Loose Parts

Of course, sometimes the natural area available to you is lacking in terms of suitable play materials for children to interact with. Landscape architect Simon Nicholson proposed the theory of loose parts in his 1971 article "How NOT to Cheat Children: The Theory of Loose Parts." By *loose parts*, he means materials that can be moved, carried, combined, redesigned, lined up, and taken apart and put back together in multiple ways. Nicholson contended that people are drawn to environments that they can interact with and that children in particular "love to interact with variables" (Nicholson 1971, 30). He emphasized that the greater the amount of loose parts, the greater the inventiveness and creativity that can result. Legos are the classic manufactured toy that capitalizes on the loose parts idea. A forest with moveable dead branches, pine needles, pinecones, stones, dig-able soil, pill bugs, and the like provides a panoply of loose parts. Most conventional playgrounds with fixed equipment provide very few loose parts, except in the wood chips spread out underneath the equipment. Therefore, one strategy for enhancing your play yard is to import loose parts.

A wonderful Canadian guide entitled *Forest and Nature School in Canada: A Head, Heart, Hands Approach to Outdoor Learning* includes a useful beginning list of possible loose parts to introduce on the playground.

As you consider other possible loose parts, note that the National Toy Hall of Fame inducts great new toys every year and two recent inductees have been the stick and the cardboard box. Sometimes the best toys are the simplest toys. This was aptly illustrated by a child attending a Forest School in Canada. When asked what he was grateful for one day at snack, he responded, "sticks and love" (Carruthers Den Hoed 2014, 19).

LOOSE PARTS

- natural materials sourced sustainably on your site, such as sticks, rocks, pine needles, flowers, acorns, stumps, branches, logs, and fallen bark (Note: bringing in nonnative or foreign objects from other sites can be disruptive to local habitats)

- tools for building, making, and creating (used in a timely, safe, and purposeful manner, with appropriate training to support its use, and only when elicited by a child's interest)

- handmade wooden mallets, stakes, and tree cookies (can be made by educators and/or adults)

- buckets, trowels, pulleys, rope, natural fibers, and tarps of varying sizes

- identification books and tools for plants, animals, and birds

- clay, charcoal, wax crayons, pencil, paper, and twine (for documentation, reflection, and/or making learning journals) (Carruthers Den Hoed 2014, 35)

Natick Organic Community Farm. Construction materials transformed into a set of "loose parts" for nature play.

Site Preservation: Learning from Canada

Finally, it's important to recognize that lots of little feet and hands in a small natural area on a daily basis are going to have an impact. We've talked earlier about the importance of tolerating some impact for the benefit of supporting children's play. And it's important to differentiate between utilization play and destructive play. Utilization play, such as collecting Indian poke leaves to make fairy boats in Greenland needs to be supported within limits. Destructive play, wanton thrashing of wildflowers for no good reason, needs to be discouraged. Therefore, as we support constructive play and utilization of natural resources, we should also cast an eye toward preserving our natural resources.

Our Forest Schools Canada colleagues provide the following guidelines to shape our thinking about the environmental impact of nature preschool and forest kindergarten programs. They recommend that it should be an integral aspect of forest kindergarten planning to assess the Environmental Impact of your activities on your site. Before and during a group's visit to a site, the educator should work with staff and children to assess the risk, ecological sensitivity, and play value of the site. In addition to choosing rich natural places for children to engage with, they also act as stewards of the place, conscious of the group's interactions with it and their impact on it over time. This process will help students to develop a relationship with the land, the wider community, and with each other.

Whether you've just got access to the public park down the block, or the ratty little thicket in between the back of the garage and the fence, or the woods at the edge of the playground that are normally off limits, you have many choices. Maybe it's just one day a week, like they're doing in Quechee and Burlington, Vermont. Or perhaps it's your Family Nature Club of parents and toddlers going on outings in different parks in your region once a month. One step off the trail and into the woods is a step in the right direction. The children will appreciate it. As one Forest School Canada five-year-old student said, "I love Forest School! Forest School is better than candy. The only thing better than Forest School is MORE Forest School" (Carruthers Den Hoed 2014, 19).

Does the site already have a management plan? Consider using this as a building block for determining activities and locations of these activities.

Who are your stakeholders and partners for FNS? Engaging community partners is key to building a supportive framework and can enhance programming. We do this by identifying community stakeholders and partners even prior to launching programs and by holding public forums or more informal coffee or fireside chats. . . .

How will you measure your impact? A Forest and Nature School site will be used season after season, year after year. Therefore it is important to ensure that measures are in place to ensure that the site is used sustainably.

How often will you monitor & assess your impact? Regular site monitoring and impact assessments should be part of daily risk assessment. Watch, in particular, for evidence of negative impact on the site. If possible, move sites periodically to avoid degradation and negative impacts.

Does the site come with unique concerns? Some sites come with unique species and habitats that need special care. Research the site carefully before and throughout your use of it for a FNS program. (Carruthers Den Hoed 2014, 39)

CHAPTER 10

Best Practices in Nature-Based Early Childhood Education

PATTI ENSEL BAILIE

Providing a nature-based program for young children requires a significant investment in time, staffing, and resources. If the preschool is located at a nature center, it seems as though it should be easy to implement, but few nature centers know how to provide a high-quality program, as there are no official guidelines and nature center directors typically do not have the expertise needed. It's not enough to have a great outdoor space because integrating early childhood and environmental education requires planning developmentally appropriate activities, as well as experiences in natural habitats and contact with animals. How do we provide an excellent program that includes the best of early childhood education and the best of environmental education? Where do we find best practices for nature-based early childhood programs? We should start by looking at high-quality practices in early childhood education and environmental education and then look at the overlap to see what emerges.

High-Quality Practices of Early Childhood Education

High-quality practices in early childhood education are clearly articulated by the National Association for the Education of Young Children (NAEYC) as those that are developmentally appropriate. Developmentally appropriate practice (DAP) in early childhood education is about meeting children where they are according to what is known about child development, the individual child, and the social and cultural contexts in which the child lives (Copple and Bredekamp 2009). Central to DAP are the integrated curriculum, attention to the whole child, child-centered and play-based curriculum, and intentional teaching practices.

These practices are based on extensive research in child development. In *Developmentally Appropriate Practice in Early Childhood Programs,* early childhood specialists Carol Copple and Sue Bredekamp articulate twelve major principles in human development and learning that form a basis for decision making in early education. They contend that children's learning and development follow specific sequences, but proceed at varying rates from child to child. Learning is influenced by the dynamic interaction between biological maturation and experience, and by early experiences and social and cultural contexts. Secure, consistent relationships are important, as are opportunities for children to be challenged and to practice new skills. And finally, the principles also suggest that there are optimal periods for certain types of development and that development proceeds toward greater complexity. Children learn in a variety of ways, play is important, and children's experiences shape their motivation and approaches to learning (Copple and Bredekamp 2009).

High-Quality Practices of Environmental Education

The most comprehensive approach for establishing best practices in the field of environmental education is provided by the North American Association for Environmental Education (NAAEE) in the National Project for Excellence in Environmental Education. The project initiated several interrelated efforts from 1996 to 2010 and created guidelines in the areas of excellence for environmental education material in kindergarten through grade twelve programs, preparation of environmental educators, nonformal programs, and, most recently, early childhood environmental education. These guidelines provide standards for the profession. The most recent early childhood guidelines, which were created by a collaborative group of early childhood educators and environmental educators, identify six key areas: program philosophy, purpose, and development; developmentally appropriate practices focused on nature and the environment; a curriculum framework for environmental learning; play and exploration; places and spaces; and educator preparation (NAAEE 2010).

Comparison of Approaches

These two sets of principles and guidelines represent the high-quality practices in both early childhood education and environmental education. Looking at them side by side provides a comparison and opportunity to identify what is best for nature-based early childhood programs. In order to better understand these practices, principles, and guidelines, the table below compares the ideas inherent in each.

The resonance of these two sets of principles and guidelines is instructive. Both address the whole child in some way. DAP refers to all domains of early childhood, and Early Childhood Environmental Education (ECEE) guidelines can be used to plan programs "with the whole child in mind" (NAAEE 2010, 21). Play is important for

Comparison of NAEYC Developmentally Appropriate Practices and NAAEE Early Childhood Environmental Education Guidelines	
NAEYC developmentally appropriate practices (DAP)	**NAAEE early childhood environmental education guidelines (ECEE)**
Whole child focus	Whole child focus
Play-based	Play- and exploration-based
Age, individual, culturally appropriate	Address individual capabilities, culturally appropriate
Intentional practices	Authentic experiences
Meet children where they are	Make connections to previous experience
Child-centered	Child-directed and inquiry-based
Need for professional development and preparation	Need for educator preparation
Research-based child development practices	Need for practice based on research, theory, primary experience
	Curriculum framework for environmental learning
	Outdoor places and spaces

young children, and programs that provide opportunities for play are emphasized in both contexts. The ECEE guidelines go beyond DAP to advocate for exploration of the outdoor world as a fundamental part of the guidelines. Understanding that programs for children are fundamentally different from those provided for adults, both frameworks address the age, individual, and cultural needs of children. Each framework encourages either intentional practices, intentional programs, or authentic experiences, and puts forward the understanding that meeting children where they are and relating to their past experiences is important. Clearly both sets of guidelines agree that we need early childhood programming that connects children to the local, natural world rather than locks them up inside.

No Current Existing Standards

My research suggests that no quality standards exist for nature preschools (Bailie 2012). Nature center directors, who often do not have experience in early childhood education or age-appropriate practices for early childhood environmental education, usually rely on the nature preschool director to put the program together and set the policies. Many of the directors have created their own nature-based curriculum and most are not even written down. Therefore, each nature preschool, although allied with the natural world, runs by a separate set of rules, policies, expectations, and practices closely aligned with the experience and background of the nature preschool director.

When the director has experience with quality practices in early childhood and environmental education, the preschool program is of high quality. If the director's experience is limited, the program suffers, and, although there are early childhood licensing quality measures to adhere to, they often do not go far enough to help improve the overall quality and integrate nature. Subsequently, all areas of the program suffer. Because of the lack of quality standards in this field, the preschool director wields a lot of power over the program and should therefore be required to have a dual background in both early childhood and environmental education and knowledge of high-quality practices of each.

Identifying Best Practices for Nature Preschools

As part of this multiple case study of nature preschools (Bailie 2012), I interviewed nature preschool directors, observed classes, and examined relevant documents. Using the Early Childhood Environmental Education Guidelines (NAAEE 2010) as a filter, I identified high-quality practices inherent in the nature-based early childhood programs that I studied. These high-quality practices can be divided into five categories:

1. Program goals, curriculum, and practices
2. Staffing qualifications, including the teacher's role and professional development
3. Environments and physical space, both indoors and outdoors
4. Nature center resources and leadership
5. Parents and community

These categories of practice are described below and then form the framework for a rubric for identifying quality programs. It is my hope that this rubric can serve as the beginning of a comprehensive approach to establishing best practices for nature-based early childhood programs. (See Self-Assessment Rubric on pp. 223–228)

Family Nature Play. Connecting children to the local, natural world rather than locking them up inside.

1. Program Goals, Curriculum, and Practices

Although developing the whole child is the aim of early childhood education, developing an ecological identity and an environmental ethic is brought to the forefront when the preschool is placed in a nature center setting. Nature and daily nature explorations are used as the central organizing concept of the program and curriculum, based on local, seasonal, and natural occurrences. Nature is not just a topic or activity center, but the integrating thread that intentionally ties all the parts of the program together, including preschool philosophy, classroom design, methodologies, outdoor spaces, and public identity. Since nature is the main focus, academics are integrated in a meaningful way in the context of reality. The curriculum focuses on environmental interactions and authentic experiences. There are clear goals for both early childhood education and environmental education, and these are communicated clearly to staff, parents, and the nature center administration. The program is grounded in environmental and sustainable living practices.

Programs put a priority on nature by spending at least half their time outside (often starting their day outside), which includes both playing in naturalized play areas and hiking in diverse natural habitats. Child-initiated outdoor investigations and unstructured nature play is fostered, enabling children to know a place deeply and develop a sense of place.

2. Staffing Qualifications

Finding excellent teachers who have a background in both early childhood education and environmental education can be difficult. Until recently, there were no higher education programs that combined these two disciplines in one degree. Antioch University New England now offers a certificate program in Nature-based Early Childhood Education.

Often, nature center directors will look for a preschool director who has a background in early childhood education because they assume that the nature center staff can provide the environmental education portion of the program. However, it is the combination of both disciplines that reinforces the basis of the curriculum. One way to include early childhood and environmental education expertise is by hiring two teachers for each class, one with early childhood experience and the other with environmental education experience.

Typically, environmental education and nature center programs have focused on the K–12 ages at formal schools and nonformal education centers (such as museums and nature centers). Although preschool-aged children often take field trips to nature centers, the environmental educators are not usually trained to provide age appropriate programs. The third-grade field trip with a focus on constructing a food web for the animals and plants at the nature center meadow just doesn't work for preschoolers. For instance, bird programs for preschoolers should focus on having the children become birds rather than observing them. Therefore, the nature-based preschool teachers need to be trained to be facilitators of children's experiences in the natural world rather than teachers about the natural world. They act as guides and mentors, giving children time to explore the natural world and ask questions in order to solve problems they encounter in their explorations.

However, it is not enough to engage the children. Teachers must be fully engaged as well. A key part of high-quality practices includes a commitment to professional development. (Look at the wonderful 2013 book *To Look Closely* by Laurie Rubin, which describes her nature-based literacy curriculum with second graders. In it, she includes excerpts from her own nature journal, created independently of the classroom, which demonstrates her ongoing personal professional development in nature studies.) The director and teachers are educated and trained in both early childhood and environmental education and have a working knowledge of quality standards in both. There is ongoing professional development of both early childhood education and environmental education that should include field trips to model programs and cultivation of the teachers' own interest in nature.

3. Environment

Nature becomes the third teacher in a nature preschool classroom. Setting up the classroom environment requires an intentional approach that integrates nature in every area—dramatic play, library, art, housekeeping, block play, sensory table, science, and math. Dramatic play could become a veterinarian office, farmer's market, or maple sugar camp. The book area could include field guides and picture books about the forest, pond, or animals. Feathers or evergreen branches can be used for painting and tree cookies can be part of the block-building area. Natural materials are included in the sensory table (such as sunflower heads with seeds to pull, soil, snow, shelling corn, water with shells, the list is endless). There is extensive use of natural lighting, windows that can be opened with expansive outdoor views, real wood furnishings, natural materials for play and artistic expression, innovative use of classroom animals and live plants. Immediate access to the outdoors is possible with a door from the classroom that opens out to a naturalized play area so the children can be indoors or outdoors at any given time.

The outdoor areas are designed to be natural, where children plant and harvest gardens, pile and move rocks, dig in sand and soil, crawl through hollow logs, climb trees, balance on logs, build forts and fairy houses, and have access to loose parts and water. These naturalized outdoor play spaces should provide a "density of diversity," multiple habitats and landforms that are accessible and provide transitions to the nature center habitats such as wetlands, forests, ponds, shorelines, and prairies. These diverse habitats provide opportunities to explore in "wild nature."

4. Nature Center Resources and Leadership

One of the benefits of having a nature preschool associated with a nature center is access to the natural history artifacts and access to naturalists. Naturalists visit the classes on a regular basis, bringing in live animals or taking hikes on the nature center property. Special programs, such as maple sugaring, meeting live raptors, apple cidering, access to a greenhouse, gardening, and visiting an apiary, are provided, and children have access to wild and domestic animals. If not located at a nature center, then the program could be associated with one so the children are able to access these resources on a regular basis (weekly, monthly, or seasonally). Nature centers such as Schlitz Audubon in Milwaukee and Boston Nature Center in Boston have initiated programs so other urban early childhood programs can visit them, and their staff visit these other programs to naturalize them.

Of equal importance, when the program is operated by a nature center, is that the leadership and administration of the nature center supports the nature preschool program and philosophy (including a commitment for the resources needed to provide professional development for preschool staff and regularly scheduled naturalist programs).

5. Parents and Community

Probably one of the most difficult aspects of the nature-based early childhood program is convincing parents and the general public that this approach is as good (or better) than a traditional preschool. Where academics have become the norm and reading in kindergarten a necessity, parents often feel that playing in nature is a luxury that their children can't afford. Home visits, parent-teacher conferences (one, two, or three times a year), and daily communication are important. Documentation of children's experiences in the form of pictures and children's words is also used for reflection, planning, and communication. Special seasonal nature programming that includes the entire family strengthens the children's connection to nature as they share their knowledge and experience with their families.

Reaching out to the community and being a model for other preschools and kindergartens allow the nature preschool teachers to share the benefits of this approach with other professionals in the education field. This helps to disseminate nature-based early childhood practices and educate licensing specialists about the necessity of having animals in the classrooms, taking children to the pond or other body of water, allowing children to climb trees, and hiking to the diverse habitats in all weather. These are not typically covered by the policies and rules prescribed by the state for child care facilities. Clear communication and education are often required to overcome objections.

Wedding Best Practices at Schlitz Audubon Nature Preschool

One of the nature centers that has opened a nature preschool in the last decade is the Schlitz Audubon Nature Center in 2003. As the founding director of this preschool, I used my experience as a naturalist and early childhood educator to create the program. Located fifteen minutes north of Milwaukee, Wisconsin, the center borders on Lake Michigan, with 185 acres of diverse habitats, including prairie, wetlands and ponds, forests, and Lake Michigan beach. In this setting, children have the opportunity to visit the different habitats on a daily basis. Early childhood educators work with environmental educators to provide a nature-based curriculum.

In designing the program, we consciously aspired to the combination of early childhood education and environmental education. The curriculum is emergent, following the children's interests, based on seasonal happenings outside and the ways that the children respond to these changing environments. Nature activities include catching insects, following animal tracks in the snow, maple sugaring, planting trees, observing animals at the pond, and unstructured play in natural play areas. These activities in the natural world combine with developmental goals as the children become more confident and independent, even learning self-regulation skills as they explore the habitats. All domains of development (physical, social, emotional, cognitive, and spiritual) are met through nature-based activities. And by spending time outside, they develop an increased awareness of the environment that contributes to their ecological identity. Ann Pelo (2008), a writer and early childhood educator in Seattle, Washington, describes the meaning of an ecological identity:

> As a teacher, I want to foster in children an ecological
> identity, one that shapes them as surely as their cultural
> and social identities. I believe that this ecological identity,
> born in a particular place, opens children to a broader
> connection with the earth; love for a specific place makes

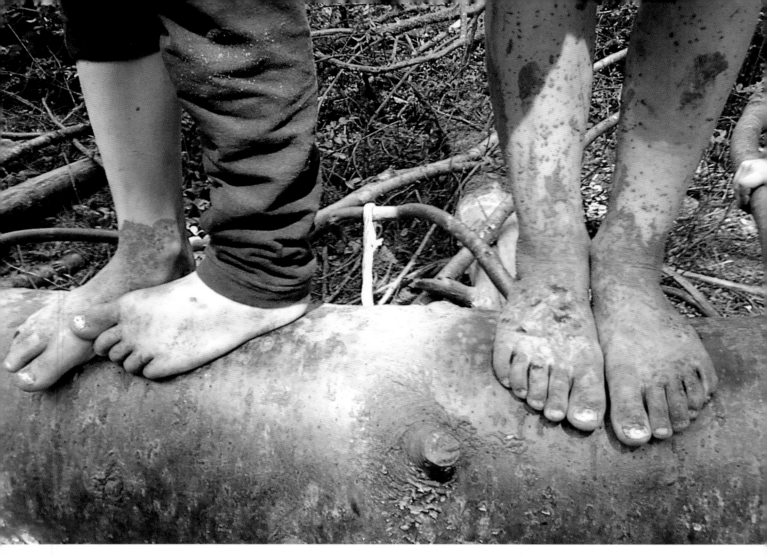

Family Nature Play. "An ecological identity allows us to experience the earth as our home ground."

possible love for other places. An ecological identity allows us to experience the earth as our home ground, and leaves us determined to live in honorable relationship with our planet. (124)

She further suggests a "handful of principles . . . [to] cultivate this love of place in young children's hearts and minds . . . [that include] walk the land, learn the names, embrace sensuality, explore new perspectives, learn the stories, [and] tell the stories" (Pelo 2008, 125).

The Schlitz Audubon Nature Preschool (SANP) aspires to these ideals. The goals of the nature curriculum include developing curiosity about the natural world, observation skills, appreciation of the beauty of nature, a willingness to use all the senses to make discoveries, an understanding of self and one's relationship to the natural world, an understanding of natural phenomena and concepts and a drive to experiment, and an ability to communicate about nature (Schlitz Audubon Nature Preschool 2006). But establishing the curriculum, communicating the benefits of this approach to the parents, and putting the program together was challenging, because few guidelines existed to provide a road map for the program.

Challenges

Even though early childhood programs had been offered at the nature center, the process of starting a nature preschool was more complex. Nature center early childhood programs are often "mom and me" types of programs where three- to four-year-olds and an adult (usually mom, but sometimes dad, grandparents, or a nanny) come once a season (or once a month) to do a one-hour program (hike, meet an animal, do a craft, etc.). Even the programs that were offered at nature centers in the past, such as the Rye Nature Center in New York or the Nature Center at Shaker Lakes in Cleveland, Ohio, where parents signed their children up for a ten-week two-hour session each season (without adult partners) seemed likely candidates to start nature preschools. But even these programs were naturalist led and often not developmentally appropriate because of a lack of early childhood experience on the part of the naturalist.

We moved beyond this episodic model to create well-integrated, immersive programs with the following efforts:

1. Hiring competent staff who were fluent in EC and EE, training teachers in this type of methodology, and providing a higher staff-to-child ratio than is found in other preschools
2. Defining goals that addressed both child development and environmental literacy and learning and creating an appropriate curriculum to blend both types of goals
3. Creating the environment, inside and out, that included nature in all areas of the classroom and supported unstructured nature play and exploration in natural areas
4. Consciously educating parents and the public on the value of this type of program
5. Addressing all state licensing requirements for early childhood centers and creating exemplary registration and administrative policies

Finally, after a number of years of implementation, we documented our work in a policy and procedures manual, created an extensive handbook, and assembled a curriculum guide, *Partnering with Nature: A Nature-Focused, Discovery-Based, Preschool Curriculum*. This creation of foundational documents is an essential part of developing an exemplary program. You'll need to create these in draft forms early on and then commit to evolving them into finished form within the early years of your program.

Assessment Rubrics for High-Quality Practices

The following rubrics were developed as indicators of high-quality practices for nature-based early childhood programs. The ideas described above undergird the rubrics, and the rubrics can serve as a set of guidelines when developing or implementing nature-based early childhood programs. Wherever a program fits on the continuum, there is always more that can be done to increase the quality and better integrate nature into existing early childhood programs.

You'll find that some of these rubric elements are specific to programs based at nature centers, such as Section IV, Nature Center Resources. Feel free to omit some of these components, or use them to assess your collaboration with nature centers and other environmental education programs in your area. As suggested above, all early childhood programs benefit from collaborations with environmental programs and professionals in their regions to extend the comprehensiveness of their engagement with nature.

We have provided both an overview assessment and a more comprehensive assessment for different uses. The overview assessment gives you a quick, at-a-glance sense of your program's nature-ness. The comprehensive assessment is probably more useful for in-depth, engaged conversations with your full staff and board. For questions or consultation regarding the use of the rubrics, please contact Patti Ensel Bailie at the University of Maine, Farmington, or David Sobel at Antioch University New England.

Elements	1	2	3	4
NATURE CENTER PRESCHOOL: Overview Self-Assessment Rubric				
Program Goals, Curriculum, Practices Dual goals for ECE and EE where nature is the central organizing concept. Program is child centered, play and inquiry based	◆ Program focus is on academics ◆ Teacher directed ◆ Few nature topics, but basic ones (i.e. leaves changing)	◆ Program focus is child development ◆ Mix of teacher and child directed ◆ Some nature topics are incorporated	◆ Goals are focused on child development, and some nature ◆ Child centered ◆ Nature topics are inquiry based and often	◆ Goals for the program are integrated, both child development and EE ◆ Play based, child-focused ◆ Nature is central concept of curriculum
Staffing Teacher's role is facilitator and is trained in both ECE and EE where PD is supported and teachers cultivate own interest in nature	◆ Director and teachers have only ECE or EE expertise ◆ PD is not supported ◆ Teacher directed	◆ Teachers are ECE, but have visiting naturalists ◆ PD is allowed, but minimal	◆ Teachers with backgrounds in ECE or EE work together to combine expertise in classroom	◆ Director and teachers have background in both ECE and EE ◆ PD is supported ◆ Teacher as facilitator, nature guide
Environment Indoors is infused with nature and natural light. Outdoors includes nature play and diverse habitats for wild nature experiences	◆ Indoor areas do not include nature ◆ Outdoor area is traditional playground	◆ Indoor area sometimes includes nature ◆ Outdoor area contains gardens	◆ Indoor area includes natural materials ◆ Outdoor area has natural play features but no wild areas	◆ Classroom is infused with nature, animals, plants, and natural light ◆ Outdoor natural play areas and diverse habitats
Nature Center Resources include access to naturalists, special programs, animals, and artifacts Leadership supports the nature preschool philosophy and PD	◆ Program is not at a nature center and has no access to those resources	◆ Program has access to a city park or other natural area that they visit monthly or seasonally	◆ Program has a relationship with a nature center that provides weekly programming at either site	◆ Program is at a nature center and has access to all resources available ◆ Nature center leadership supports PD and preschool philosophy
Parents & Community Communication with parents of benefits of nature, family programs, sharing nature-based approach	◆ Poor parent communication ◆ No family programs or teacher workshps	◆ Fair parent communication (1 mtg) ◆ Annual family program ◆ Willing to share	◆ Good parent communication (2 mtg) ◆ 2 family programs ◆ Conference pres	◆ Excellent parent communication (3 mtg) ◆ Seasonal family programs ◆ Educator workshops

NATURE CENTER PRESCHOOL: Comprehensive Self-Assessment Rubric

Section I: Program Goals, Curriculum Practices

Indicators	1	2	3	4
Program Goals Dual goals for both child development and conservation values, based on high-quality practices of ECE and EE, grounded in sustainable practices	◆ Program focuses on early literacy and math ◆ Teacher directed ◆ Topics are learned by direct instruction and memorization ◆ No sustainable practices or in planning stage	◆ Program focus is on child development ◆ Mix of teacher- and child-directed learning ◆ Mix of play and direct instruction ◆ 1 sustainable practice evident*	◆ Goals are focused on child development with some nature engagement ◆ Primarily child directed ◆ Some topics are learned through play ◆ 2 sustainable practices evident*	◆ Goals of the program are integrated, both child development and conservation values—whole child focus ◆ Place-based orientation ◆ Play based, child directed ◆ Integrated learning guided by interest ◆ 3+ sustainable practices evident*
Curriculum Central organizing concept is nature, based on local, seasonal, authentic experiences, academically integrated, learning in the context of reality	◆ Nature included as part of a science corner or other limited area (not available at all times) ◆ No "choice time" provided for children to choose activities in which to participate	◆ Mix of local and nonlocal nature included in classroom activities ◆ Units of study are mix of local/seasonal and other ◆ "Choice time" for children is provided for 25% of indoor class time or less	◆ Focus on nearby nature play and engagement ◆ Authentic experiences are evident— some projects in response to children's interests ◆ "Choice time" is provided for 26–50% of indoor class time	◆ Authentic experiences are locally and seasonally based ◆ Weekly themes/ units of study/ projects are nature-based (inside and outside) ◆ "Choice time" is a large part (51% or more) of the indoor time ◆ Experientially based activities
Program Practices Start outside, child initiated, unstructured nature play, exploration in wild areas, inquiry based	◆ Day starts inside ◆ Daily outdoor time is up to 15% of class time ◆ No hikes in semi-wild areas ◆ Nature is present via books and videos ◆ Use of worksheets	◆ Start day inside ◆ Daily outdoor time 15–30% of class time ◆ Visit natural habitat once a month ◆ Science involves direct teaching primarily	◆ Start day inside ◆ Daily, unstructured outdoor time in natural area 30–45% of class time ◆ Visit natural habitats at least once a week ◆ Inquiry-based science	◆ Begin the day outside ◆ Daily, unstructured outdoor time in natural area is at least 45% of the class time ◆ Daily hikes to explore in a variety of natural habitats (wild areas) ◆ Children reflect on their experiences/ documentation ◆ Inquiry-based activities ◆ Project-based learning present

Examples of sustainable practices include using real plates, utensils, cloth napkins, recycling, composting, rain barrels, etc.

Section II: Staffing

Indicators	1	2	3	4
Teacher's Role Authentic engagement of teacher, facilitator, provides "nature time" for children and play in natural environments	◆ Teachers direct learning and provide small amounts of nature time either indoors or outdoors ◆ Staff does not show comfort w/ nature immersion (e.g. lack of suitable outdoor clothing, does not interact with natural environment) ◆ Teachers complain about the weather	◆ Teachers provide monthly opportunities for play in natural environments ◆ Staff shows some comfort w/nature immersion by wearing mostly suitable outdoor clothing, interacting with the natural environment in 1 way* ◆ Teachers do not complain about or praise the weather	◆ Teachers provide weekly opportunities for play in natural environments ◆ Staff shows moderate comfort w/nature immersion by wearing suitable outdoor clothing, interacting with natural environments in 2 ways* ◆ Teachers are mostly positive about the weather	◆ Teachers provide daily opportunities for child-centered learning through play in natural environments ◆ Staff shows comfort w/ nature immersion by dressing appropriately for the weather, interacting with natural environments in 3+ ways* ◆ Teachers express positive aspects of the weather and communicate these to the children
Professional Development Cultivation of own interest in nature, visit model programs, attend workshops and training to develop ECE and/or EE skills	◆ Teachers have little interest in nature and do not attend workshops or trainings related to nature topics	◆ Teachers are interested in nature but do not cultivate own interests and rarely attend workshops or trainings related to nature topics	◆ Teachers have cultivated own interests in nature and attend workshops and trainings related to nature at least once a year	◆ Teachers have cultivated own interests in nature, visit model programs and attend workshops and trainings at least twice a year
Formal Education Directors and teachers are trained in both ECE and EE with an integration of methods	◆ Teachers not trained in either ECE or EE ◆ Teachers appear disinterested in work environment	◆ Teachers have either ECE or EE background with the other discipline not represented in the classroom	◆ Teachers have either ECE or EE background and both disciplines are represented in the classroom	◆ Directors and teachers have formal training in ECE and EE and are able to integrate the methods associated with each

Examples of interacting with natural environments include lying on the ground, raking leaves, catching insects, picking up worms, catching tadpoles and frogs, turning over logs, planting and/or harvesting gardens, tapping maple trees, etc.

Section III: Environment

Indicators	1	2	3	4
Indoors Nature is infused into all areas of the classroom, plenty of natural light, wood and natural materials, animals and plants	◆ No natural light ◆ Difficult transition to outdoors ◆ Few natural materials ◆ Plastic furnishings and toys ◆ No plants or animals in the classroom ◆ No nature-based books	◆ Little natural light ◆ No door to outside from classroom ◆ Photos of natural materials ◆ Small, dedicated space includes natural materials ◆ Mix of plastic and wood furnishings ◆ Either plants or animals in the classroom, but not both ◆ Few books are nature based	◆ Some natural light ◆ Easy transition to outdoors, but not from classroom ◆ Natural materials in two areas of the classroom ◆ Primarily wood furnishings, but some plastic ◆ One plant and animal in the classroom ◆ Some books are nature based	◆ Plenty of windows and natural light ◆ Door from class-room to outdoors ◆ Natural materials present in all areas of the classroom and reflect a variety of nature (not stereotypes) ◆ Animal puppets, manipulatives, dramatic play based on nature ◆ Diverse textures/earth-based colors ◆ Organized play areas/collections ◆ Wood and natural furnishings ◆ Two or more plants and animals in the classroom ◆ Most books are nature based/field guides present *(At least 7 of the above are evident)*
Outdoors Natural play area with loose parts, climbing areas, digging sand and soil, gardening, water	◆ Traditional playground with simple climbing structures, sandbox, few natural features	◆ Traditional playground with some trees and bushes, sand area, water table	◆ Naturalized outdoor area with some traditional playground equipment ◆ Trees, bushes, sand area, gardens, water table ◆ Loose parts include logs and sticks	◆ Garden/quiet areas ◆ Sensory rich environment ◆ All natural objects (loose parts), including logs, sticks, rocks, etc. ◆ Trees for climbing ◆ Sand and soil for digging ◆ Water feature ◆ Logs for balancing ◆ Hills and open spaces
Diverse Habitats Wild areas of natural habitats for exploration outside of the play area—woods, prairie, wetlands, ponds, etc.	◆ No access to natural habitats* outside play area	◆ Access to 1 natural habitat* nearby to explore	◆ Access to 2 natural habitats* nearby to explore	◆ Variety of trees, plants and wildlife to interact with ◆ Access to 3+ natural habitats* nearby to explore ◆ Stewardship to remove invasives and introduce balance

Examples of natural habitats include pond, river, wetland, marsh, meadow, field, prairie, lake/beach, woodlands, etc.

NATURE CENTER PRESCHOOL: Comprehensive Self-Assessment Rubric

Section IV: Nature Center Resources

Indicators	1	2	3	4
Naturalists Naturalists provide special programs and regularly scheduled visits to classes	• Little regular interaction with naturalists • Few special programs	• Naturalist visits seasonally and brings animals for special programs	• Naturalist visits once a month and brings animals for special programs	• Naturalist visits at least once a week and hikes with the children; visit includes an outdoor activity • Special programs at least twice a month
Special programs/ Resources Such as maple sugaring, raptors, animals, gardening, collections, greenhouses, etc.	• Limited habitats • Few extra resources • Few special programs offered	• Yearly field trip to nature center for special program (i.e. maple sugaring or animal program and hike)	• Seasonal field trip to nature center for special program (i.e. fall hike, winter animal tracks, spring maple sugaring)	• Diverse habitats, greenhouses, apiary, raptors, sugarhouse, gardens, etc., available as part of the program on site
Animals & Artifacts Access to wild and domestic animals and nature artifacts for education	• Little access to animals or artifacts	• Yearly access to natural artifacts through nature trunks that are borrowed • Wild and domestic animals seen during seasonal naturalist visit or yearly field trip	• Collections of nature artifacts available through a nature trunk on a monthly basis • Wild and domestic animals seen on field trips seasonally or naturalist visits monthly	• Collections of nature artifacts available on an ongoing basis to support seasonal nature topics such as bird parts, animals bones, bird nests, tree seeds, etc. • Wild and domestic animals available on a regular basis to support programs

NATURE CENTER PRESCHOOL: Comprehensive Self-Assessment Rubric

Section V: Parents and Community

Indicators	1	2	3	4
Parents Clear communication and education with parents of benefits of nature for young children, resources for parents to provide nature experiences for their children	◆ No parent manual ◆ Infrequent newsletter or resource list ◆ No parent/teacher conferences ◆ No parent workshops ◆ Little documentation	◆ Parent manual provided, but incomplete ◆ Annual parent newsletter ◆ Seasonal reports of classroom activities ◆ One parent/ teacher conference per year ◆ One parent workshop but not on nature	◆ Parent manual provided* ◆ Seasonal parent newsletter ◆ Monthly reports of classroom activities ◆ Two parent/ teacher conferences per year ◆ Two parent workshops (one on nature) ◆ Photo documentation	◆ Parent manual provided* ◆ Monthly parent newsletter ◆ Weekly reports of classroom activities to parents ◆ Seasonal (3) parent/teacher conferences ◆ Seasonal parent workshops of benefits of nature for children ◆ Photo documen- tation of projects posted
Family Programs Seasonal programs allow children to share nature with their families	◆ No family day visits ◆ No family gatherings	◆ One family program per year but might not be focused on nature	◆ Two family programs per year with one focused on nature	◆ Seasonal (3) family programs (all nature based) such as owl hikes, camping, catching frogs or insects
Sharing Knowledge Program models appropriate nature-based early childhood practices for other educators and is a resource for the community	◆ No educator classes ◆ No volunteer calendar ◆ No community calendar	◆ One workshop per year for educators in the community on various topics (not necessarily nature) ◆ Volunteer calendar for opportunities to volunteer occasionally ◆ Little connection to the community is apparent	◆ Two workshops per year for educators in the community where one is focused on providing nature for young children ◆ Volunteer calendar for opportunities to volunteer monthly ◆ Connection to the community is through a calendar	◆ Seasonal (3) workshops provided for educators in the community to learn about nature-based approach ◆ Volunteer calendar for opportunities to volunteer weekly ◆ Connection to the community is evident (calendar, notices, community reps visit, etc.)

Parent manual includes mission statement and program philosophy related to nature and appropriate clothing to wear for the weather.

CHAPTER 11

An Autumn Day in the Life: A West Coast Nature Preschool and Forest Kindergarten

ERIN K. KENNY

It is a drippy late autumn day at Cedarsong Forest Kindergarten on Vashon Island in Washington's Puget Sound. The woods are silent except for the patter of the raindrops on the leaves, and we drink in the ambience before the atmosphere explodes with the arrival of excited children.

As cars begin to pull up the driveway, we three teachers wait in anticipation to see what the day will bring. At Cedarsong's Forest Kindergarten, we never know what to expect. We try not to have any expectations because we are committed to the interest-led, child-driven flow of each day. We have no set agenda, structure, or curriculum prepared; we simply allow each day to unfold according to the children's energy, interests, and curiosity.

The parents spend time dressing each child in appropriate clothing for this chilly autumn day: Bogs boots, Oakiwear rain pants, and Columbia Omni-Tech jackets. The children chatter excitedly, calling to each other and to the teachers wondering what adventures the day will bring. As we walk in with the group of twelve children, the teachers ask leading questions: What do you think the puddle will look like today? Do you think there will be more or less water than yesterday? Each child makes a guess, and one child responds, "I think there will be water in the puddle because, *look*, there is water in the birdbath." These are the kinds of synaptic leaps we witness every day as children extrapolate their learning from one situation to another.

As we approach the mud puddle in Main Camp, some of the children run to the edges and explore whether there are animal footprints

The map contains the following labels: Driveway, Compost Toilet, The Unicorn, Climbing Logs, Clara, Hemlock Camp, Parking Area, Main Camp, Fire Pit, Squirrel Camp, Echo Castle, Mud Puddle, Monkey Tree, Hazelnut Camp, The Loop, Butterfly Trail, Gremlin Trail, Heart Trail, Lending Library, Red Yarn Camp, Forest Theater, Old Marona Camp, Balancing Logs, Secret Trail

Cedarsong Nature School Trails Map

Cedarsong Nature School. Map of Cedarsong's five acres of private forest land. Cartography by Kathleen O'Brien.

in the silky mud. "Raccoon prints!" the children yell excitedly. Other children fetch the measuring sticks—tall sticks painted with different stripes of color—and proceed to the water's edge, guessing how high the water will be before putting the sticks in the water. "I think it will be up to the yellow stripe," guesses one boy. "I think it will be up to the blue stripe," guesses another. One after another, the children weigh in on how high they think the water will be. They take turns with the measuring stick, inserting it into various places around the puddle, observing where the puddle is deepest.

"Let's play Sink or Float," suggests a three-year-old girl. The children all reach down for various nature objects to toss into the puddle. Before they toss, with unexpected patience for young children, they ask one another, "Do you think this will sink or float?" This game was developed by a five-year-old boy as he experimented one day with throwing different objects into the puddle. The teachers encouraged him to stop and first ask whether he thought a particular object would sink or float. The children became captivated with guessing the outcome. Initially, they came to the conclusion that big things sink and little things float. However, as they experimented, they ended up changing their hypothesis based on their observations. Eventually they came to the conclusion that it is a matter of how much something weighs that determines whether it will sink or float.

Some of the children grab buckets and begin pouring water down the hill, noticing that it always ends up heading back down to the puddle. "Let's build a dam!" one child exclaims and the other children chime in their agreement. There is a discussion among the children about the best way to make a dam. First they try using just mud. They soon notice, however, that the water breaks through easily. Next they collect sticks, dry dirt, and debris gathered from the forest and place them in layers on the dam. "I'll get the sticks,"

Cedarsong Nature School. The mud puddle in Main Camp.

one yells. "I'll get the dry dirt," another shouts. The evolution of teamwork and cooperation happens organically without teacher direction or suggestion. In fact, the teachers have not yet said much of anything on this morning. Instead, they observe the free flow of experimentation and learning that transpires.

Another group of children has settled into making mud cakes by collectively gathering dry dirt, sticks, and fir needles, and then mixing in muddy water so that the batter attains the right consistency. As they dig up dirt for their cake mix, they notice that the dirt is different colors and have soon identified red, yellow, brown, and even black dirt. They scoop up shovels full of each type of dirt and place them each on one of the stumps around our fire pit to compare the difference in color and also the differing textures and smells of each sample. The children also experiment with making mud balls to see which type of mud holds together better. They throw the mud balls against a tree trunk and notice that very wet mud balls splatter and drier mud balls stick. A couple of the kids begin painting each other's faces with mud, finding the perfect specific consistency for the face paint.

The children who are still mixing their buckets of mud call to those making the dam saying, "We made cement for your dam!" The dam grows taller and sturdier as all the children now collaborate on this project. After a while, they decide it is time to test out their dam. The children gather buckets of water and agree to pour all of them at the same time. "One, two, *three*!" they all shout and then pour. "Teacher, I noticed that the water made a sound when we poured it fast," observes one three-year-old boy. All the children then begin experimenting with the changing sound of the water as they alternately pour it slowly and quickly down the hill.

Almost as if on cue, several of the children begin calling out, "I'm ready to go on an adventure!" When I then ask who wants to head out on an adventure, most of the children chime in, and it is decided that eight children want to go and four children want to stay, continuing their mud and water play at Main Camp. Two teachers head to the top of the trail and encourage the children to count how many are heading out on the adventure. Since Cedarsong is located on five acres of unfenced private forestland, one of the most important rules is that all children need to be able to see a teacher, and be seen by a teacher, at all times. We invite the children to help us count the eight children who have decided to go on the adventure down Heart Trail.

I grab the thermos of hot water, letting the children know I have it and ask, "Who wants to help make the forest tea today?" Most of the kids chime in, "I want to!" So I wander more slowly with the children who want to add native foraged plants to our hot water. Teacher Kristen heads down the trail with the kids who feel like running, and Teacher Ginger stays behind with those four kids who wanted to stay at Main Camp. Committing to a 1:4 teacher to student ratio allows us to honor more completely our interest-led programming as the children get to decide which activity appeals more to their energy level at any point in time. The group of children walking with me begins to grab huckleberry leaves, red cedar tips, salal leaves, and "forest candy" (Douglas fir buds), confidently nibbling some and adding the rest to the hot water for our forest tea, which we will drink later. Some children lick raindrops off the leaves and giggle as they give themselves a "shower" by shaking the branches of each bush they walk under.

Eventually we end up at the hazelnut grove, where Teacher Kristen's group of kids is climbing. The children immediately notice that some of the other kids are barefoot and begin to remove their boots. The children who are climbing explain how they noticed that it was slippery

Cedarsong Nature School. Going on an adventure down the trail.

Cedarsong Nature School. Foraging native plants to make forest tea.

on the climbing limbs today because of the rain. "That's why we took our shoes off," articulates a three-year-old. As Kristen keeps an eye on the kids who are climbing, I wander over to our Forest Theater—a tarp strung between two trees—where some of the children are creating a spontaneous performance. There is a lot of negotiation about who is going to play what character and what the scenario is going to be. One child begins to hand out "popcorn" (huckleberry leaves) to the kids who have decided to be in the audience. Another child stands at a tall old stump pretending it is the microphone and begins to tell the story as each child emerges from behind the curtain when their character is introduced. On this day we are introduced to the snow fairy, a unicorn, and a dog named Biscuit. Each child is encouraged to choose her own character and no one may dictate another child's character.

About this time, some of the children mention that they are hungry. I encourage them to check in with their friends about whether anyone else is hungry, knowing that it is indeed snack time. The children begin to ask around, "Are you hungry?" and soon all the children agree that it is time for snack. I begin to sing our snack song:

It's time for snack, woo-woo,
Time for snack, woo-woo,
Let's head on back to Main Camp and have our snack,
It keeps us strong and in a good mood.

Cedarsong Nature School. A tarp strung between two trees creates the Forest Theater.

All the children join in by the second line, and we are singing loudly as we trundle back up Heart Trail to Main Camp, alerting those kids who are still at the mud puddle that we are on our way.

When we arrive at Main Camp, the rest of the group is loudly singing the snack song too, and two teachers head over to the wash stand with the group of kids to rinse off their hands. After all the visible loose dirt has been removed from the children's hands with water and non-antibacterial soap, we head to the snack table under a freestanding picnic shelter. One of the teachers has already arranged placemats and the kids' water bottles on the table, and the children all take their places. Coats, hats, and mittens come off as the children realize they are quite warm from all of the morning activity.

Before handing out the snack, I talk about how lucky we are to have enough food to eat each day and how important it is to be thankful for that. We all sing our blessing song before eating our food.

Give thanks to the Mother Gaia,
Give thanks to the Father Sun,
Give thanks for the plants in the garden,
Where the Mother and the Father are one.

Snack consists of mostly organic choices, including raisins, apricots, sunflower seeds, pumpkin seeds, almonds, rice or corn cakes, and fresh apple and carrot. We do not serve meat, dairy, wheat, peanuts, or anything with artificial colors or flavors or refined sugars. I ask each child if they want a particular food item before putting it on their placemat to reduce waste.

As soon as we show up to the snack table, our bird friends gather nearby. Some have become quite bold, coming close enough that the children can easily identify them now. "There's the towhee," says one two-year-old girl. "And there's the song sparrow," chimes a three-year-old boy. Many adults don't even know the names of these common native birds. However, the children get so close to them that they can tell a male from a female towhee because of subtle differences in their coloration.

"I see Teacher Kristen has the nature journal out; who would like to add something to the journal?" I say. All of the children's hands shoot up and then they take turns making suggestions for entries into our ongoing nature journal. They recount the following memories from the day:

- how they made the perfect cement for the dam
- how they discovered the best way to make a solid dam
- how they noticed water makes a different sound depending on how fast it is poured
- how there are different colors of dirt and how they feel and smell differently
- what ingredients went into the tea
- the slipperiness of the branches and the need to be more aware
- the millipede they saw
- the earthworms and the salamander we discovered
- the play they created at Forest Theater
- how some of their friends were barefoot

As the children excitedly relate their morning adventures, their observations, how they played, and what they discovered, the teacher records their responses in the nature journal.

A NOTE ON DOCUMENTING LEARNING

As fall deepens, the children notice evidence of the changing season, and there is a lot of discussion during snacktime centered around these changes. Where have all the insects gone? Why is it foggy in the mornings? Why is it darker in the forest? Why can we see our breath? Why are the leaves falling? Why are there so many mushrooms now? Why is there so much mold on the ground? Forest kindergarten children are acutely aware of the seasonal changes because they are immersed in the natural world all year long. Their minds are continuously processing the changes they notice, and the children come up with their own unique answers—some of them correct, some of them adorable. One day when we asked the children for their ideas about why the fog was dripping from the trees, one four-year-old child answered, "Because the sun is crying."

At the end of each month, I compile these notes into a newsletter and distribute it to the parents so that the learning becomes visible. In a culture that expects measurable learning from even our youngest children, these newsletters give the parents a way to understand the very real natural science lessons that occur every day at the forest kindergarten. Besides the hard sciences of botany, biology, chemistry, ornithology, entomology, physics, and engineering, the children are learning important lessons in social skills through play negotiation and practice at conflict resolution. These forest kindergarten children are also learning respect for all aspects of the natural world, and they're given important opportunities to practice empathy and compassion. I was so touched one day to hear a three-year-old boy say to another child, "I feel upset when you break my fairy house," rather than lashing out in anger.

After snack the children begin to complain about being cold, and some whining voices rise above the conversation. I respond, "I can't understand you when you whine; can you please use another voice to let me know what you need?" The children change their voices and even the youngest, at two years old, begins to clearly express his needs. All three teachers get busy helping children put their coats, mittens, and hats back on and fill each child's water bottle with the warm forest tea. The chillier autumn temperatures mean the teachers have to focus more on keeping the children warm. Besides the occasional barefoot child, most everyone is bundled up these days in their required winter clothing. When kids complain about being cold we ask, "What are some of the things you can do if you feel cold?" The children respond with suggestions such as, "put on more clothes, run, dance, and hop." Although having a campfire might seem like a good strategy, I have actually found that it is not because it causes the kids to sit still in one place. It is much better to get those kids moving!

The children begin to head back to Main Camp as the rain increases in intensity and a loud raven caws overhead. As we walk back, I encourage the children to stop, stand still, and listen. "What do you hear?" I ask. The children answer "rain," "the raven," "the wind." We stand for a few moments, silent and still, listening. "Can you see the wind?" I ask. The children hesitate before answering. Half of the children answer yes and the other half answer no. There is a pause as the children absorb the question. I say, "If you can't see the wind, how do you know it's there? What are your clues?" "I can see the trees dancing," answers one four-year-old. "I can feel it on my cheek," answers another. Several of the children mentioned that they could also smell the wind and notice how it made the light in the forest shift and change. We stand for a moment more before the children spontaneously continue on their path.

As we approach Main Camp, the children begin to break into groups, some heading up to a play area they have named the Unicorn, others heading to a space named Echo Castle, and a third group heading to Clara, one of our beloved red cedar trees. The teachers each tag along behind one of the groups, carefully keeping a distance so the social group consists of the children. I follow the group up to Clara and the children begin talking about needing the rakes to clear more of the area behind the cedar tree. Two of the children run to retrieve the rakes and the others grab the bowl of chunky chalk to color the bark of the trees, decorating this special area.

This tree has become the place where children ask to go when they are feeling out of sorts or need emotional balance. On this day, the children begin to clear out space under some neighboring huckleberry bushes using rakes, and I hear one three-year-old girl say, "This can be my place to come when I am feeling sad and I don't want anyone watching me." Quite often we observe that children, like all of us, just need to sit quietly on the ground in a natural area slightly removed from the group to process their feelings of sadness or anxiety. When our children are given this opportunity, they learn that nature is the perfect venue to self-soothe and return to emotional balance. We have noticed that often children don't want to "talk it out." Rather, they just need to be left alone in a safe, nurturing place on the earth.

The children notice a lot of exposed roots during winter months as a result of erosion, and on this day they begin to discuss it again as they are raking around Clara. I ask the leading question, "Where do the roots of plants like to live?" The children all answer, "Under the ground." I follow up with, "So how do you think these roots feel when they are above the ground?" The answers I received from the three- and four-year-olds were "sick," "sad," and "they might hurt." One four-year-old boy elaborated, "If I was a tree and my roots were uncovered all of the time, I would feel really sad." Acting on these feelings, the children spend time deeply engaged in transporting mud, dirt, and debris to cover the roots of this favorite tree.

After a time, one of the children calls out, "Let's play What's Missing!" The kids all begin to pick up nature objects from the ground—fir cones, lichen, sticks, rocks, leaves, and branches—and then lay them out in a line on the forest floor. Once they have gathered about ten to twelve objects, we identify each one and then together count how many items we have. As the others close their eyes or turn their heads toward the sky, one child picks an object from the line and hides it behind his/her back, letting us know when they are ready. "What's missing?" the child then asks, and everyone tries to guess what has been taken from the line. In the middle of this game, the other two groups of children and their teachers wander over, intrigued by the excitement generated by the game.

After many rounds, the children notice that we are sitting in a circle and begin to suggest storytelling. I ask, "Who wants to tell a story?" Inevitably, several children have a story they want to relate and we listen as each story evolves. Sometimes we gather leaves and make a pretend book by piercing one side of the leaf bundle with a stick to

Cedarsong Nature
School. Leaf art
is simple but so
compelling.

make a binding. Each child then takes a turn "reading" from the book, making up his or her own story as they go along.

Some of the children wander off with a teacher and bring back musical instruments from the storage bin we leave out on the forest floor for them to grab from. This leads to some wonderful spontaneous song and dance as the kids call out their requests from our Cedarsong originals song list, and we all begin a raucous sing-along. One of the kids suggests a parade to Squirrel Camp, and we take off in that direction, banging our instruments and singing loudly.

Squirrel Camp has developed into a wonderful "camp-out" place. We often end up here playing that we are having a cookout. The children go through the motions of gathering wood for the fire, arranging logs around the campfire, and then lighting the fire, all in their elaborate, detailed, make-believe way. Each child grabs a stick and puts leaves or cones on the end of it to pretend they are roasting marshmallows. Eventually a couple of children announce that it is nighttime and they put out the fire with their stick hoses. The children go through the motions of setting up a tent and then invite each other inside. All the children lay down, calm and quiet, on the wet ground. I have noticed that children will often voluntarily lie still on the forest floor and gaze up at the forest canopy. Generally, they are motionless and appear to be in quiet meditation. This kind of stillness is not usually an option in a chaotic, indoor preschool. Eventually, a five-year-old spontaneously announces, "Morning!" and they all get up and start the camp day game over again.

Cedarsong Nature School. A simulated camp-out at Squirrel Camp.

Since the forest is so damp, the children find a lot of what we call "chicken wood." This is the very decayed wood of the alder tree. It becomes so soft as it decomposes that the children can literally squeeze water out of handfuls of the wood; the resulting product looks a lot like shredded chicken meat. Several of the four-year-olds set up an imaginary food stand and serve this chicken wood rolled up in a salal leaf, calling it a burrito. As the children begin to line up, the servers announce that a burrito costs one salal leaf. Before the kids begin to just pluck living leaves off the bushes for this part of the play, the teachers remind them to choose leaves that are already on the ground. Part of our philosophy is to teach these young children to respect and appreciate all aspects of the natural world.

The imagination of children involved in free play never ceases to astonish me. With little more than a few buckets and shovels as props, kids create many wonderful scenarios. For example, after mixing in a bucket, one four-year-old informed me, "We put sprinkled dirt in mud with leaves and it turned to chocolate." One day, a five-year-old showed the other kids how to make telescopes out of rolled salal leaves. Another day, several of the children created tiny dolls out of fir cones with huckleberry leaves stuck in them. Douglas fir boughs are often used as tools or as pretend household implements. One three-year-old showed the other children how to use a bough as a dust mop as she swept the forest floor. Sword fern crowns and skirts are often crafted into costumes for spontaneous plays at our Forest Theater.

At some point, all twelve children decide collectively that they want to head back to Main Camp from Squirrel Camp. As we walk back together, a three-year-old asks, "What does *hibernate* mean anyway?" In autumn the subject of hibernation comes up quite a bit, as it had during the course of this day, and it seemed like this young boy was still processing it. Instead of answering him directly, true to our inquiry-based teaching style, I ask, "Hey kids, your friend wants to know what hibernate means." One four-year-old responds, "It means sleeping through the winter." I then prompt further, "What are some examples of things that hibernate?" to which several children answer, "Bears." "Insects." "Millipedes." "Flowers." Later on this day, some children are picking at a decomposing log with sticks and discover a bald-faced hornet in hibernation. We all get a chance to look at it with our handheld microscopes before carefully placing it in an out-of-the-way place where it can continue its slumber undisturbed.

As we approach Main Camp, children begin to peel off and head to different areas to play. Some wander back to the puddle for mud and water play. Others grab the chalk and start coloring the tree bark, making observations about the different textures of each. Others begin some imaginative play under what they call the "talking bush." The teachers stand slightly away from the kids to give them a sense of freedom. We are removed yet available if a child truly needs help. One four-year-old who is struggling with a very full bucket of water yells, "Hey, I need some teamwork over here." Several children run to his aid, and they work together to haul the heavy bucket to the top of the hill so they can pour it down the river he has dug.

As parents begin to arrive, the children respond in various ways. Some run to their parents, excited and flushed, jabbering about all of the fun they had today at Cedarsong. Other kids look disappointed as they spot their parents because they are not ready to leave. One

Cedarsong Nature School. Do millipedes hibernate?

Cedarsong Nature School. Parents support full-on immersion for their children.

three-year-old girl begins to cry as she announces, "I don't want to go now." Her friend picks up a small rock and says, "Here. You can take this home with you and then you have a piece of Cedarsong until you come back." The first girl stops crying and beams at her friend and then at her mom. I could not have thought of a better strategy myself!

These parents are all genuinely glad to see their children so muddy. Some of the children, upon seeing their parents, decide it is time for a mud bath and begin to jump, sit, and roll in the mud puddle. Thankfully, our parent community supports this full-on immersion for their children. In fact, I have received much complimentary feedback over the years from parents who report that having their child enrolled at Cedarsong's forest kindergarten has improved their family bonds. They tell me that their children now play longer outside without needing adult direction and without complaint. Parents have also told me that they can no longer use the excuse that it is raining to resist going outdoors when their children are begging them to play outside. Many families say that having their child in the forest kindergarten has increased their own nature time and reduced their family's media time.

At the end of the day, many parents stay and chat with us teachers, asking about what their children did and how they played. This is an opportunity for us to connect as a community in sharing our love of this particular early childhood education model, while the children continue to play happily and lovingly. As I stand and watch the group, I feel deliciously tired and yet energized at the same time. I notice the children laughing, the parents chatting, the raven above, the wind in the trees, and the rain still dripping, and I am filled with gratitude for this experience.

References

Aleccia, JoNel. 2012. "Hurt on the Stairs: A Child Is Treated Every 6 Minutes in the U.S." *MSNBC*. March 12. http://childinjurypreventionalliance .org/resources/1/NewsArticles/MSN.com-Hurt-on-the-Stairs-A-Child-is-Treated-Every-6-Minutes-in-the-U.S.-06.12.12.pdf.

Anderson, Sarah, and Robert Whitaker. 2009. "Prevalence of Obesity Among US Preschool Children in Different Racial and Ethnic Groups." *Archives of Pediatrics and Adolescent Medicine* 163 (4): 344–48.

Armitage, Kevin C. 2009. *The Nature Study Movement: The Forgotten Popularizer of America's Conservation Ethic.* Lawrence, KS: University Press of Kansas.

Ashton-Warner, Sylvia. 1963. *Teacher.* New York: Simon & Schuster.

Bailey, Liberty Hyde. 1903. *The Nature-Study Idea: Being an Interpretation of the New School Movement to Put the Child in Sympathy with Nature.* New York: Doubleday, Page.

Bailie, Patti E. 2012. "Connecting Children to Nature: A Multiple Case Study of Nature Preschools." PhD diss., University of Nebraska–Lincoln.

Bailie, Patti E., H. Bartee, and M. Oltman. 2009. *The State of Nature Center-Based Preschools in the United States 2007–2008.* Report to National Audubon Society and Kalamazoo Nature Center.

Banning, Wendy, and Ginny Sullivan. 2011. *Lens on Outdoor Learning.* Saint Paul, MN: Redleaf Press.

Bennett, Rosemary. 2009. "Lessons in Life at the Forest School." *Times* (London). October 6. http://www.thetimes.co.uk/tto/education /article1801036.ece

Bodrova, Elena, and Deborah Leong. 2005. "Uniquely Preschool." *Educational Leadership* 63 (1): 44–47.

Brown, William H., Karin A. Pfeiffer, Kerry L. McIver, Marsha Dowda, Cheryl L. Addy, and Russell R. Pate. 2009. "Social and Environmental Factors Associated with Preschoolers' Nonsedentary Physical Activity." *Child Development* 80 (1): 45–58.

Brussoni, Mariana, Lise L. Olsen, Ian Pike, and David A. Sleet. 2012. "Risky Play and Children's Safety: Balancing Priorities for Optimal Child Development." *International Journal of Environmental Research and Public Health* 9 (9): 3134–48.

Burdette, Hillary L., and Robert C. Whitaker. 2005. "Resurrecting Free Play in Young Children: Looking Beyond Fitness and Fatness to Attention, Affiliation, and Affect." *Archive of Pediatrics and Adolescent Medicine* 159 (1): 46–50.

Carroll, Alicia, and Bisse Bowman. 2006. "Learning to Read Nature's Book: An Interdisciplinary Curriculum for Young Children in an Urban Setting." *Community Works Journal* 7 (3): 19–25; 32. http://www.communityworksinstitute.org/cwjonline/cwjarchive/cwjwinter06-fullcolor.pdf.

Carruthers Den Hoed, Rebecca, ed. 2014. *Forest and Nature School in Canada: A Head, Heart, Hands Approach to Outdoor Learning*. Ottawa: Forest School Canada. http://www.forestschoolcanada.ca/wp-content/themes/wlf/images/FSC-Guide_web.pdf?date=july72014.

Carson, Rachel. 1965. *The Sense of Wonder*. New York: Harper and Row.

Centers for Disease Control and Prevention. 1998. "Guidelines for School and Community Programs to Promote Lifelong Physical Activity among Young People." Centers for Disease Control and Prevention. http://www.cdc.gov/mmwr/preview/mmwrhtml/00046823.htm.

Chawla, Louise. 1999. "Life Paths into Effective Environmental Action." *The Journal of Environmental Education* 31 (1): 15–26.

Cobb, Edith. 1959. "The Ecology of Imagination in Childhood." *Daedalus* 88 (3): 537–48. Boston: MIT Press.

Cobb, Edith. 1977. *The Ecology of Imagination in Childhood*. New York: Columbia University Press.

Comstock, Anna Botsford. 1911. *Handbook of Nature Study*. Ithaca, NY: Cornell University Press.

Connors, Margaret, and Bill Perkins. 2005. "Learning from Nature in the Urban Wilds." *Community Works Journal* 7 (2): 29–31.http://www.communityworksinstitute.org/cwjonline/cwjarchive/cwjsummer05-web.pdf.

Copeland, Kristen A., Susan N. Sherman, Cassandra A. Kendeigh, Heidi J. Kalkwarf, and Brian E. Saelens. 2012. "Societal Values and Policies May Curtail Preschool Children's Physical Activity in Child Care Centers." *Pediatrics* 129 (2): 265–74. http://pediatrics.aappublications.org/content/early/2012/01/02/peds.2011-2102.full.pdf.

Copple, Carol, and Sue Bredekamp, eds. 2009. *Developmentally Appropriate Practice in Early Childhood Programs: Serving Children from Birth through Age 8*. Washington, DC: NAEYC.

Cornell, Joseph. 2015. "About the Founder." Sharing Nature Worldwide. Accessed June 7. http://www.sharingnature.com/about-us/joseph-cornell.php.

Danks, Fiona, and Jo Schofield. 2011. *The Stick Book: Loads of Things You Can Make or Do with a Stick*. London: Frances Lincoln.

De Roo, Ana C., Thiphalak Chounthirath, and Gary A. Smith. 2013. "Television-Related Injuries to Children in the United States, 1990–2011." *Pediatrics* 132 (2): 267–74. DOI: 10.1542/peds.2013-1086.

Doolan, Paul. 2011. "Forest Kindergarten." *ThinkShop* (blog). December 7. http://www.pauldoolan.com/2011/12/for-two-years-my-little-girl-went-to.html.

Duckworth, Angela Lee, and Lauren Eskreis-Winkler. 2013. "True Grit."

Observer 26 (4). http://www.psychologicalscience.org/index.php
/publications/observer/2013/april-13/true-grit.html.

Duffin, Michael, Chris Hardee, George Tremblay, and PEER Associates.
2012. *Shades of Green: Boston School's Environmental Initiative (BSEI),
2009–2012, Summary Report on the Third Multi-Year Cycle of a
Comprehensive, Ongoing Program Evaluation.* Richmond, VT: PEER
Associates. http://www.peecworks.org/peec/peec_research
/01B8EE18-001D0211.3/BSEI%20Evaluation%202009-2012.pdf.

Eastman, Charles. 1902, 1971. *Indian Boyhood.* New York: Dover
Publications.

Elkind, David. 2009. Introduction to *The Wisdom of Play: How Children Learn
to Make Sense of Their World.* Ulster Park, NY: Community Playthings.
http://elf2.library.ca.gov/pdf/WisdomOfPlay.pdf.

Egle, Anita. 2013. "Waldkindergarten: Forest Kindergarten in
Germany." Creative STAR Learning Company. Aberdeenshire,
Scotland. http://creativestarlearning.co.uk/early-years-outdoors
/waldkindergarten-forest-kindergarten-in-germany.

Flood, Alison. 2015. "Oxford Junior Dictionary's Replacement of
'Natural' Words with 21st-Century Terms Sparks Outcry." *The Guardian,*
January 13. http://www.theguardian.com/books/2015/jan/13
/oxford-junior-dictionary-replacement-natural-words.

Fröebel, Friedrich. 2009. *The Education of Man.* Edited by Josephinetr Jarvis.
Charleston, SC: BiblioLife.

Gill, Tim. 2007. *No Fear: Growing Up in a Risk Averse Society.* London:
Calouste Gulbenkian Foundation.

Golden, Anna. 2010. "Exploring the Forest: Wild Places in Childhood."
Voices of Practitioners 5 (1): 1–11. https://www.naeyc.org/files/naeyc
/file/vop/VOP_Anna_Golden(1).pdf.

Grahn, Patrik, F. Martensson, B. Lindblad, P. Nilsson, and A. Ekman. 1997.
"Ute pa Dagis." *Stad and Land,* 145.

Gray, Peter. 2012. "As Children's Freedom Has Declined, So Has
Their Creativity." *Psychology Today* (blog). September 17. https://
www.psychologytoday.com/blog/freedom-learn/201209/
children-s-freedom-has-declined-so-has-their-creativity.

Hopeman, Riley, and David Sobel. 2014. "Taking the Classroom to the
Forest: A School's Forest Fridays Program." *Community Works Journal.*
http://www.communityworksinstitute.org/cwjonline/essays
/a_essaystext/sobel_forestfridays.html.

Jackman, Wilbur S. 1891. *Nature Study for the Common Schools.* New York:
Henry Holt.

Kenny, Erin. 2013. *Forest Kindergartens: The Cedarsong Way.* Vashon, WA:
Cedarsong Nature School.

Kilpatrick, William H. 1951. Introduction to *The Education of Man: Aphorisms,*
by Heinrich Pestalozzi. New York: Philosophical Library.

Langer, Susanne. 1942. *Philosophy in a New Key: A Study in the Symbolism of
Reason, Rite, and Art.* Cambridge, MA: Harvard University Press.

Lear, Linda. 1997. *Rachel Carson: Witness for Nature*. New York: Henry Holt.

Louv, Richard. 2008. *Last Child in the Woods: Saving Our Children from Nature-Deficit Disorder*. Chapel Hill, NC: Algonquin Books.

Maine Department of Education. 2015. "Key Points in English Language Arts." Maine Department of Education. Accessed June 16. http://www.maine.gov/doe/ela/professional/module-one/keypoints.html.

Malaguzzi, Loris. 2011. "History, Ideas, and Basic Philosophy: An Interview with Lella Gandina." In *The Hundred Languages of Children: The Reggio Emilia Experience in Transformation*, 3rd ed., edited by Carolyn Edwards, Lella Gandini, and George Foreman, 27–72. Santa Barbara, CA: Praeger.

Marcon, Rebecca A. 2002. "Moving Up the Grades: Relationship between Preschool Model and Later School Success." *Early Childhood Research & Practice* 4 (1). http://ecrp.uiuc.edu/v4n1/marcon.html.

Martin, Keith J., Thiphalak Chounthirath, Huiyun Xiany, and Gary Smith. 2014. "Pediatric Shopping Cart-Related Injuries Treated in US Emergency Departments, 1990–2011." *Clinical Pediatrics* 53 (3): 277–85. http://dx.doi.org/10.1177/0009922813513322.

Merrill, Jenny. 1916. "The Kindergarten of To-day." In *Paradise of Childhood* by Edward Wiebe. Springfield, MA: Milton Bradley Company.

Miller, Edward, and Joan Almon. 2009. *Summary and Recommendations of Crisis in the Kindergarten: Why Children Need to Play in School*. College Park, MD: Alliance for Childhood. http://www.nj.gov/education/ece/k/mod1/Crisis.pdf.

Mills, Enos A. 1920. *The Adventures of a Nature Guide*. New York: Doubleday, Page.

Molomot, Lisa, and Rona Richter. 2013. *School's Out: Lessons from a Forest Kindergarten*. New Haven, CT: Linden Tree Films. DVD, 36 min.

Montessori, Maria. 1964. *The Montessori Method*. New York: Schocken Books.

Nicholson, Simon. 1971. "How NOT to Cheat Children: The Theory of Loose Parts." *Landscape Architecture* 62 (1): 30–34.

Noddings, Nel. 2002. Preface to *Teaching Children to Care: Classroom Management for Ethical and Academic Growth, K–8*, rev. ed., by Ruth Sidney Charney, 1–2. Greenfield, MA: Northeast Foundation for Children.

The North American Association for Environmental Education. 2010. *Early Childhood Environmental Education Programs: Guidelines for Excellence*. Washington DC: The North American Association for Environmental Education. http://resources.spaces3.com/c518d93d-d91c-4358-ae5e-b09d493af3f4.pdf.

Pappano, Laura. 2010. "Kids Haven't Changed; Kindergarten Has: New Data Support a Return to 'Balance' in Kindergarten." *Harvard Education Letter* 26 (5).

Pelo, Ann, ed. 2008. *Rethinking Early Childhood Education*. Milwaukee, WI: Rethinking Schools.

Pyle, Robert Michael. 1998. *The Thunder Tree: Lessons from an Urban Wildland*. New York: Lyons Press.

———. 2002. "Eden in a Vacant Lot: Special Places, Species, and Kids in the Neighborhood of Life." In *Children and Nature: Psychological, Socio-cultural, and Evolutionary Investigations*, edited by Peter H. Kahn, Jr. and Stephen R. Kellert, 305–327. Cambridge, MA: MIT Press.

Ransome, Arthur. 1930. *Swallows and Amazons*. London: Jonathan Cape.

Robertson, Juliet. 2008. *I Ur Och Skur "Rain or Shine": Swedish Forest Schools*. Creative STAR Learning Company. Aberdeenshire, Scotland. http://creativestarlearning.co.uk/wp-content/uploads/2013/06/Rain-or-shine-Swedish-Forest-Schools.pdf.

Robertson, Juliet, Penny Martin, Lynnette Borradaile, and Steven Alker. 2009. *Forest Kindergarten Feasibility Study*. Creative STAR Learning Company and Forestry Commission Scotland. Aberdeenshire, Scotland. http://www.educationscotland.gov.uk/Images/Forest%20 Kindergarten%20Feasibility%20studyApril%202009_tcm4-597032.pdf.

Rubin, Laurie. 2013. *To Look Closely: Science and Literacy in the Natural World*. Portland, ME: Stenhouse.

Sandseter, Ellen Beate H. 2007. "Risky Play among Four and Five Year-old Children in Preschool." In *Vision into Practice: Making Quality a Reality in the Lives of Young Children*, edited by Sharon O'Brien, Peadar Cassidy, and Heino Shonfeld, 248–56. Conference. Dublin: Centre for Early Childhood Development and Education. http://www.cecde.ie/english/pdf/Vision%20into%20Practice/Vision%20into%20Practice.pdf.

Sax, Leonard. 2001. "Reclaiming Kindergarten: Making Kindergarten Less Harmful to Boys." *Psychology of Men & Masculinity* 2 (1): 3–12.

Schlitz Audubon Nature Center Preschool. 2006. *Policy and Procedures Manual*. Milwaukee, WI.

Shepard, Paul. (1982) 1998a. *Nature and Madness*. Athens, GA: University of Georgia Press.

———. 1998b. *The Tender Carnivore and the Sacred Game*. Athens: University of Georgia Press.

Silber, Kate. 1965. *Pestalozzi: The Man and His Work*. London: Routledge and Kegan Paul.

Smith, Gregory, and David Sobel. 2010. *Place- and Community-based Education in Schools*. New York: Routledge.

Sobel, David. 1996. *Beyond Ecophobia: Reclaiming the Heart in Nature Education*. Great Barrington, MA: The Orion Society.

———. 2011. *Wild Play: Parenting Adventures in the Great Outdoors*. San Francisco: Sierra Club Books.

Sobel, David, Rachel Becker-Klein, and Patti Bailie. 2015. "Nature-based Preschool Education: Final Research Report to the Storer Foundation." Keene, NH: Antioch University New England.

Stires, Anne. 2013. *The Chocolate River Bakery Cookbook*. Alna, ME: Wabi Sabi Cottage and Juniper Hill School.

Teale, Edwin Way, ed. 1954. *Wilderness World of John Muir*. New York: Houghton Mifflin.

Tough, Paul. 2012. *How Children Succeed: Grit, Curiosity, and the Hidden Power of Character*. New York: Houghton Mifflin.

Turner, Frederick Jackson. 1921. "The Significance of the Frontier in

American History." In *The Frontier in American History*, 1–38. New York: Henry Holt.

Vitale, Susan, Robert D. Sperduto, Frederick L. Ferris. 2009. "Increased Prevalence of Myopia in the United States between 1971–1972 and 1999–2004." *Archives of Ophthalmology* 127 (12): 1632–39. DOI:10.1001 /archophthalmol.2009.303.

Warden, Claire. 2012a. *Nature Kindergartens and Forest Schools: An Exploration of Naturalistic Learning within Nature Kindergartens and Forest Schools*. 2nd ed. Crieff, Scotland: Mindstretchers.

———. 2012b. *Talking and Thinking Floorbooks: Using 'Big Book Planners' to Consult Children*. Crieff, Scotland: Mindstretchers.

———. 2013. *Outdoor Learning: A Year at Auchlone*. Crieff, Scotland: Mindstretchers. DVD, 220 min.

Wilson, David McKay. 2009. "Developmentally Appropriate Practice in the Age of Testing: New Reports Outline Key Principles for PreK–3rd Grade." *Harvard Education Letter* 25 (3) 1–3.

Wilson, Ruth A. 1996. *Starting Early: Environmental Education during the Early Childhood Years*. ERIC Clearinghouse for Science, Mathematics, and Environmental Education. ERIC identifier ED402147. http://files.eric .ed.gov/fulltext/ED402147.pdf.

Index

costs, 43
curriculum, 87–89
experimentation, 15–16
indoor activities, 20–22
language development, 108,
117–118
sacred fire circle, 13–14
setting, 4, 5–7
STEM learning, 16–18
traditions, 18–20, 25–26

K

Kenny, Erin K., 40, 229–245
Kilpatrick, William H., 76
kindergarten
as balance of child-initiated
play and experiential
learning guided by
teacher, 85–86
current American, 34–35
early, 30–31
original emphasis, 27
"kindergarten readiness,"
148–149

L

Laissez-Faire, Loosely Struc-
tured Classroom model, 86,
87–89, 97–101
Langer, Suzanne, 113, 114
language development
alphabet books, 119–120
by early humans, 113–114
examples
Beebe Environmental and
Health Sciences Magnet
School, 119–120
Bradford Elementary
School, 120
Juniper Hill School, 108,
117–118
Pathways to Nature
Preschool, 120–121
Rise, 115–117
Young Achievers Science
and Math Pilot School,
127–130

Floorbooks, 124–126
"talking local," 110–113,
127–130
wedding dance with song,
114–118
Larimore, Rachel, 56
"Learning from Nature in the
Urban Wilds" (Connors and
Perkins), 203
learning readiness, 41, 63
"Learning to Read Nature's
Book: An Interdisciplin-
ary Curriculum for Young
Children in an Urban Set-
ting" (Carroll and Bowman),
127–130
Leila Day Nurseries, 203
Lens on Outdoor Learning
(Banning and Sullivan), 41,
123–124, 126
Linde, Siw, 32
literacy
natural world as source for,
127–130, 132–135
teaching through
alphabet books, 119–120
movement and song,
114–118
organic reading, 110–111,
127–130
litigation fears, 35
Live and Learn Early Learning
Center, 197
location of school. See site
selection
loose parts, 207–208

M

magical thinking, 32
Mariposa, 197
mathematics
literacy component, 127–130
as part of STEM learning,
16–18, 28–29
Merrill, Jenny, 31
Miller, Edward, 83, 85–86
Mills, Enos, 52–53, 54

Minnucci, Eliza, 130–132
Montessori, Maria, 49
Muir, John, 202

N

Natick Community Organic
Farm, 61
See also Forest Gnomes
program
National Association for the
Education of Young Children
(NAEYC), 211–212
National Project for Excellence
in Environmental Education,
212
Naturally Curious (Holland),
131–132
Natural Start (website), 56
natural world
American versus European
concept of, 72
as basis for inquiry by children, 50–51
benefits of education based
in, 201–202
absence of attention deficit
disorder, 40
cognitive, 143–144
creative, 144–145
physical, 146–148
social and emotional,
148–149
spiritual, 150–151
as central organizing principle of nature preschools,
215
child's interpenetrating relationship with, 29–30
development of empathy
between children and, 12
importance in historical
educational movements,
49–51
literacy and
as basis for taxonomy of
language, 123–124
effectiveness, 132–135

David Sobel is an education author and has been a faculty member in the Education Department at Antioch University New England for forty years. He consults and speaks widely on child development and place-based education and has authored seven books and more than seventy articles focused on children and nature for educators, parents, environmentalists, and school administrators.